SIDE BY SIDE
TEACHER'S GUIDE

SIDE BY SIDE TEACHER'S GUIDE

1A

Steven J. Molinsky

Bill Bliss

Illustrated by

Richard E. Hill

Contributing Authors

Mary Ann Perry
Christine Harvey
with
Elizabeth Handley

Editorial Development
Tina B. Carver

PRENTICE HALL REGENTS, Englewood Cliffs, NJ 07632

Printed in the United States of America

10

ISBN 0-13-809491-8

Prentice-Hall International, Inc., *London*
Prentice-Hall of Australia Pty. Limited, *Sydney*
Editora Prentice-Hall do Brasil, Ltda., *Rio de Janeiro*
Prentice-Hall Canada Inc., *Toronto*
Prentice-Hall of India Private Limited, *New Delhi*
Prentice-Hall of Japan, Inc., *Tokyo*
Prentice-Hall of Southeast Asia Pte. Ltd., *Singapore*
Whitehall Books Limited, *Wellington, New Zealand*

Contents

INTRODUCTION

I. The Philosophy and Spirit of SIDE BY SIDE

SIDE BY SIDE is a conversational English series. Its goal is to help students learn to *use* the language grammatically, through practice with meaningful conversational exchanges. To achieve this goal, all exercises throughout the texts are designed so that students will *speak to* and *interact with* each other.

Grammatical structures are usually isolated and drilled through a variety of traditional structural exercises such as repetition, substitution, and transformation drills. These exercises effectively highlight particular grammatical structures . . . but they are usually presented as a string of single sentences, not related to each other in any unifying, relevant context.

Traditional dialogs, on the other hand, may do a fine job of providing examples of real speech, but they don't usually offer sufficient practice with the structures being taught. Teachers and students are often frustrated by the lack of a clear grammatical focus in these meaningful contexts. And besides that, it's hard to figure out what to *do* with a dialog after you have read it, memorized it, or talked about it.

Through the methodology of Guided Conversations, SIDE BY SIDE attempts to combine the best features of traditional grammatical drills and contextually rich dialogs. The aim is to actively engage students in *meaningful conversational exchanges within carefully structured grammatical frameworks*, and then encourage students to break away from the textbook and *use* these frameworks to create conversations *on their own*. Through the Guided Conversation approach, students are presented with a model conversation that highlights a specific aspect of the grammar. In the exercises that follow the model, students pair up and work "side by side," creating new conversations based on the structure of the model. In this way, *all* of the language practice which is generated through the texts results in active communication taking place between students . . . practicing and speaking together, SIDE BY SIDE.

II. SIDE BY SIDE Overview

A. Chapter Highlights

1. Grammatical Paradigms

Each chapter covers one or more specific grammatical structures. A new structure appears first in the form of a grammatical paradigm, or grammar box—a simple schema of the structure.

These paradigms are meant to be a reference point for students as they proceed through the lesson's conversational activities. While these paradigms highlight the structures being taught, we don't intend them to be goals in themselves.

Students are *not* expected to memorize or parrot back these rules. Rather, we want students to take part in conversations that show they can *use* these rules correctly.

2. Model Guided Conversations

Model Guided Conversations serve as the vehicles for introducing new grammatical structures, as well as many communicative uses of English. Since the model becomes the basis for all of the exercises which follow, it is essential that students be given sufficient practice with it before proceeding with the lesson.

3. SIDE BY SIDE Exercises

In the numbered exercises that follow the model, students pair up and work "side by side," placing new content into the given conversational framework. These exercises form the core learning activity of each lesson.

4. ON YOUR OWN

An important component of each chapter is the "On Your Own" activity. These student-centered exercises reinforce the grammatical structures of the lesson while breaking away from the text and allowing students to contribute content of their own.

These activities take various forms: role-plays, interviews, extended guided conversations, and questions about the students' real world. In these exercises, students are asked to bring to the classroom new content, based on their interests, their backgrounds, and their imaginations.

5. Classroom Dramas

"Classroom Dramas" are the full-page comic strip dialogs that appear every once in a while throughout the text. The goal of these dialogs is to tackle a specific grammatical structure and give students the opportunity to rehearse this structure in a short, playful conversation.

B.   Ancillary Materials

1. SIDE BY SIDE Activity Workbooks

Activity Workbooks provide additional reading, writing, listening, and pronunciation practice with the structures presented in the student texts. Periodic check-up tests are also included.

2. SIDE BY SIDE Tapes

Audio-cassette tapes, fully coordinated with the texts, have been designed so that the student doesn't simply listen and repeat, but actively engages the taped voices in genuine conversations. All model conversations and SIDE BY SIDE exercises are included on the tapes.

3. SIDE BY SIDE Dialog Visual Cards

These poster-size illustrations depict the characters and settings of all model dialogs. Their use during introduction of the model helps to assure that students are engaged in active listening and speaking practice during this important stage in the lesson.

4. SIDE BY SIDE Picture Cards

SIDE BY SIDE Picture Cards illustrate key concepts and vocabulary items. They can be used for introduction of new material, for review, for extra-enrichment exercises, and for role-playing activities.

Suggestions for coordinating these ancillary materials with the SIDE BY SIDE student texts are provided in each lesson of the Teacher's Guide.

III. Format of the Teacher's Guide

A. Chapter Overview

Introductory notes for each chapter offer information on the following:
1. FOCUS of the chapter.
2. COMMUNICATIVE SKILLS.
3. NEW VOCABULARY.
4. LANGUAGE NOTES, including comments on pronunciation, spelling, and language usage.
5. CULTURE KEY, including cultural information about U.S. life and customs.

B. Step-by-Step Guide for Teaching Each Lesson in the Chapter

Included here are the following:
1. FOCUS of the lesson.
2. GETTING READY: suggestions for introducing the new concepts in the lesson.
3. PRESENTING THE MODEL: steps for introducing the model conversation.
4. SIDE BY SIDE EXERCISES: suggestions for practicing the exercises, as well as a listing of new vocabulary.
5. OPTIONAL WRITING PRACTICE: suggestions for assigning optional written homework of selected SIDE BY SIDE exercises.
6. WORKBOOK: page references in the Activity Workbook which correspond to the particular lesson.
7. EXPANSION ACTIVITIES: optional activities for review and reinforcement of the content of the lesson.

C. WORKBOOK PAGES

At the end of each chapter are found the corresponding workbook pages with notes to the teacher and the key to listening exercises.

IV. General Teaching Strategies

A. Introducing The Model

Since the model conversation forms the basis of each lesson, it is essential that students practice the model several times in a variety of ways before going on to the exercises.

The following 8 steps are recommended for introducing model conversations: .

1. Have students look at the model illustration in the book or on the SIDE BY SIDE Dialog Visual Card. This helps to establish the context of the conversation.
2. Set the scene. For every model, one or two lines are suggested in the Teacher's Guide for you to use to "set the scene" of the dialog for your students.
3. Present the model. With books closed, have students listen as you present the model or play the tape one or more times.

   If you are using the Dialog Visual Cards, point to the people in the illustration as you present the model. If you are not using the Dialog Visual Cards, you might want to draw two stick figures on the board to represent the speakers in the dialog. (You can also show that two people are speaking by changing your position or by shifting your weight from one foot to the other as you present the model.)

   The goal here is to make the presentation of the dialog as realistic as possible.
4. Full-Class Choral Repetition. Model each line and have the whole class repeat in unison.
5. Have students open their books and look at the dialog. Ask if there are any questions and check understanding of new vocabulary. (All new vocabulary in the model is listed here. The illustration and the context of the dialog normally help to clarify the meaning of the new words.)
6. Group Choral Repetition. Divide the class in half. Model line A and have Group 1 repeat; model line B and have Group 2 repeat. Continue this with all lines of the model.
7. Choral Conversation. Groups 1 and 2 practice the dialog twice, without teacher model. First Group 1 is Speaker A and Group 2 is Speaker B; then reverse.
8. Call on one or two pairs of students to present the dialog.

In steps 6, 7, and 8 you should encourage students to look up from their books and "say" the lines rather than read them. (Students can of course refer to their books when necessary.) *The goal here is not memorization or complete mastery of the model.* Rather, students should be familiar with the model and feel comfortable saying it.

At this point, if you feel that additional practice is necessary before going on to the SIDE BY SIDE exercises, you can do Choral Conversation in small groups or by rows.

B. SIDE BY SIDE Exercises

The numbered SIDE BY SIDE exercises which follow the model form the core learning activity in each lesson. Here students use the pictures and word cues provided to create conversations based on the structure of the model. Since all language practice in the text is conversational, you will always call on a pair of students to do each exercise. *Your* primary role for the SIDE BY

SIDE exercises is to serve as a resource to the class—for help with the structures, new vocabulary, intonation, and pronunciation.

The following 3 steps are recommended in each lesson for practicing the SIDE BY SIDE exercises. (Students should be given thorough practice with the first two exercises before going on.)

1. Exercise 1. Introduce any new vocabulary in the exercise. Call on two students to present the dialog. Then do Choral Repetition and Choral Conversation Practice.
2. Exercise 2. Same as for exercise 1.
3. For the remaining exercises, there are two options: either Full-Class Practice or Pair Practice.

FULL-CLASS PRACTICE

Call on a pair of students to do each exercise. Introduce new vocabulary one exercise at a time. (For more practice, call on other pairs of students, or do Choral Repetition or Choral Conversation.)

PAIR PRACTICE

Introduce new vocabulary for all the exercises. Next have students practice all of the exercises in pairs. Then have pairs present the exercises to the class. (For more practice, do Choral Repetition or Choral Conversation.)

The choice of Full-Class Practice or Pair Practice should be determined by the content of the particular lesson, the size and composition of the class, and your own teaching style. In any case, you might wish to vary your approach from lesson to lesson.

Suggestions For Pairing Up Students

Whether you use Full-Class Practice or Pair Practice, you can select students for the pairs in various ways. You might want to pair students by ability. For example, students of similar ability might work more efficiently together. On the other hand, you might wish to pair a weaker student with a stronger one. The slower student benefits from this pairing, while the more advanced student also strengthens his or her abilities by helping the partner.

You should also encourage students to *look at* each other when speaking. This makes the conversational nature of the language practice more realistic.

Presenting New Vocabulary

Many new vocabulary words are introduced in the SIDE BY SIDE exercises. The illustration normally helps to convey the meaning, and the new words are written for students to see and use in their conversations. In addition, you might

1. write the new word on the board or on a word card;
2. say the new word several times and ask students to repeat chorally and individually;
3. help clarify the meaning with SIDE BY SIDE Picture Cards or your own visuals (pictures from magazines, newspapers, or your own drawings).

Students might also find it useful to keep a notebook in which they write each new word, its meaning, and a sentence using that word.

Open-Ended Exercises (The "Blank Box")

In many lessons, the final SIDE BY SIDE exercise is an open-ended one. This is indicated in the text by a blank box. Here the students are expected to create conversations based on the structure of the model, but with vocabulary which they select themselves. This provides students with an opportunity for creativity, while still focusing on the particular structure being practiced. These open-ended exercises can be done orally in class and/or assigned as homework for presentation in class the next day.

Reviewing SIDE BY SIDE Exercises

Some or all of the SIDE BY SIDE exercises in each lesson should be reviewed in class the day after they are presented. Whenever possible, you should try to review the exercises with books closed (although some lessons require that students refer to the written and picture cues in the text). When reviewing a lesson, encourage students to use expressive language and look at and talk to each other when practicing.

Other Uses for SIDE BY SIDE Exercises

While SIDE BY SIDE exercises are intended primarily for practice in conversation, they can also be used to provide writing practice. In every lesson several exercises are suggested for assignment as optional written homework.

The illustrations in the text can also have many uses. They can be used as a springboard for discussion of students' own interests, experiences, and cultural attitudes. In addition, many illustrations are rich sources of new vocabulary which might not be specifically taught in the lesson, but which can be discussed as that exercise is practiced by the class.

C.   ON YOUR OWN

"On Your Own" activities offer students the opportunity to contribute content of their own within the grammatical framework of the lesson. These activities take the form of role-plays, interviews, extended guided conversations, and questions about the student's real world.

You should introduce these activities in class and assign them as homework for presentation the next day. In this way, students will automatically review the previous day's grammar while contributing new and inventive content of their own.

"On Your Own" activities are meant for simultaneous grammar reinforcement and vocabulary building. Students should be encouraged to use a dictionary in completing the "On Your Own" activities. In this way, they will not only use the words they know, but the words they would *like* to know in order to really bring their interests, backgrounds, and imaginations into the classroom.

As a result, students will be teaching each other new vocabulary and also sharing a bit of their lives with others in the class.

D.   Classroom Dramas

These playful classroom conversations can be treated in a variety of ways. Some teachers will simply want to read through these dramas with their students. Others might want to act them out, using students in the class as the characters.

Students enjoy memorizing these dramas and using them frequently throughout the course. In fact, they often break into these conversations spontaneously, without any prompting from the teacher. (Many students, for example, like to impress visitors to their class by confidently performing these dramas as though they were really happening for the first time.)

E.   Expansion Activities

Each lesson contains ideas for optional review and reinforcement activities. Feel free to pick and choose or vary the activities to fit the particular needs and learning styles of students in your class. These ideas are also meant to serve as a springboard for developing your own learning activities.

V.   General Guiding Principles

1. In doing the exercises throughout the book, students should practice *speaking* to each other, rather than *reading* to each other. Therefore, while students will need to refer to the text to be able to practice the conversations, they shouldn't read the lines word by word. Rather, they should practice scanning a full line, then looking up from the book and *speaking* the line to another person.

2. Throughout, teachers should be using the book to teach proper intonation and gesture. (Capitalized words are used through the text to indicate spoken emphasis.) Students should be encouraged to truly "act out" the dialogs in a strong and confident voice.

3. Use of the text should be as *student-centered* as possible. Modeling by the teacher should be efficient and economical, but students should have every opportunity to model for each other as they are capable of doing that.

4. Vocabulary can and should most effectively be taught in the context of the conversation being practiced. Very often it will be possible to grasp the meaning from the conversation or its accompanying illustration. Teachers should spend time drilling vocabulary in isolation *only* if they feel it is absolutely essential.

5. Students need not formally study or be able to produce grammatical rules. The purpose of the text is to engage students in active conversational practice that gets them to *use* the language according to these rules.

6. Writing practice can be an effective supplement to the conversational practice, but it should not *precede* the conversational practice for a given dialog, nor should it be seen as required.

7. Finally, students should be given every opportunity to apply their own lives and creative contributions to the exercises. This is directly provided for in the blank boxes at the end of many exercises as well as in the "On Your Own" activities, but teachers can look to *all* exercises with an eye toward expanding them to the real world of the classroom or the students' real lives.

VI. LINE BY LINE: English Through GrammarStories

LINE BY LINE is the reading/writing companion text to SIDE BY SIDE. After completing each chapter of the SIDE BY SIDE Student Book and Activity Workbook, you should assign the corresponding chapter in LINE BY LINE. Suggestions for presenting and practicing the stories in LINE BY LINE are given in the introduction to the text.

SIDE BY SIDE
TEACHER'S GUIDE

CHAPTER 1 OVERVIEW

TEXT PAGES 1-3

FOCUS

Introduction of the following forms of the verb *to be*:

am	*I am from Mexico City.*
are	*Where are you from?*
is	*What is your phone number?*

COMMUNICATIVE SKILLS

1. Asking for information about another person:
   What is your name?

2. Giving information about oneself:
   My name is Maria.

VOCABULARY

address	phone number	one	1	six	6
am	Thank you very much.	two	2	seven	7
are	you	three	3	eight	8
from	your	four	4	nine	9
I	You're welcome.	five	5	ten	10
is	what				
name	where				

LANGUAGE NOTES

The verb *to be* is commonly contracted in speech and informal writing. The contracted forms, such as *I'm*, are taught in Chapter 2.

CULTURE KEY

On text page 3, a TV talk show host is interviewing a famous person. Talk shows are popular in the U.S. and usually feature a well-known host talking with famous people.

GETTING READY

1. Teach the first question and answer in the conversation before students open their books. Teach:

> What is your name? My name is _____.

Begin by saying *your* name: "My name is _____." Then ask individual students: "What is your name?" Students answer: "My name is _____." Next, signal individual students to ask each other.

2. Teach the numbers zero to 10. (See CHAPTER OVERVIEW, Vocabulary.)
    a. Write the numbers on the board or large cards. Point to each number and have students repeat after you several times.
        After some practice, point to the numbers more rapidly—first in order, then out of order. Have students say the numbers as you point.
    b. Have a student go to the board and point to numbers. Have that student or the whole class say the numbers.

PRESENTING THE MODEL

1. Have students look at the model illustration in the book or on the SBS (SIDE BY SIDE) Dialog Visual Card.

2. Set the scene: "A teacher and students are talking."

3. With books closed, have students listen as you present the model or play the tape one or more times.

4. **Full-Class Choral Repetition**: Model each question and answer in the dialog and have students repeat.

5. Have students open their books and look at the dialog. Ask students if they have any questions and check understanding of vocabulary.

6. **Group Choral Repetition**: Divide the class in half. Model the 1st question of the dialog and have Group 1 repeat; model the answer and have Group 2 repeat. Continue this way with the other questions and answers in the dialog.

7. **Choral Conversation**: Groups 1 and 2 practice the dialog twice, without teacher model. First Group 1 asks the questions and Group 2 gives the answers; then reverse.

8. Call on one or two pairs of students to present the dialog.

    (For additional practice, do Choral Conversation in small groups or by rows.)

SIDE BY SIDE EXERCISES

In the section **Answer These Questions**, students use the questions of the model to give their own names, addresses, phone numbers, and where they are from.

Call on pairs of students to present the dialog, using information about themselves in the answers. You can also use pair practice: have students practice the dialog in pairs, and then present their dialogs to the class.

Note that the numbers in the students' addresses may be higher than the ones they have learned. For this exercise you can have students read each digit in their address: For example, *232* might be read as *two, three, two,* rather than *two thirty two*. (Higher numbers will be taught in Chapter 5.)

OPTIONAL WRITING PRACTICE

Have students write the questions and answers on text page 2 for homework.

WORKBOOK

Students can now do pages 1, 2, 3.

ON YOUR OWN

This is a role-play exercise which reviews the questions on text page 2. Students pretend to be famous celebrities who are being interviewed on television. (See CHAPTER OVERVIEW, Culture Key.) One student is the interviewer and asks the questions. Another pretends to be the famous person.

1. Have students think of famous people in the categories suggested at the bottom of text page page 3. If they have difficulty with this, make some suggestions.

2. Introduce the new vocabulary: *Thank you very much, You're welcome.*

3. Have pairs of students practice and then role-play these interviews in front of the class, making up addresses and phone numbers for the famous people.

A. WHAT ARE THEY SAYING?

what	my	name	from	I
is	your	address	thank	you
am		phone number		

1. What is your name?
2. What is your address?
3. What is your phone number?
4. Thank you.

My name is Betty Jones.
My address is 333 Main Street.
My phone number is 868-2766.
You're welcome.

5. What is your name?
My name is Harry Ross.

6. What is your address?
My address is 10 River Street.

Harry Ross
10 River Street

1

7. What is your phone number?
My phone number is 723-1576.

8. Where are you from?
I am from Chicago.

B. NAME/ADDRESS/PHONE NUMBER

STUDENT IDENTIFICATION CARD

Name: _Maria_ _Gonzalez_
      First Name Last Name

Address: _235 Main Street_
      Number   Street

Phone Number: _741-8906_

My name is Maria Gonzalez.
My address is 235 Main Street.
My phone number is 741-8906.

My name is _____

What is YOUR name, address, and phone number?

STUDENT IDENTIFICATION CARD

Name: _____
      First Name Last Name

Address: _____
      Number   Street

Phone Number: _____

2

Students practice asking and answering: *What is your name? What is your address? What is your phone number? Where are you from?* (text page 2)

one	two	three	four	five	six	seven	eight	nine	ten

C. WRITE

1 = _one_
2 = _two_
3 = _three_
4 = _four_
5 = _five_
6 = _six_
7 = _seven_
8 = _eight_
9 = _nine_
10 = _ten_

D. WHAT'S THE NUMBER?

1. My address is four Main Street.

2. My address is ten Main Street. [10]

3. My address is seven Main Street. [7]

4. My address is five Main Street. [5]

5. My address is nine Main Street. [9]

6. My address is eight Main Street. [8]

E. LISTEN   Listen and write the missing number.

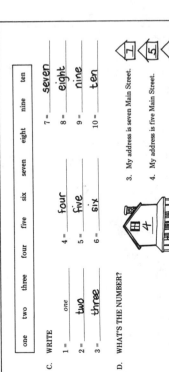

1. What is your phone number? My phone number is 231-496 _5_.

2. What is your phone number? My phone number is 743-529 _6_.

3. What is your phone number? My phone number is 492-71 _8_ 5.

4. What is your phone number? My phone number is 637-89 _7_ 6.

F. LISTEN

Listen and put a circle around the number you hear.

1. 1 ③ 5   3. ④ 5 6
2. 6 7 ⑧   4. 5 ⑦ 10
                     5. 6 8 ⑨
                     6. 2 3 ⑥

3

Students practice writing and listening to numbers 1-10. (text page 2)

TEACHER'S NOTES

CHAPTER 2 OVERVIEW

2

TEXT PAGES 5-9

FOCUS

1. The verb *to be.*
2. Subject pronouns.
3. Contractions with the verb *to be.*
4. *Where* questions.

COMMUNICATIVE SKILLS

Asking for and giving information about location:
> *Where's Helen?*   *Where's Albert?*
> *She's in the living room.*   *He's in the restaurant.*

VOCABULARY

and	he	monkey	the
at home	he's	movie theater	they
bank	hospital	Mr.	they're
basement	I	Mrs.	we
bathroom	I'm	newspaper	we're
bedroom	it	park	where
car	it's	post office	where's
cat	kitchen	restaurant	yard
dining room	library	she	you
dog	living room	she's	you're
garage		supermarket	zoo

LANGUAGE NOTES

The contracted forms of the verb *to be* should be used in the chapter whenever possible. For example,
> *Where's Tom?*
> *He's in the kitchen.*

CULTURE KEY

1. **Yard** (text page 6)
   Many U.S. families relax, plant gardens, and play sports in this grassy area around the house.

2. **Basement** (text page 6)
   Basements are common in buildings located in colder climates. The heating system is often located there.

3. **Forms of address** (text page 7)
   Mr.   refers to both married and single men.
   Mrs. refers to married women.
   Miss refers to single women. (See Chapter 3.)
   Ms.   has been used in recent years to refer to all women, whether they are married or single.

4. **Dog, cat** (text page 7)
   Dogs and cats are very popular as pets in the U.S. The pet often becomes a beloved family member. We may refer to pets as *he, she,* or *it. He* or *she* is used when we refer to the pet by name. For example, *Where's Rover? **He's** in the living room. It* is used when we ask, *Where's the dog (or cat)? **It's** in the living room.*

TEXT PAGES 6-7
FOCUS

The grammar box at the top of the page summarizes all the structures that are taught on text pages 7-9. Below are the structures which are presented on text page 7:

Where are you?	I'm } in the _____. We're }
Where are they?	They're in the _____.

Teach the vocabulary on text page 6. Point to each part of the house and say the new word. Have students repeat after you—first chorally, then individually.

Or present this vocabulary using your own visuals, the SBS Dialog Visual Card, or SBS Picture Cards 1-8. Point to one visual at a time, say the word, and have students repeat.

PRESENTING THE MODEL

There are 3 model conversations. **Introduce and practice each model before going on to the next.** For each model:

1. Have students look at the model illustration in the book or on the SBS Dialog Visual Card.
2. Set the scene: "People are talking at home."
3. With books closed, have students listen as you present the model or play the tape one or more times.
4. **Full-Class Choral Repetition**: Model each line and have students repeat.
5. Have students open their books and look at the dialog. Ask students if they have any questions and check understanding of new vocabulary:
   - 1st model: *where, are, you, I'm, in, the*
   - 2nd model: *we're*
   - 3rd model: *Mr., and, Mrs., they're*
6. **Group Choral Repetition**: Divide the class in half. Model line A and have Group 1 repeat; model line B and have Group 2 repeat.
7. **Choral Conversation**: Groups 1 and 2 practice the dialog twice, without teacher model. First Group 1 is Speaker A and Group 2 is Speaker B; then reverse.
8. Call on one or two pairs of students to present the dialog.
   (For additional practice, do Choral Conversation in small groups or by rows.)
9. Expand each model with further substitution practice.
   a. After students practice the model, *Where are you? I'm in the kitchen,* cue other substitutions, such as:

Teacher cue:	bedroom	Teacher cue:	living room
Teacher:	Where are you?	Teacher:	Where are you?
Student:	I'm in the bedroom.	Student:	I'm in the living room.

   b. This practice can be done chorally, or you can call on individual students.

   When practicing *we're,* you can make this more realistic by asking about two of your students. For example,

Teacher cue:	dining room
Teacher:	Where are you and (John)?
Student:	We're in the dining room.

c. When practicing *they're*, use names of students in your class. For example,
    Teacher cue: garage
    Teacher: Where are (John) and (Bill)?
    Student: They're in the garage.

SIDE BY SIDE EXERCISES

Examples:

1. A. Where are you?
   B. I'm in the bedroom.
	2. A. Where are you?
	   B. I'm in the dining room.

3. A. Where are you? B. We're in the kitchen.	

1. **Exercise 1:** Call on two students to present the dialog. Then do Choral Repetition and Choral Conversation Practice.

2. **Exercise 2:** Same as above.

3. **Exercises 3-9:**
   Either

   Full-Class Practice: Call on a pair of students to do each exercise. (For more practice, call on other pairs of students, or do Choral Repetition or Choral Conversation.)
   or
   Pair Practice: Have students practice all of the exercises in pairs. Then have pairs present the exercises to the class. (For more practice, do Choral Repetition or Choral Conversation.)

OPTIONAL WRITING PRACTICE

Have students write sentences 1, 3, 5, 7, 8 for homework.

WORKBOOK

Students can now do page 4.

EXPANSION ACTIVITIES

1. *Practice With Visuals*
   Use your own visuals, word cards, or SBS Picture Cards 1-8 to review the structures on text page 7. Have students pretend to be in various places, and ask and answer questions. For example,
   a. To practice *I'm*, give a visual of the living room to Student A and ask: "Where are you?" Student A answers: "I'm in the living room."
   b. Practice *I'm* this way with other students using other locations.
   c. Call on pairs of students to practice both the question and answer with *I'm* as you give a visual to one student.
   d. To practice *we're*, give a visual to Student A and Student B and ask Student A: "Where are you and Student B?" Student A answers: "We're in the _____."
   e. Practice *we're* with other students using other locations; then call on pairs of students to practice both the question and answer.
   f. To practice *they're*, give a visual to Student A and Student B and ask another Student C, "Where are A and B?" Student C answers: "They're in the _____." Continue this practice with other students and locations.

2. *Pronunciation Practice*
   Practice contractions with the verb *to be*. Have students repeat after you chorally and individually. Say the full form and have students say the contracted form. For example,
       Teacher: I am
       Students: I'm

FOCUS

Introduction of: *Where's* _____ ? $\left.\begin{array}{l}\textit{He's}\\\textit{She's}\\\textit{It's}\end{array}\right\}$ *in the* _____ .

GETTING READY

Review the vocabulary on text page 6. Use SBS Picture Cards 1-8 or the illustration in the text to practice these words. Point to a place and have students say the name. Have students respond chorally, then individually. Practice each word several times.

PRESENTING THE MODEL

There are 3 model conversations. **Introduce and practice each model before going on to the next.** For each model:

1.   Have students look at the model illustration in the book or on the SBS Dialog Visual Card.

2.   Set the scene: "People are talking at home."

3.   With books closed, have students listen as you present the model or play the tape one or more times.

4.   **Full-Class Choral Repetition**: Model each line and have students repeat.

5.   Have students open their books and look at the dialog. Ask students if they have any questions and check understanding of new vocabulary:

     1st model: *where's, he's*
     2nd model: *she's*
     3rd model: *car, it's*

6.   **Group Choral Repetition**: Divide the class in half. Model line A and have Group 1 repeat; model line B and have Group 2 repeat.

7.   **Choral Conversation**: Groups 1 and 2 practice the dialog twice, without teacher model. First Group 1 is Speaker A and Group 2 is Speaker B; then reverse.

8.   Call on one or two pairs of students to present the dialog.

     (For additional practice, do Choral Conversation in small groups or by rows.)

9.   Expand the first 2 models with further substitution practice.
     a.   After students practice the model, *Where's Bob? He's in the living room,* cue other substitutions using names of male students in the class. For example,

Teacher cue:	kitchen	Teacher cue:	basement
Teacher:	Where's (Tom)?	Teacher:	Where's (John)?
Student:	He's in the kitchen.	Student:	He's in the basement.

     b.   Similarly, after presenting the second model, cue other substitutions using names of female students in the class. For example,

Teacher cue:	dining room
Teacher:	Where's (Maria)?
Student:	She's in the dining room.

SIDE BY SIDE EXERCISES

Examples:

1. A. Where's Tom?
   B. He's in the bedroom.

3. A. Where's Helen?
   B. She's in the living room.

5. A. Where's the newspaper?
   B. It's in the kitchen.

1. **Exercise 1:** Call on two students to present the dialog. Then do Choral Repetition and Choral Conversation Practice.

2. **Exercise 2:** Same as above.

3. **Exercises 3-9:**

> **New vocabulary:** 5. *newspaper*   6. *cat*   7. *dog*

Either

Full-Class Practice: Call on a pair of students to do each exercise. Introduce the new vocabulary as you do exercises 5, 6, 7. (For more practice, call on other pairs of students, or do Choral Repetition or Choral Conversation.)

or

Pair Practice: Introduce all the new vocabulary. Next have students practice all of the exercises in pairs. Then have pairs present the exercises to the class.

(For more practice, do Choral Repetition or Choral Conversation.)

OPTIONAL WRITING PRACTICE

Have students write exercises 2, 4, 5, 7, 9 for homework.

WORKBOOK

Students can now do pages 5, 6.

EXPANSION ACTIVITIES

1. *Practice With Visuals*

   You can review the structures on text page 8 by using your own visuals or SBS Picture Cards 1-8. Use the same method you used on text page 7. Again, use visuals to show the location of students in a house. Ask questions about students in your class. For example,

   "Where's Student A?"
   "He's/She's in the _____."

   Next, have students ask each other questions about the person holding a visual for location. Practice both *he* and *she* this way. For practicing *it*, you can use objects, such as a newspaper, along with the visuals.

2. *Listening Exercise*

   Tell your students the following story. (This story is not found in the book.) You can use visuals if you wish. You can pause as you tell the story to ask the questions below, or you can wait until the end.

   The Wilson Family

   The Wilson family is at home today. Mr. and Mrs. Wilson are in the kitchen. Mary Wilson is in the living room. Fred Wilson is in the bathroom. The cat and the dog are in the garage.

   Questions: Where are Mr. and Mrs. Wilson?
   Where's Mary Wilson?
   Where's Fred Wilson?
   Where are the cat and the dog?

FOCUS

1. Review of: *Where's* _____? *Where are* _____?
2. Introduction of: *Where am I?*

SIDE BY SIDE EXERCISES

Examples:

1. A. Where's Albert?
   B. He's in the restaurant.

2. A. Where's Carmen?
   B. She's in the bank.

1. **Exercise 1:** Introduce the new word: *restaurant.* Call on two students to present the dialog. Then do Choral Repetition and Choral Conversation Practice.

2. **Exercise 2:** Introduce the new word: *bank.* Same as above.

3. **Exercises 3-9:**

New vocabulary: 3. *supermarket*   4. *library*   5. *park*   6. *movie theater*
7. *post office*   8. *zoo*   9. *hospital*

Either

Full-Class Practice: Call on a pair of students to do each exercise. Introduce new vocabulary one exercise at a time.

(For more practice, call on other pairs of students, or do Choral Repetition or Choral Conversation.)

or

Pair Practice: Introduce new vocabulary for all the exercises. Next have students practice all these exercises in pairs. Then have pairs present the exercises to the class.

(For more practice, do Choral Repetition or Choral Conversation.)

OPTIONAL WRITING PRACTICE

Have students write exercises 1, 2, 3, 4, 5, 9 for homework.

ON YOUR OWN

In this exercise, students practice questions and answers using the patterns:

   Where's _____? Where are _____? Where am I?

Students can use any names and any places they wish. The object of the exercise is to get students to practice the structures with vocabulary of their choice in order to talk about real-life places and people. Although there are only 3 exercises indicated in the book, you may want your students to do more. Encourage students to use dictionaries to learn new words.

This exercise can be done orally in class or for written homework. If you assign it for homework, you should do one example in class to make sure students understand what's expected. Have students present their questions and answers in class the next day.

WORKBOOK

Students can now do pages 7, 8.

EXPANSION ACTIVITY

Practice With Visuals
Use SBS Picture Cards 9-17, or your own visuals or word cards for the vocabulary on text page 9. Practice asking and answering questions about these locations as you did for places in the home. Use this method to practice all the subject pronouns and forms of the verb *to be*. Pay special attention to the use of contractions and pronunciation of the final *s* in *she's*, *he's*, and *it's*.

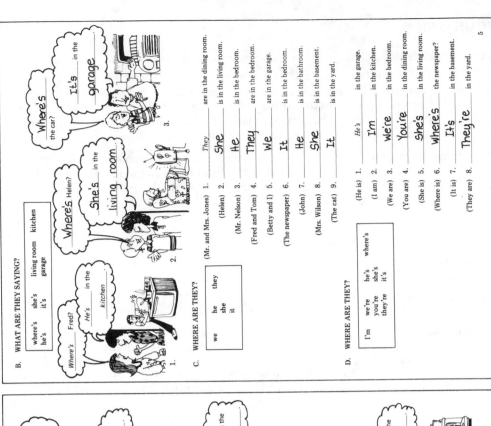

A. WHAT ARE THEY SAYING?

I'm	you	basement	living room
we're	are	bedroom	yard
they're	where	kitchen	

1. Where are you? / I'm in the garage.
2. Where are you? / We're in the living room.
3. Where are Harry and Betty? / They're in the yard.
4. Where are you and Tom? / We're in the bedroom.
5. Where are John and Bill? / They're in the basement.
6. Where are you? / I'm in the kitchen.

B. WHAT ARE THEY SAYING?

| where's | she's | living room | kitchen |
| he's | it's | garage | |

1. Where's Fred? / He's in the kitchen.
2. Where's Helen? / She's in the living room.
3. Where's the car? / It's in the garage.

C. WHERE ARE THEY?

we	he	they
	she	
	it	

1. (Mr. and Mrs. Jones) _They_ are in the dining room.
2. (Helen) She is in the living room.
3. (Mr. Nelson) He is in the bedroom.
4. (Fred and Tom) They are in the bedroom.
5. (Betty and I) We are in the garage.
6. (The newspaper) It is in the bedroom.
7. (John) He is in the bathroom.
8. (Mrs. Wilson) She is in the basement.
9. (The cat) It is in the yard.

D. WHERE ARE THEY?

I'm	he's	where's
we're	she's	
you're	it's	
they're		

1. (He is) _He's_ in the garage.
2. (I am) I'm in the kitchen.
3. (We are) We're in the bedroom.
4. (You are) You're in the dining room.
5. (She is) She's in the living room.
6. (Where is) Where's the newspaper?
7. (It is) It's in the basement.
8. (They are) They're in the yard.

Students practice the present tense of *to be* with the subject pronouns *I, we, they, you*. Also students practice the interrogative *where*. (text pages 6-7)

Students practice changing nouns to subject pronouns and practice forming contractions. (text page 8)

18   CHAPTER TWO

G. WHAT'S THE SIGN?

Fill in the signs. Then complete the sentences.

LIBRARY

1. Tom and Mary _are in the library_ .

HOSPITAL

2. Albert is _in the hospital_ .

PARK

3. Fred and Helen are _in the park_ .

RESTAURANT

4. Betty _is in the restaurant_ .

BANK

5. Rita _is in the bank_ .

POST OFFICE

6. Bob and Jane _are in the post office_ .

MOVIE THEATER

7. Jane _is in the movie theater_ .

SUPERMARKET

8. John and Martha _are in the supermarket_ .

This exercise is a review of *to be* + locations. (text page 9)

THE FRANKLIN FAMILY

E.

The Franklin family is at home today. (1) Mr. Franklin is _in_ the _kitchen_ . (2) Mrs. Franklin is _in_ the _yard_ . (3) Tom and Jane are _in_ the _bedroom_ . (4) Betty _is_ _in_ the _living room_ . (5) The dog _is_ _in_ the _dining room_ . (6) The cat _is_ _in_ the _bathroom_ .

F.

he's	they're
she's	
it's	

He's in the kitchen.

1. Where's Mr. Franklin? _He's in the kitchen._
2. Where's Mrs. Franklin? _She's in the yard._
3. Where are Tom and Jane? _They're in the living room._
4. Where's Betty? _She's in the bedroom._
5. Where's the dog? _It's in the dining room._
6. Where's the cat? _It's in the bathroom._

Exercise E can be done for homework or in class as a dictation.
In Exercise F, students answer questions based on the paragraph in Exercise E. (text page 8)

Key to Exercise H
Read or play the tape.

1. Where are they? They're in the hospital.
2. Where are they? They're in the supermarket.
3. Where's Mary? She's in the bank.

Key to Exercise I
Read or play the tape.

1. Where are you?
2. I'm in the car with Mrs. Jones.
3. Where's Mr. Jones?
4. He's in Mexico City.
5. Where are you?
6. I'm in the bathroom.
7. Where's the newspaper?
8. It's in the living room.

Exercise H gives listening practice combined with vocabulary from Chapter 2. (text page 9)

TEACHER'S NOTES

CHAPTER 3 OVERVIEW

TEXT PAGES 11-15

FOCUS

Introduction of the present continuous tense:
What's John doing?   *What are you doing?*
He's cooking.   *I'm studying?*

COMMUNICATIVE SKILLS

1. Asking for and giving information about location:
   Where's Walter?
   He's in the kitchen.

2. Asking for and giving information about people's activities:
   What are Fred and Mary doing?
   They're studying English.

VOCABULARY

baseball	discotheque*	lunch	sleeping
breakfast	doing	mathematics†	studying
cards	drinking	piano	TV
coffee	eating	playing	watching
cooking	English	radio	what
dancing	guitar	reading	what's
dinner	lemonade	singing	
	listening to		

*A discotheque is often called a *disco*.
†Mathematics is often referred to as *math*.

LANGUAGE NOTES

The contraction *what is* → *what's* is common in spoken English.

CULTURE KEY

1. **Baseball** (text page 14)
   Along with football and basketball, baseball is a very popular spectator sport in the U.S.

2. **Breakfast, lunch, dinner** (text page 14)
   In general, people in the U.S. like to eat three meals a day: breakfast, before work or school; lunch, around noon; and dinner, in the early evening.

TEXT PAGES 12-13

FOCUS

| Introduction of the present continuous tense. |

GETTING READY

Review contractions of the verb *to be.* Say the full forms and have students tell you the correct contracted forms:

I am → I'm   we are → we're
he is → he's   you are → you're
she is → she's   they are → they're
it is → it's

PRESENTING THE MODEL

There are 6 model conversations. **Introduce and practice each model before going on to the next.** For each model:

1. Have students look at the model illustration in the book or on the SBS Dialog Visual Card.
2. Set the scene: "Neighbors are talking."
3. With books closed, have students listen as you present the model or play the tape one or more times.
4. **Full-Class Choral Repetition:** Model each line and have students repeat.
5. Have students open their books and look at the dialog. Ask students if they have any questions and check understanding of new vocabulary:

     1st model: *what, doing, reading*
     2nd model: *cooking*
     3rd model: *studying English*
     4th model: *what's, eating*
     5th model: *watching TV*
     6th model: *sleeping*

6. **Group Choral Repetition:** Divide the class in half. Model line A and have Group 1 repeat; model line B and have Group 2 repeat.
7. **Choral Conversation:** Groups 1 and 2 practice the dialog twice, without teacher model. First Group 1 is Speaker A and Group 2 is Speaker B; then reverse.
8. Call on one or two pairs of students to present the dialog.
    (For additional practice, do Choral Conversation in small groups or by rows.)
9. After all of the models have been introduced, go back to the first and practice it again by cuing the substitution of other verbs. For example,

     Teacher cue: cooking   Teacher cue: sleeping
     Teacher: What are you doing?   Teacher: What are you doing?
     Student: I'm cooking.   Student: I'm sleeping.

Continue this with the next four models to practice *we're, they're, he's, she's.*

SIDE BY SIDE EXERCISES   (text page 13)

Examples:

| 1. A. What are you doing? | 2. A. What are Mr. and Mrs. Jones doing? |
| B. I'm reading the newspaper. | B. They're eating dinner. |

1. **Exercise 1:** Call on two students to present the dialog. Then do Choral Repetition and Choral Conversation Practice.
2. **Exercise 2:** Introduce the new word: *dinner*. Same as above.
3. **Exercises 3-7:**

> | **New vocabulary:** | 7. *playing the piano* |

Either

Full-Class Practice: Call on a pair of students to do each exercise. Introduce the new vocabulary before doing exercise 7.

(For more practice, call on other pairs of students, or do Choral Repetition or Choral Conversation.)

or

Pair Practice: Introduce the new vocabulary. Next have students practice all of the exercises in pairs. Then have pairs present the exercises to the class.

(For more practice, do Choral Repetition or Choral Conversation.)

4. **Exercise 8:** In this exercise, the window is *blank*. Ask students to imagine they are living in the building, and have them answer using any vocabulary they wish. Call on several pairs of students to practice this exercise.

OPTIONAL WRITING PRACTICE

Have students write exercises 1, 3, 4, 6 for homework. Also have them write three dialogs for exercise 8.

WORKBOOK

Students can now do page 9.

EXPANSION ACTIVITIES

1. *Practice With Real Objects*

   Use real objects to represent on-going activities that students can talk about. Some suggested objects are:

   - a pot and spoon for *cooking*
   - a newspaper for *reading*
   - a textbook for *studying*
   - an eating utensil (such as a fork or chopsticks) for *eating*.

   Use one object at a time to practice *What _____ doing?*, using all the pronouns. For example,
   a. Hold a pot and spoon and say, "I'm cooking." Have students repeat.
   b. Give the objects to Student A and ask, "What are you doing? Student A answers, "I'm cooking."
   c. Ask another student, "What's *(Student A)* doing?" ("He's/She's cooking.") Ask several other students. Give the objects to different students in order to practice *he's* and *she's*.
   d. Practice *we're*. Give the objects to 2 students. Ask each one, "What are you and _____ doing?" ("We're cooking.") Practice *we're* with several pairs of students.
   e. Practice *they're*. Give the objects to two students. Ask another student, "What are they doing?" Give the visual to several pairs of students; call on other pairs of students to ask and answer, "What are they doing?"
   f. Practice *you're*. Hold an object and ask, "What am I doing?"

   Practice this way using other objects. Be sure to have students practice asking as well as answering.

2. *Practice With Visuals*

   Use your own visuals, word cards, or SBS Picture Cards 18-24 to practice the present continuous tense. Use the same method as in 1 above, but use visuals in place of objects.

FOCUS

> Review and contrast of: *Where _____? and What _____ doing?*

GETTING READY

Review vocabulary for places in the home and community. Use SBS Picture Cards or your own visuals, or the illustrations on text pages 6 and 9. Indicate a place and have students say the name.

PRESENTING THE MODEL (Exercise 1)

1. Have students look at the model illustration in the book or on the SBS Dialog Visual Card.

2. Set the scene: "Two people are talking about Walter."

3. Present the model.

4. Full-Class Choral Repetition.

5. Ask students if they have any questions; check understanding of new vocabulary: *breakfast.*

6. Group Choral Repetition.

7. Choral Conversation.

8. Call on one or two pairs of students to present the dialog.

   (For additional practice, do Choral Conversation in small groups or by rows.)

SIDE BY SIDE EXERCISES

Examples:

2.	A. Where's Betty?		3.	A. Where are Mr. and Mrs. Smith?
	B. She's in the park.			B. They're in the dining room.
	A. What's she doing?			A. What are they doing?
	B. She's eating lunch.			B. They're eating dinner.

1. **Exercise 2:** Introduce the new word: *lunch.* Call on two students to present the dialog. Then do Choral Repetition and Choral Conversation Practice.

2. **Exercise 3:** Introduce the new word: *dinner.* Same as above.

3. **Exercises 4-14:**

New vocabulary:	4. *guitar* 5. *cards* 6. *baseball* 7. *Miss, drinking, coffee*
	8. *cafeteria, lemonade* 10. *classroom, mathematics*
	11. *discotheque, dancing* 12. *singing* 13. *listening to, radio*

Either
Full-Class Practice: Call on a pair of students to do each exercise. Introduce the new vocabulary one exercise at a time.

(For more practice, call on other pairs of students, or do Choral Repetition or Choral Conversation.)

or

Pair Practice: Introduce all the new vocabulary. Next have students practice all of the exercises in pairs. Then have pairs present the exercises to the class.

(For more practice, do Choral Repetition or Choral Conversation.)

OPTIONAL WRITING PRACTICE

Have students write exercises 3, 7, 8, 14 for homework.

ON YOUR OWN

Here students practice these structures with vocabulary of their own choice. They can use any names, places, and activities they wish. Although there are only 2 exercises in the book, you may want your students to do more. Encourage students to use dictionaries to learn new words.

This exercise can be done orally in class or for written homework. If you assign it for homework, you should do one example in class to make sure students understand what's expected. Have students present their ON YOUR OWN conversations in class the next day.

WORKBOOK

Students can now do pages 10, 11, 12.

EXPANSION ACTIVITIES

1. *Practice With Visuals or Real Objects*
   Review *Where _____?* and *What _____ doing?* by using a combination of visuals and objects as cues for oral practice. Use two cues at a time: one represents a *location*, such as *park, kitchen,* or *library*; the other represents an *on-going activity*, such as *eating* or *studying English*. For locations, use your own visuals, word cards, or SBS Picture Cards 1-17. For activities, use your own visuals, word cards, SBS Picture Cards 18-30, or objects such as:
   >   a few cards—for *playing cards*
   >   an eating implement, such as a knife or chopsticks—for *eating lunch*
   >   a cup—for *drinking coffee*
   >   a book—for *studying English*
   >   a ball—for *playing baseball*
   a. Hold up a cue for *park* and *eating*; say, "I'm in the park. I'm eating lunch." Give these cues to a student; ask: "Where are you?" and "What are you doing?"
   b. Use these two cues (either visuals or a combination of visuals and objects) to practice all the other pronouns:
   >   Where am I? What am I doing?
   >   Where is _____? What is he/she doing?
   >   Where are _____ and _____? What are they doing?
   >   Where are you and _____? What are you doing?
   c. As you practice each pronoun, call on pairs of students to ask and answer whenever possible.

2. *Picture Card Game*
   Use SBS Picture Cards for *locations* and *on-going activities* that the students know. Place the cards in two separate piles, face down. Have a student take the top card from each pile; that student must use the location and activity shown on the cards to answer the questions, "Where are you?" and "What are you doing?" Have students take turns asking the questions. Give each student a turn at drawing cards. You can play this game in teams, keeping score for correct or incorrect answers.

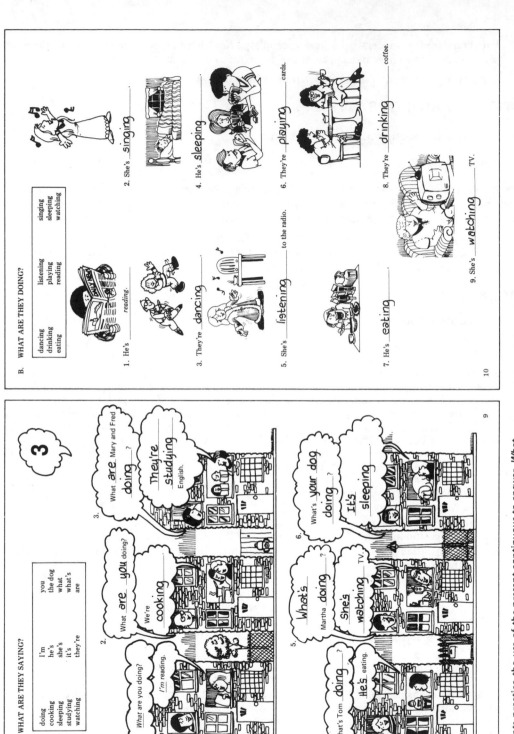

A. WHAT ARE THEY SAYING?

doing	I'm	you
cooking	he's	the dog
sleeping	she's	what
studying	it's	what's
watching	they're	are

1. *What are you doing?* I'm reading.

2. What are you doing? We're cooking

3. What are Mary and Fred doing? They're studying English.

4. What's Tom doing? He's eating.

5. What's Martha doing? She's watching TV.

6. What's your dog doing? It's sleeping

9

B. WHAT ARE THEY DOING?

dancing	listening	singing
drinking	playing	sleeping
eating	reading	watching

1. He's reading.

2. She's singing

3. They're dancing

4. He's sleeping

5. She's listening to the radio.

6. They're playing cards.

7. He's eating

8. They're drinking coffee.

9. She's watching TV.

10

Students practice the use of the present continuous to answer. *What doing?* (text pages 12-13)

Students practice the present continuous. (text pages 14-15)

28　CHAPTER THREE

11

Key to Exercise C
Read or play the tape.

1. The cat is in the garage.
2. What's she doing?
3. They're reading.
4. I'm playing the guitar.
5. He's listening.
6. You're in the cafeteria.
7. What are they doing?
8. He's in the classroom.

C. **LISTEN**

Listen to each sentence. Put a check (√) next to the appropriate picture.

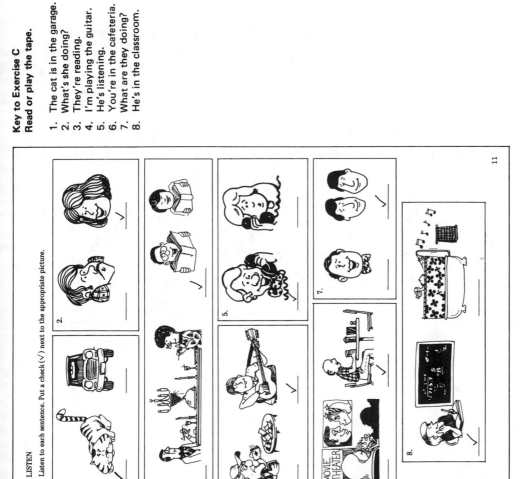

This listening exercise focuses on subject pronouns and new vocabulary in Chapter 3. (text pages 14-15)

D. WHAT'S THE QUESTION?

| Where is | he she it | ? | What's | he she it | doing? |

| Where are | you they | ? | What are | you they | doing? |

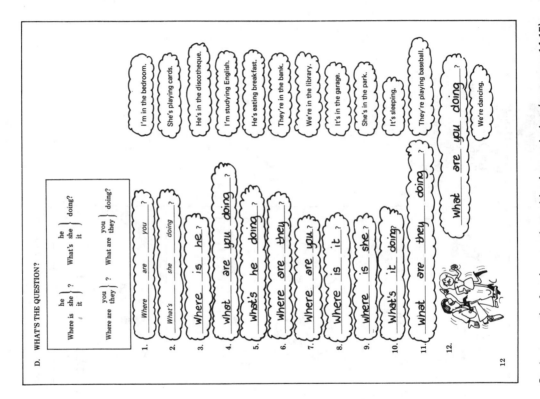

1. Where _____ are _____ you _____ ?   I'm in the bedroom.
2. What's _____ she _____ doing _____ ?   She's playing cards.
3. Where _____ is _____ he _____ ?   He's in the discotheque.
4. What _____ are _____ you _____ doing _____ ?   I'm studying English.
5. What's _____ he _____ doing _____ ?   He's eating breakfast.
6. Where _____ are _____ they _____ ?   They're in the bank.
7. Where _____ are _____ you _____ ?   We're in the library.
8. Where _____ is _____ it _____ ?   It's in the garage.
9. Where _____ is _____ she _____ ?   She's in the park.
10. What's _____ it _____ doing _____ ?   It's sleeping.
11. What _____ are _____ they _____ doing _____ ?   They're playing baseball.
12. What _____ are _____ you _____ doing _____ ?   We're dancing.

12

Students practice forming questions with *where* and *what*. (text pages 14-15)

Key to Exercise D
Read or play the tape.
Example: 547-2631

1. 695-3352
2. 496-8577
3. 724-0681
4. 358-9677
5. 582-4196

CHECK-UP TEST: Chapters 1-3

A. Answer the questions.

Ex. What's your telephone number?

My _telephone number is 236-2558_.

1. What's your name?

My _name is_ ( ).

2. What's your address?

My _address is_ ( ).

3. Where are you from?

I am from ( ).

B. Put a circle around the correct answer.

Ex. The car is in the [**garage** / hospital / supermarket].

1. Walter is eating [restaurant / coffee / **breakfast**].

2. Where's Tom? [**He's** / You're / She's] in the bedroom.

3. The monkey is in the [bank / post office / **zoo**].

4. Where are you? [They're / **We're** / He's] in the living room.

5. Albert is in the library. He's [cooking / dancing / **reading**].

6. Miss Jackson is drinking [dining room / cafeteria / **coffee**].

7. Jane is playing [**cards** / car / yard].

C. Fill in the blanks.

Ex. They're _in_ the bedroom.

1. _Where_ are you? I'm in the yard.

2. What's Helen _doing_? She's sleeping.

3. Tom is _in_ the garage.

4. What's Miss Jones doing? _She's_ singing.

5. Where's the newspaper? _It's_ in the kitchen.

6. Walter _and_ Mary are in the bank.

7. She's _watching_ TV.

8. Bobby is _listening_ to the radio.

9. _What_ are Mr. and Mrs. Smith doing?

10. Where are you and Tom? _We're_ in the park.

D. Listen and write the number you hear.

Ex. 547-2 _6_ 31

1. 695-33 _5_ 2

2. 49 _6_ -8577

3. 7 _2_ 4-0681

4. 358-967 _7_

5. 582-41 _9_ 6

13

CHAPTER 4 OVERVIEW

TEXT PAGES 17-21

FOCUS

1. Short answers with the verb *to be: Yes, I am. Yes, they are.*
2. Possessive adjectives: *my, his, her, its, our, your, their*

COMMUNICATIVE SKILLS

1.   Asking for and giving information about people's activities:
    What are you doing?
    I'm fixing my sink.

2.   Asking whether someone is busy:
    Are you busy?
    Yes, I am.

3.   Indicating possession:
    my sink, his car, their homework

VOCABULARY

apartment	cleaning	her	my	teeth
bar	clothes	hi	our	their
bicycle	exercises	his	painting	washing
brushing	feeding	homework	parking lot	window
busy	fixing	its	room	your
children	hair	laundromat	sink	

LANGUAGE NOTES

1.   Some students have difficulty distinguishing *his* from *he's* and *watching* from *washing.*

2.   The homonyms *it's* and *its* are easily confused in writing.

3.   *Yes* can be pronounced *yuh* and *yeah* in informal speech.

CULTURE KEY

1. Traditional U.S. culture assigns household chores to women and repairs or outdoor jobs to men. The illustrations in this chapter reflect the fact that many people in the U.S. are breaking from these traditional patterns.

2. **Laundromat** (text page 21)
   In the U.S. many people take their laundry to a *laundromat*—a place where they pay to use machines to wash and dry their clothes.

FOCUS

1. Possessive adjectives.
2. Practice with the present continuous tense.

GETTING READY

1. Read the forms in the grammar box at the top of the page. Have students repeat after you.

2. Demonstrate the idea of possession: Point to your book and say, *my book*. Point to a male student's book and say, *his book*. Point to a female student's book and say, *her book*.

PRESENTING THE MODEL

There are 5 model conversations. **Introduce and practice each model before going on to the next.** For each model:

1. Have students look at the model illustration in the book or on the SBS Dialog Visual Card.

2. Set the scene: "People are talking on the telephone."

3. Present the model.

4. Full-Class Choral Repetition.

5. Ask students if they have any questions; check understanding of new vocabulary:

1st model:	*hi, fixing, my, sink*
2nd model:	*his*
3rd model:	*cleaning, her, room*
4th model:	*our, apartment*
5th model:	*children, doing, their, homework*

6. Group Choral Repetition.

7. Choral Conversation.

8. Call on one or two pairs of students to present the dialog.

   (For additional practice, do Choral Conversation in small groups or by rows.)

WORKBOOK

Students can now do page 14.

EXPANSION ACTIVITIES

1. *Practice With Students' Names*
    Have pairs of students practice the model conversations again. This time have students pretend to call other students on the telephone and use names of people in the class in place of those in the book.

2. *Practice With Visuals*
    Use visuals to practice *What _____ doing?* and answers with possessive adjectives. Use your own visuals or SBS Picture Cards 31-33 to represent: a broken sink, car, or TV. Hold a visual and say, "I'm fixing my *(sink/car/TV)*." Give the visual to a student and ask, "What are you doing?" Ask another student, "What's he/she doing?" Call on a pair of students to talk about the student holding the visual. Expand this activity so that students ask and answer many questions about broken objects, using the possessive adjectives. For added realism you can bring a wrench or other tool to class and give it to students along with the visual.

FOCUS

1. Yes/No Questions:	*Is Nancy busy?*
2. Short answers:	*Yes, she is.*
3. Present continuous tense:	*She's washing her car.*

GETTING READY

1. Have students listen and repeat as you read the short answers in the grammar box at the top of the page.

2. Review contractions with the verb *to be*. Say the full form and have students give the contracted form.

PRESENTING THE MODEL

1. Have students look at the model illustration in the book or on the SBS Dialog Visual Card.

2. Set the scene: "People are talking on the telephone."

3. Present the model.

4. Full-Class Choral Repetition.

5. Ask students if they have any questions; check understanding of new vocabulary: *busy, washing—hair.*

6. Group Choral Repetition.

7. Choral Conversation.

8. Call on one or two pairs of students to present the dialog.

   (For additional practice, do Choral Conversation in small groups or by rows.)

SIDE BY SIDE EXERCISES

Examples:

1. A. Is Nancy busy?
   B. Yes, she is.
      She's washing her car.
		2. A. Is Ted busy?
		   B. Yes, he is.
		      He's feeding his dog.	

3. A. Are you busy?
   B. Yes, we are.
      We're cleaning our yard.
		4. A. Are Mr. and Mrs. Jones busy?
		   B. Yes, they are.
		      They're painting their kitchen.	

1. **Exercise 1:** Call on two students to present the dialog. Then do Choral Repetition and Choral Conversation Practice.

2. **Exercise 2:** Introduce the new word: *feeding.* Same as above.

3. **Exercises 3-14:**

New vocabulary:	4. *painting*	6. *exercises*	7. *bicycle*	9. *windows*
	11. *clothes*	14. *brushing–teeth*		

   Either Full-Class Practice or Pair Practice.

4. **Culture Note:**
   Many of these exercises can be a springboard for a discussion of men's and women's responsibilities in the home. (See CHAPTER OVERVIEW, Culture Key)

OPTIONAL WRITING PRACTICE

Have students write exercises 1, 4, 5, 7, 8, 11, 12 for homework.

WORKBOOK

Students can now do pages 15, 16, 17.

EXPANSION ACTIVITIES

1. *Practice With Word Cards*

   a. Make word cards for:

car	apartment	exercises	TV
dog	bicycle	teeth	garage
yard	clothes	windows	hair
kitchen	homework	cat	

   b. Create a conversation according to the model:
      A. Are you busy?
      B. Yes, I am.
      A. What are you doing?
      B. I'm _____.

   Each student must answer using an appropriate verb (such as *cleaning* or *fixing*) and the object on the card. For example, for the card *bicycle* a student can answer: "I'm washing my bicycle" or "I'm fixing my bicycle."

   c. You can also practice other pronouns. For example,
      A. Is _____ busy?
      B. Yes (he/she) is.
      A. What's (he/she) doing?
      B. (He's/She's) _____.

2. *Practice With Visuals*
   Use your own visuals or SBS Picture Cards 31-41 to review the conversations on text pages 19-20.

ON YOUR OWN

FOCUS

> Review of: present continuous tense and possessive adjectives.

The illustration for this exercise shows people in various places around town involved in different activities. Students use the model conversation at the bottom of the page to talk about the illustration.

PRESENTING THE MODEL

1. Have students look at the model illustration in the book or on the SBS Dialog Visual Card.
2. Introduce the new words: *parking lot, bar, laundromat.*
3. Present the model.
4. Full-Class Choral Repetition.
5. Ask students if they have any questions; check understanding of new vocabulary.
6. Group Choral Repetition.
7. Choral Conversation.
8. Call on one or two pairs of students to present the dialog.

SIDE BY SIDE EXERCISES

Examples:

> A. Where's Mr. Nathan?
> B. He's in the park.
> A. What's he doing?
> B. He's reading the newspaper.
>
> A. Where's Bobby Davis?
> B. He's in the library.
> A. What's he doing?
> B. He's studying.
>   or
> He's reading.
>   or
> He's doing his homework.

Call on pairs of students to ask and answer questions about the people in the illustration.

For the [?] location, next to the bar, students can choose any vocabulary to answer the question.

This exercise can be done as either Full-Class Practice or Pair Practice. You can also assign it as written homework.

WORKBOOK

Students can now do page 18.

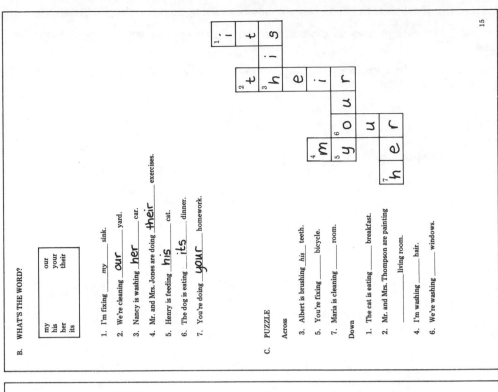

A. ON THE PHONE

what	her	my	cleaning	children
what's	his	our	doing	homework
are		their	fixing	sink

1. Hi! _What_ are you doing? I'm fixing _my_ sink.

2. What's Bob _doing_? He's fixing _his_ car.

3. _What's_ Mary doing? She's cleaning _her_ room.

4. _What_ _are_ you doing? We're _cleaning_ _our_ apartment.

5. What are your _children_ _doing_? They're doing _their_ _homework_.

Students practice possessive adjectives. Also, there is a review of the present continuous. (text page 18)

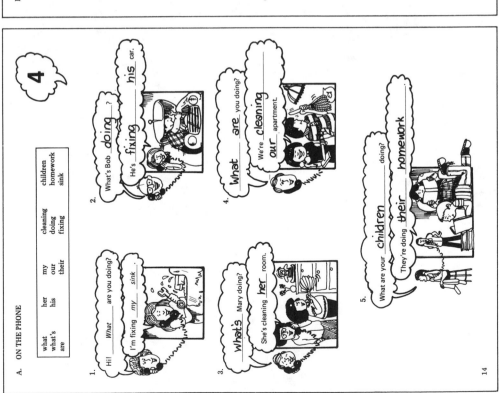

B. WHAT'S THE WORD?

my	our
his	your
her	their
its	

1. I'm fixing _my_ sink.
2. We're cleaning _our_ yard.
3. Nancy is washing _her_ car.
4. Mr. and Mrs. Jones are doing _their_ exercises.
5. Henry is feeding _his_ cat.
6. The dog is eating _its_ dinner.
7. You're doing _your_ homework.

C. PUZZLE

Across

3. Albert is brushing _his_ teeth.
5. You're fixing _____ bicycle.
7. Maria is cleaning _____ room.

Down

1. The cat is eating _____ breakfast.
2. Mr. and Mrs. Thompson are painting _____ living room.
4. I'm washing _____ hair.
6. We're washing _____ windows.

Students have further practice with possessives. (text pages 19-20)

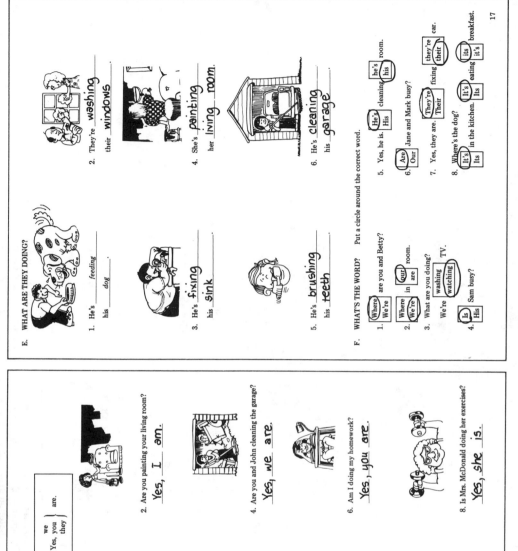

D. SHORT ANSWERS

Yes, I am.	Yes,	he she it	is.
		Yes, we you they	are.

1. Is Peggy fixing her car?
   Yes , *she* is.

2. Are you painting your living room?
   Yes, I *am.*

3. Are your children cooking breakfast?
   Yes, they *are.*

4. Are you and John cleaning the garage?
   Yes, we *are.*

5. Is Michael feeding his cat?
   Yes, he *is.*

6. Am I doing my homework?
   Yes, you *are.*

7. Are Carol and Dan washing their clothes?
   Yes, they *are.*

8. Is Mrs. McDonald doing her exercises?
   Yes, she *is.*

16

E. WHAT ARE THEY DOING?

1. He's *feeding*
   his *dog* .

2. They're *washing*
   their *windows* .

3. He's *fixing*
   his *sink* .

4. She's *painting*
   her *living room* .

5. He's *brushing*
   his *teeth* .

6. He's *cleaning*
   his *garage* .

F. WHAT'S THE WORD? Put a circle around the correct word.

1. (Where) / We're are you and Betty?

2. Where / We're in Our / (are) room.

3. What are you doing? We're washing / watching TV.

4. Is / His Sam busy?

5. Yes, he is. He's / His cleaning his / (His) room.

6. Are / Our Jane and Mark busy?

7. Yes, they are. They're fixing they're / their car.

8. Where's the dog? It's / Its in the kitchen. Its / It's eating its / it's breakfast.

17

Students give short answers to questions in the present continuous. Also, students review vocabulary of the chapter. (text pages 19-20)

Students practice the vocabulary of activities at home. In Exercise F, students must discriminate between words that look and sound similar. (text pages 19-20)

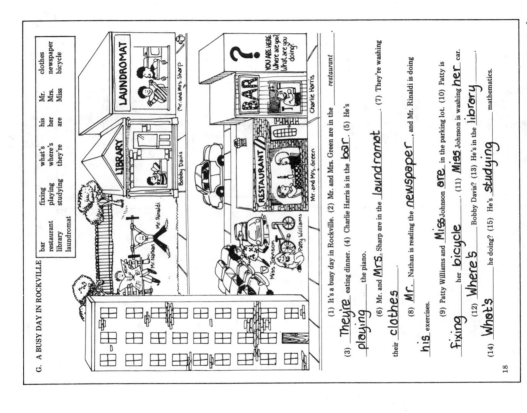

G. A BUSY DAY IN ROCKVILLE

bar	fixing	what's	his	Mr.	clothes
restaurant	playing	where's	her	Mrs.	newspaper
library	studying	they're	are	Miss	bicycle
laundromat					

(1) It's a busy day in Rockville. (2) Mr. and Mrs. Green are in the _restaurant_. (3) They're playing the piano. (4) Charlie Harris is in the _bar_. (5) He's (6) Mr. and Mrs. Sharp are in the _laundromat_. (7) They're washing their _clothes_. (8) Mr. Nathan is reading the _newspaper_, and Mr. Rinaldi is doing his exercises. (9) Patty Williams and Miss Johnson _are_ in the parking lot. (10) Patty is fixing her _bicycle_. (11) Miss Johnson is washing her car. (12) Where's Bobby Davis? (13) He's in the _library_. (14) What's he doing? (15) He's _studying_ mathematics.

18

Exercise G is a fill-in drill which reviews the vocabulary and structures of Chapter 4. Students can do this for homework or you can do this exercise as a dictation in class. (text page 21)

TEACHER'S NOTES

CHAPTER 5 OVERVIEW

TEXT PAGES 23-30

FOCUS

1. Yes/No questions:	*Are you married?*
2. Short answers:	*No, I'm not.*
3. Adjectives:	*I'm single.*
4. Possessive nouns:	*Stanley's Restaurant*
	Henry's cat, Fred and Sally's dog

COMMUNICATIVE SKILLS

1. Asking for and giving information about people and things:
    Tell me about your boss. Is he old?
    No, he isn't. He's young.

    Tell me about your new car. Is it large?
    No, it isn't. It's small.

2. Expressing regret:
    I'm sorry to hear that.

3. Talking about the weather:
    How's the weather?
    It's sunny.

VOCABULARY

beautiful	large	quiet	cloudy
big	little	rich	cold
cheap	loud	short	cool
difficult	married	single	hot
easy	new	small	raining
expensive	noisy	tall	snowing
fat	old	thin	sunny
handsome	poor	ugly	warm
heavy	pretty	young	

aren't	genius	neighbors	teacher
ask	having a good time	no	telephone call
boss	here	not	tell me about
brother	Hi, _____. This is _____.	on vacation	terrible
calling	house	or	today
champagne	How's the weather?	questions	weather
chapter	I'm sorry to hear that.	Santa Claus	
city	isn't	sister	
	long-distance	tea	

LANGUAGE NOTES

Beautiful and *pretty* are commonly used to refer to women and things; *handsome* is commonly used for men.

CULTURE KEY

Santa Claus (text page 27) is a legendary man who is traditionally associated with Christmas celebrations (December 25th) in the U.S. Children believe he lives in the North Pole and brings Christmas gifts to their homes every year.

FOCUS

1. Yes/No questions with the verb *to be*.
2. Questions with *or*.
3. Possessive nouns: *Albert's*

GETTING READY

1. Introduce possessive nouns:
   a. Point to a few students and name some of their possessions. Have students repeat after you. For example,

      "Jane"   "Bob"
      "Jane's pencil"   "Bob's pen"

   b. Write the possessive forms on the board. For example,
      Jane's pencil   *Joe's book*

2. Demonstrate the idea of opposites:
   a. Draw and label 2 stick figures on the board:

   Say, "Bob is *tall*."
   "Bill is *short*."

   Have students repeat.

   b. Draw 2 more stick figures on the board:

   Say, "Herman is *heavy*."
   "David is *thin*."

   Have students repeat.

PRESENTING THE MODEL

1. Have students look at the model illustration in the book or on the SBS Dialog Visual Card.
2. Set the scene: "Two people are talking about Bob and Bill."
3. Present the model.
4. Full-Class Choral Repetition.
5. Ask students if they have any questions; check understanding of new vocabulary: *tall, short, or.*
6. Group Choral Repetition.
7. Choral Conversation.
8. Call on one or two pairs of students to present the dialog.

   (For additional practice, do Choral Conversation in small groups or by rows.)

SIDE BY SIDE EXERCISES

Examples:

1.	A.	Is Alice young or old?	2.	A.	Is Margaret young or old?
	B.	She's young.		B.	She's old.
5.	A.	Is Herman's car new or old?	6.	A.	Is David's car new or old?
	B.	It's new.		B.	It's old.

1. **Exercises 1 and 2**: Introduce the new words: *young, old*. Call on two students to present each dialog. Then do Choral Repetition and Choral Conversation Practice.

2. **Exercises 3 and 4**: Introduce the new words: *heavy, fat, thin*. Same as above.

3. **Exercises 5-22**:

> **New vocabulary:**   5-6. *new, old*   7-8. *beautiful, pretty, ugly*
> 9-10. *handsome, ugly*   11-12. *rich, poor*   13-14. *big, little, house*
> 15-16. *noisy, quiet, neighbors*   17-18. *expensive, cheap, champagne, tea*
> 19-20. *married, single*   21-22. *easy, difficult, questions*

Either Full-Class Practice or Pair Practice.

OPTIONAL WRITING PRACTICE

Have students write exercises 1, 2, 3, 4, 13, 14, 15, 16 for homework.

WORKBOOK

Students can now do page 19.

EXPANSION ACTIVITIES

1. *Practice With Visuals*
   You can review the structures and vocabulary on text pages 24-25 using visuals of opposite adjectives. Use your own visuals, stick figures on the board, or SBS Picture Cards 42-50.
   a. Point to visuals of a tall person and a short person. Ask, "Is he/she tall or short?" Students answer. "He's/She's tall" or "He's/She's short."
   b. Practice other adjectives this way.
   c. Give visuals to students or have students point to visuals; have them ask each other questions.

2. *Picture Story*
   Review the structures and vocabulary by telling a story using the board.

   a. Draw a fat man.
      Say: "Herman is heavy."
             "He's young."

   b. Draw a house.
      Say: "His house is old."
             "It's large."

   c. Draw a car.
      Say: "His car is new."
             "It's expensive."

   d. Have students tell you about Herman using the pictures as cues. You can also ask students *or* questions, such as "Is Herman thin or heavy?" Students can ask each other questions about Herman.

   Another Picture Story:

   a. "Helen is tall."
      "She's beautiful."

   b. "Her apartment building is big."
      "Her neighbors are noisy."

   c. "Her bicycle is old."

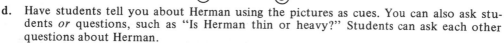

TEXT PAGES 26-27

FOCUS

> Yes/No questions with *to be* and negative short answers:
> *Are you married?*   *Is he tall?*
> *No, I'm not.*   *No, he isn't.*

GETTING READY

Write these structures on the board and have students repeat after you: (Read from left to right.)

Am I tall?	Yes, I am.	No, I'm not.
Is he tall?	Yes, he is.	No, he isn't.
Is she tall?	Yes, she is.	No, she isn't.
Are we tall?	Yes, we are.	No, we aren't.
Are you tall?	Yes, you are.	No, you aren't.
Are they tall?	Yes, they are.	No, they aren't.

PRESENTING THE MODEL

There are 3 model conversations. **Introduce and practice each model before going on to the next.** For each model:

1. Have students look at the model illustration in the book or on the SBS Dialog Visual Card.
2. Set the scene: "Two people are talking."
3. Present the model.
4. Full-Class Choral Repetition.
5. Ask students if they have any questions; check understanding of new vocabulary: *tell me about.*
6. Group Choral Repetition.
7. Choral Conversation.
8. Call on one or two pairs of students to present the dialog.
   (For additional practice, do Choral Conversation in small groups or by rows.)

SIDE BY SIDE EXERCISES

Examples:

> 1. A. Tell me about your brother. Is he tall?
>   B. No, he isn't. He's short.
> 2. A. Tell me about your sister. Is she single?
>   B. No, she isn't. She's married.

1. **Exercise 1:** Introduce the new word: *brother.* Call on two students to present the dialog. Then do Choral Repetition and Choral Conversation Practice.
2. **Exercise 2:** Introduce the new word: *sister.* Same as above.
3. **Exercises 3-10:**

> **New vocabulary:**   4. *boss*   9. *questions, book*   10. *Santa Claus*

Either Full-Class Practice or Pair Practice.

OPTIONAL WRITING PRACTICE

Have students write exercises 2, 4, 5, 6, 9 for homework.

WORKBOOK

Students can now do pages 20, 21, 22.

EXPANSION ACTIVITIES

1. **Sentence Game**
   Use the words in the grammar boxes at the top of text page 26 to have students make as many new sentences as possible. For example,
   Am I tall?
   I am tall./I'm tall.
   I'm not tall.
   Here are some alternative ways to set up the game:
   a. Students can work individually, in pairs, or in small groups.
   b. Students can write the sentences or say them. (One student could write them on the board.)
   c. Students can limit themselves to only the words at the top of text page 26 or they can use additional verbs (cooking, studying...), additional adjectives (thin, rich...), and additional prepositional phrases (in the kitchen, in the restaurant...).

2. **Practice With Visuals**
   Use visuals of opposite adjectives for people and things:
   a. Point to a visual and say, "Tell me about _____." For example,
      "Tell me about Bill."   "Tell me about your house."
      ("He's thin.")   ("It's large.")
      Suggestion: when you refer to a visual of a person, give that person a name.
   b. Have students ask each other Yes/No questions about visuals. For example,
      "Is he tall?"   "Is he short?"
      ("No, he isn't. He's short.")   ("Yes, he is.")

3. **Students Talk About Themselves**
   Write these words on the board:

brother	boss	cat	young	cheap	quiet	single
sister	apartment	dog	new	fat	noisy	married
neighbors	house	car	rich	thin	beautiful	big
			old	expensive	handsome	
			poor	loud	ugly	

Practice according to the pattern:

A. Tell me about your *(car)*.
   Is *(it old)*?
B. Yes, *(it is)*.
   or
   No, *(it isn't)*. *(It's new)*.

This can be done as Full-Class Practice or Pair Practice.

If Pair Practice, have students report back to the class. For example,
   "Bill's car is new."
   "His house is old."
   "His dog is little."

TEXT PAGE 28 (TOP) THE WEATHER

GETTING READY

1. Teach the numbers 10-100. See the suggestions for teaching numbers on page 4 of this *Teacher's Guide*. These numbers are given on text page xii of SIDE BY SIDE Book 1 A.

2. Contrast difficult numbers. Put this list on the board:

A	B
13	30
14	40
15	50
16	60
17	70
18	80
19	90

Listening Practice: Say a number from column A or column B. Have students indicate the correct column by saying or writing *A* or *B*.

Pronunciation Practice: Have students say a number from column A or B. Other students indicate which is the correct column.

WORKBOOK

Students can now do pages 23, 24.

PRESENTING THE MODEL

There are 8 weather expressions. Practice each one before going on to the next. (Note the use of thermometers to indicate *hot, warm, cool,* and *cold.*)

1. Have students listen as you read from the book or play the tape.

2. Have students repeat after you chorally and individually.

3. Practice conversationally by asking students, "How's the weather?" Students answer, "It's sunny." chorally and individually.

4. Call on pairs of students to ask each other.

5. Practice the other weather expressions this way.

6. When students have learned and practiced all the vocabulary, ask, "How's the weather today?"

WORKBOOK

Students can now do page 25.

EXPANSION ACTIVITIES

1. *Practice With Visuals*

    Use your own visuals or SBS Picture Cards 51-58 to review weather vocabulary.

    a. Point to visuals one by one and ask, "How's the weather?" Have students answer chorally and/or individually, "It's _____."

    b. Have students point to visuals and ask each other, "How's the weather?"

2. *Talk About the Weather*

    a. Ask students about the weather in different regions of your country or nearby countries: "How's the weather in _____ today?" "Is it sunny?"

    b. Say the following temperatures in Fahrenheit and Centigrade/Celsius. Have students tell you if they are *hot, cold, warm,* or *cool.*

0°F	40°F	50°F
90°F	20°C	0°C

ON YOUR OWN

PRESENTING THE MODEL

1. Have students look at the model illustration in the book or on the SBS Dialog Visual Card.

2. Set the scene: "Jim is on vacation in Miami, Florida. He's calling his friend Jack on the telephone. Jim is very upset."

3. With books closed, have students listen as you present the model or play the tape one or more times.

4. Full-Class Choral Repetition.

5. Have students open their books and look at the dialog. Ask students if they have any questions and check understanding of new vocabulary:

    long-distance telephone call, Hi, _____, This is _____ calling, on vacation, having a good time, having a terrible time, here, I'm sorry to hear that.

6. Group Choral Repetition.

7. Choral Conversation.

8. Call on one or two pairs of students to present the dialog.

9. Pair Practice: Have students practice the model in pairs as you walk around the room listening and helping.

SIDE BY SIDE EXERCISES

The skeletal dialog on text page 29 is the same as the one on text page 28 with key words left out. Students use the dialog as a guide for the exercises that follow. In these exercises Student A pretends to be on vacation and is calling Student B. You can add realism to the dialog by bringing a telephone to class or by having each student pretend to hold a telephone receiver to his or her ear.

Examples:

A. Hi, *(name)*. This is *(name)*. I'm calling from Switzerland.
B. From Switzerland? What are you doing in Switzerland?
A. I'm on vacation.
B. How's the weather in Switzerland? Is it cool?
A. No, it isn't. It's warm.
B. Is it snowing?
A. No, it isn't. It's raining.
B. Are you having a good time?
A. No, I'm not. I'm having a TERRIBLE time. The weather is TERRIBLE here.
B. I'm sorry to hear that.

1. Do exercises 1 and 2 in class. Either Full-Class Practice or Pair Practice.

2. Assign Exercise 3 for homework. Have students write a dialog using *weather* vocabulary about any vacation place they know. Allow students, if they wish, to expand the dialog with their own words and ideas. Have students present their dialogs in the next class.

CLASSROOM DRAMA: *YOU'RE A GENIUS*

This exercise enables students to practice short answers such as *Yes, I am.* and *No, he isn't.* in a playful context—one in which a teacher and students are contradicting each other. Note that short answers are often used for emphatic disagreement as in this *classroom drama.*

1. Review the short answers in the grammar boxes at the top of the page. Have students repeat after you chorally.

2. Have students listen and follow along in the text as you read the dialog or play the tape one or more times.

3. Check understanding of the new words: *genius, ask, teacher.*

4. Act out the *drama* with two of your most outgoing and playful students. You take the part of the teacher.

5. Have several groups of students act it out.

You can *activate* this dialog at any future time by complimenting a student with, "You're a genius!"

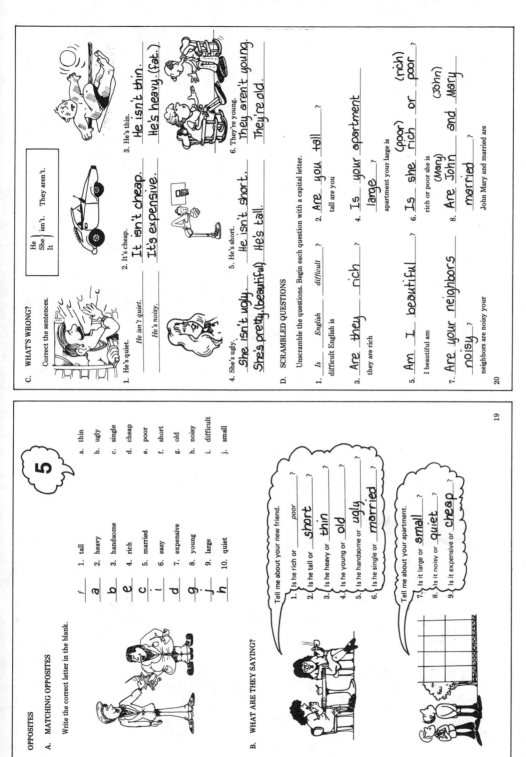

OPPOSITES

A. MATCHING OPPOSITES

Write the correct letter in the blank.

f	1. tall	a.	thin
a	2. heavy	b.	ugly
b	3. handsome	c.	single
e	4. rich	d.	cheap
c	5. married	e.	poor
i	6. easy	f.	short
d	7. expensive	g.	old
g	8. young	h.	noisy
j	9. large	i.	difficult
h	10. quiet	j.	small

B. WHAT ARE THEY SAYING?

Tell me about your new friend.

1. Is he rich or _poor_ ?
2. Is he tall or _short_ ?
3. Is he heavy or _thin_ ?
4. Is he young or _old_ ?
5. Is he handsome or _ugly_ ?
6. Is he single or _married_ ?

Tell me about your apartment.

7. Is it large or _small_ ?
8. Is it noisy or _quiet_ ?
9. Is it expensive or _cheap_ ?

19

C. WHAT'S WRONG?

Correct the sentences.

He / She / It isn't.   They aren't.

1. He's quiet. _He isn't quiet._ _He's noisy._
2. It's cheap. _It isn't cheap._ _It's expensive._
3. He's thin. _He isn't thin._ _He's heavy._ (fat.)
4. She's ugly. _She isn't ugly._ _She's pretty._ (beautiful)
5. He's short. _He isn't short._ _He's tall._
6. They're young. _They aren't young._ _They're old._

D. SCRAMBLED QUESTIONS

Unscramble the questions. Begin each question with a capital letter.

1. _Is_ _English_ _difficult_ ?
   difficult English is
2. _Are_ _you_ _tall_ ?
   tall are you
3. _Are_ _they_ _rich_ ?
   they are rich
4. _Is_ _your_ _apartment_ _large_ ?
   apartment your large is
5. _Am_ _I_ _beautiful_ ?
   I beautiful am
6. _Is_ _she_ _rich_ _or_ _poor_ ? (poor)(rich)
   rich or poor she is   (Mary)(John)
7. _Are_ _your_ _neighbors_ _noisy_ ?
   neighbors are noisy your
8. _Are_ _John_ _and_ _Mary_ _married_ ? (John)(Mary)
   John Mary and married are

20

Students practice writing adjectives. (text pages 24-25)

Students practice forming positive and negative sentences and questions with the verb *to be*. (text pages 26-27).

E. MARGARET'S PHOTOGRAPHS

Label the photographs.

bicycle	cat	house
boss	dog	piano
car	guitar	sink

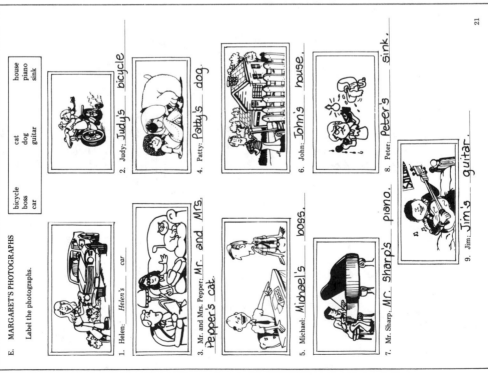

1. Helen: Helen's _car_
2. Judy: Judy's _bicycle_
3. Mr. and Mrs. Pepper: _Mr. and Mrs. Pepper's cat._
4. Patty: _Patty's dog._
5. Michael: _Michael's boss._
6. John: _John's house._
7. Mr. Sharp: _Mr. Sharp's piano._
8. Peter: _Peter's sink._
9. Jim: _Jim's guitar._

21

F. WHAT'S THE WORD?

| his | their |
| her | its |

1. (John's) _His_ sister is married.
2. (Judy's) _Her_ apartment is small.
3. (Fred and Sally's) _Their_ dog is noisy.
4. (Miss Green's) _Her_ car is new.
5. (Mr. and Mrs. Brown's) _Their_ restaurant is cheap.
6. (Sam's) _His_ neighbors are quiet.
7. (Barbara's) _Her_ brother is handsome.
8. (Mr. Larson's) _His_ cat is ugly.
9. (The dog's) _Its_ name is Fido.

Yes,	I	am.		No,	I'm	not.
	he, she, it	is.			he, she, it	isn't.
	we, you, they	are.			we, you, they	aren't.

G. MEET FRED MCQUEEN

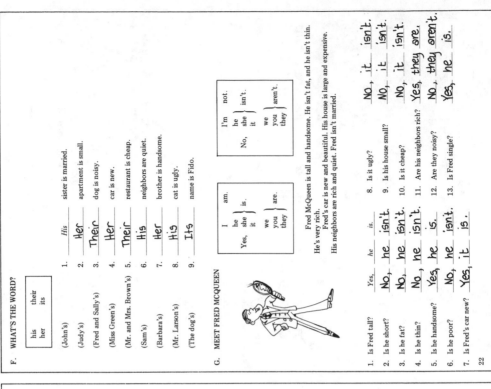

Fred McQueen is tall and handsome. He isn't fat, and he isn't thin. He's very rich. Fred's car is new and beautiful. His house is large and expensive. His neighbors are rich and quiet. Fred isn't married.

1. Is Fred tall?   _Yes, he is._
2. Is he short?   _No, he isn't._
3. Is he fat?   _No, he isn't._
4. Is he thin?   _No, he isn't._
5. Is he handsome?   _Yes, he is._
6. Is he poor?   _No, he isn't._
7. Is Fred's car new?   _Yes, it is._
8. Is it ugly?   _No, it isn't._
9. Is his house small? _No, it isn't._
10. Is it cheap?   _No, it isn't._
11. Are his neighbors rich? _Yes, they are._
12. Are they noisy?   _No, they aren't._
13. Is Fred single?   _Yes, he is._

22

In Exercise F, students change possessive nouns to possessive adjectives.
In Exercise G, students read a short story, then practice writing short answers with the verb *to be*. (text page 26-27)

Students practice forming possessive nouns. (text pages 26-27)

H. WRITING CHECKS   Complete the checks with the correct information.

0	zero
1	one
2	two
3	three
4	four
5	five
6	six
7	seven
8	eight
9	nine
10	ten
11	eleven
12	twelve
13	thirteen
14	fourteen
15	fifteen
16	sixteen
17	seventeen
18	eighteen
19	nineteen
20	twenty
21	twenty-one
22	twenty-two
23	twenty-three
24	twenty-four
25	twenty-five
26	twenty-six
27	twenty-seven
28	twenty-eight
29	twenty-nine
30	thirty
40	forty
50	fifty
60	sixty
70	seventy
80	eighty
90	ninety
100	one hundred

1.
June 17, 19 _82_
PAY TO THE ORDER OF _Johnson's Supermarket_ $ _36.00_
Thirty-six and 00/100 DOLLARS
CENTRAL BANK OHIO
Peter Nathan

2.
February 5, 19 _83_
PAY TO THE ORDER OF _City Hospital_ $ _99.00_
and 00/100 DOLLARS
CENTRAL BANK OHIO
Nancy Harris

3.
January 10, 19 _83_
PAY TO THE ORDER OF _Wilson's Supermarket_ $ _48.00_
and 0/100 DOLLARS
CENTRAL BANK OHIO
Albert Franklin

4.
19 ____
PAY TO THE ORDER OF ____ $ ____
____ DOLLARS
CENTRAL BANK OHIO

5.
19 ____
PAY TO THE ORDER OF ____ $ ____
____ DOLLARS
CENTRAL BANK OHIO

23

**Students practice writing numbers by writing checks. (text page 28)
In exercises 2 -3, students fill in just the numbers; in exercises 4-5, students write the entire check.**

I.   LISTEN

Listen to the addresses of buildings. Fill in the correct numbers on the buildings.

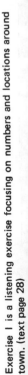

Key to Exercise I
Read or play the tape.

1.   The movie theater is at **14** Main Street.
2.   The cafeteria is at **19** Main Street.
3.   The hospital is at **22** Main Street.
4.   The library is at **27** Main Street.
5.   The post office is at **28** Main Street.
6.   The laundromat is at **31** Main Street.
7.   The zoo is at **54** Central Street.
8.   The supermarket is at **59** Central Street.
9.   The restaurant is at **62** Central Street.
10. The bank is at **65** Central Street.
11. The bar is at **73** Central Street.

Exercise I is a listening exercise focusing on numbers and locations around town. (text page 28)

Students practice writing weather expressions and then listening to and writing temperatures in Fahrenheit and Celsius. (text page 28)

Note: In Exercise J, students must use capital letters at the beginning of the answers and periods at the end.

Key to Exercise K
Read or play the tape.

1. In Moscow, it's 34° F/1° C.
2. In Cairo, it's 86° F/30° C.
3. In Caracas, it's 93° F/34° C.
4. In San Francisco, it's 72° F/22° C.
5. In Paris, it's 41° F/5° C.
6. In Athens, it's 68° F/20° C.
7. In Tokyo, it's 57° F/14° C.
8. In Rio de Janeiro, it's 98° F/37° C.

J. THE WEATHER

| it's sunny | it's warm | it's cold | it's raining |
| it's cloudy | it's cool | it's hot | it's snowing |

Tokyo 100°F/38°C   Madrid 70°F/21°C   London 50°F/10°C   Boston 32°F/0°C

San Juan   Mexico City   Hong Kong   Warsaw

1. How's the weather in Tokyo? _It's_ _sunny._
2. How's the weather in London? _It's_ _raining._
3. How's the weather in Mexico City? _It's_ _warm._
4. How's the weather in Warsaw? _It's_ _cold._
5. How's the weather in Hong Kong? _It's_ _cool._
6. How's the weather in Madrid? _It's_ _cloudy._
7. How's the weather in San Juan? _It's_ _hot._
8. How's the weather in Boston? _It's_ _snowing._
9. How's the weather in your city? _____

K. LISTEN

Listen to the temperature in Fahrenheit and Celsius. Write the numbers you hear.

1. Moscow _34°_ F/ _1°_ C
2. Cairo _86°_ F/ _30°_ C
3. Caracas _93°_ F/ _34°_ C
4. San Francisco _72°_ F/ _22°_ C
5. Paris _41°_ F/ _5°_ C
6. Athens _68°_ F/ _20°_ C
7. Tokyo _57°_ F/ _14°_ C
8. Rio de Janeiro _98°_ F/ _37°_ C

25

CHAPTER 6 OVERVIEW

6

TEXT PAGES 31-34

FOCUS

1. Review of *to be* and present continuous tense: *Who is he?*
   What's his name?
   Where is he?
   What's he doing?

2. Introduction of prepositions: *in front of, at, on.*

COMMUNICATIVE SKILLS

1. Asking for and giving information about location and activities.

2. Talking about members of one's family.

VOCABULARY

at	in front of	aunt
beach	on	brother-in-law
bed	photograph	cousin
bench	sitting	daughter
birds	soccer	father
birthday party	sofa	grandfather
crying	standing	grandmother
Eiffel Tower	Statue of Liberty	husband
favorite	swimming	mother
fireplace	Washington Monument	sister-in-law
friend	wedding	son
having dinner	who	uncle
		wife

LANGUAGE NOTES

The word *aunt* has two accepted pronunciations: [ænt] and [ant].

CULTURE KEY

1. **The Eiffel Tower** (model conversation) is a well-known landmark in Paris, France.

2. **The Statue of Liberty** (text page 32) is in New York City harbor. It is a symbol of welcome to immigrants to the U.S.

3. **The Washington Monument** (text page 34) is a famous landmark in Washington, D.C., the U.S. capital. It is dedicated to the first president of the U.S., George Washington.

GETTING READY

Introduce the vocabulary for family members. Write the words on the board and have students repeat after you:

father	husband	son	brother	grandfather
mother	wife	daughter	sister	grandmother

PRESENTING THE MODEL

1. Have students look at the model illustration in the book or on the SBS Dialog Visual Card.

2. Set the scene: "A man is talking about one of his favorite photographs."

3. Present the model.

4. Full-Class Choral Repetition.

5. Ask students if they have any questions; check understanding of new vocabulary: *favorite, photograph(s), who, Paris, standing, in front of, Eiffel Tower.*

6. Group Choral Repetition.

7. Choral Conversation.

8. Call on one or two pairs of students to present the dialog.

   (For additional practice, do Choral Conversation in small group or by rows.)

SIDE BY SIDE EXERCISES

Examples:

1.	A.	Who is she?	2.	A.	Who is he?
	B.	She's my wife.		B.	He's my son.
	A.	What's her name?		A.	What's his name?
	B.	Her name is _____.*		B.	His name is _____.*
	A.	Where is she?†		A.	Where is he?†
	B.	She's in New York.		B.	He's in the park.
	A.	What's she doing?		A.	What's he doing?
	B.	She's standing in front of the Statue of Liberty.		B.	He's playing soccer.

*Students can use any name they wish.
†The words *in this photograph* in the fifth line of the model are in parentheses to indicate that students do not need to use them in practicing the exercises. The words are there to clarify the question.

1. **Exercise 1:** Introduce the new words: *wife, Statue of Liberty.* Call on two students to present the dialog. Then do Choral Repetition and Choral Conversation Practice.

2. **Exercise 2:** Introduce the new words: *son, soccer.* Same as above.

3. Exercises 3-14:

> **New vocabulary:** 3. *daughter* 4. *at the beach, swimming* 5. *husband, fireplace*
> 6. *mother, sofa* 7. *aunt, uncle, having dinner* 8. *cousin*
> 9. *grandmother, grandfather, wedding, crying* 10. *sitting, on a bench, birds*
> 11. *friend, bed* 12. *brother-in-law, Washington Monument*
> 13. *sister-in-law* 14. *birthday party*

Either Full-Class Practice or Pair Practice.

OPTIONAL WRITING PRACTICE

Have students write exercises 6, 8, 9, 14 for homework.

ON YOUR OWN

Have students bring in photographs from home. Bring several of your own. (Note that large photographs with a limited number of people in them work best.)

1. Have students ask you questions about your photograph, using the questions from the SIDE BY SIDE exercises.

2. Have students show their photographs to the class. Have other students ask questions about the photographs.

WORKBOOK

Students can now do pages 26, 27, 28.

6

A. OUR FAMILY

husband
wife

Ted and Jane are married.

Ted   Jane

1. Ted is Jane's   husband .
2. Jane is Ted's   wife .

father
mother
son
daughter
brother
sister

Ted   Jane
Bobby   Nancy

3. Bobby is Ted and Jane's   son .
4. Nancy is their   daughter .
5. Jane is Bobby and Nancy's   mother .
6. Ted is their   father .
7. Bobby is Nancy's   brother .
8. Nancy is Bobby's   sister .

26

grandfather
grandmother
grandson
granddaughter

Fred   Hilda
Bobby   Nancy

9. Hilda is Bobby and Nancy's   grandmother .
10. Fred is their   grandfather .
11. Bobby is Fred and Hilda's   grandson .
12. Nancy is their   granddaughter .

B. WHERE ARE THEY? WHAT ARE THEY DOING?

sitting standing swimming	in front of	beach bench

1. They're   sitting   on the sofa.
2. He's at the   beach .
3. She's   swimming .
4. She's   standing .
5. They're   in front of   the fireplace.
6. She's sitting on the   bench .

C. OUT OF PLACE   Circle the word that doesn't belong.

1. car: garage, fixing, (cooking,) washing
2. beach: swimming, (sink,) hot, sunny
3. park: birds, bench, (bank,) soccer
4. living room: fireplace, television, (sink,) sofa
5. birthday party: (sleeping,) singing, dancing, eating
6. family: daughter, mother, (neighbor,) son
7. apartment: living room, bedroom, kitchen, (classroom)
8. weather: cloudy, (short,) raining, cool
9. eating: breakfast, (newspaper,) lunch, dinner
10. drinking: tea, (birds,) champagne, coffee
11. playing: guitar, baseball, piano, (car)
12. Bob: (pretty,) rich, tall, handsome
13. house: expensive, quiet, (fat,) beautiful
14. children: young, noisy, small, (cloudy)

27

Students practice vocabulary for family members. (text pages 32-34)

In Exercise B, students practice new vocabulary from Chapter 6. In Exercise C, students review vocabulary of Chapters 1-6. They circle the word that doesn't belong. (text pages 32-34)

D. A LETTER FROM NEW YORK CITY

Friday, June 10

Dear Walter,

We're on vacation in New York City, and we're having a good time. New York is beautiful. The weather is hot and sunny. It's 80°F.

Today my mother and father are at the Statue of Liberty. My sister Julie is swimming at the beach, and my brother Henry and his friends are playing soccer in the park.

I'm in Aunt Martha and Uncle Charlie's apartment. It's large and beautiful. Aunt Martha is cooking a big dinner, and Uncle Charlie is singing and playing the guitar.

Cousin Tommy and Cousin Gloria aren't on vacation. They're doing their homework in front of the TV. Their homework isn't easy.

How is the weather in Los Angeles? Is it hot?
What are you and your family doing? Are you busy studying?

See you soon,
Cousin Michael

28

E. Answer the questions in complete sentences.

1. How's the weather in New York City? _It's hot and sunny._

2. What's the temperature in New York? _It's 80°F._

3. Where are Michael's mother and father? _They're at the Statue of Liberty._

4. Who is Julie? _She's Michael's sister._

5. Where is she? _She's at the beach._

6. What's she doing? _She's swimming._

7. Who is Henry? _He's Michael's brother._

8. Where is he? _He's in the park._

9. What's he doing? _He's playing soccer._

10. Where is Michael? _He's in Aunt Martha and Uncle Charlie's apartment._

11. What's Aunt Martha doing? _She's cooking a big dinner._

12. Who is Charlie? _He's Michael's uncle._

13. What's he doing? _He's singing and playing the guitar._

14. Where are Tommy and Gloria? _They're in front of the TV._

15. What are they doing? _They're doing their homework._

16. Who is Walter? _He's Michael's cousin._

Students read a letter and then answer questions. For oral practice, have students read the letter aloud in class. (text pages 32-34)

Dictation (25 words)

Read or play the tape three times. Students listen the first time, write what they hear the second time, and correct their work the third time. Have students write this dictation on a separate piece of paper.

John isn't in his apartment. He's doing his homework in the library. John's sister and brother are busy. They're washing their car in the yard.

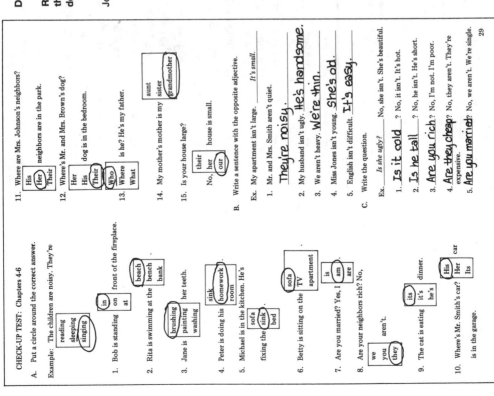

CHECK-UP TEST: Chapters 4-6

A. Put a circle around the correct answer.

Example: The children are noisy. They're [reading / sleeping / **singing**]

1. Bob is standing [**in** / on / at] front of the fireplace.
2. Rita is swimming at the [beach / **bench** / bank] in the park.
3. Jane is [**brushing** / painting / washing] her teeth.
4. Peter is doing his [sink / **homework** / room] .
5. Michael is in the kitchen. He's fixing the [sofa / **sink** / bed] .
6. Betty is sitting on the [**sofa** / TV / apartment] .
7. Are you married? Yes, I [is / **am** / are] .
8. Are your neighbors rich? No, [we / you / **they**] aren't.
9. The cat is eating [**its** / it's / he's] dinner.
10. Where's Mr. Smith's car? [**His** / Her / Its] car is in the garage.
11. Where are Mrs. Johnson's neighbors? [His / **Her** / Their] neighbors are in the park.
12. Where's Mr. and Mrs. Brown's dog? [Her / His / **Their**] dog is in the bedroom.
13. [Who / **Where** / What] is he? He's my father.
14. My mother's mother is my [aunt / sister / **grandmother**] .
15. Is your house large? No, [their / her / **our**] house is small.

B. Write a sentence with the opposite adjective.

Ex. My apartment isn't large. _It's small._

1. Mr. and Mrs. Smith aren't quiet. _They're noisy._
2. My husband isn't ugly. _He's handsome._
3. We aren't heavy. _We're thin._
4. Miss Jones isn't young. _She's old._
5. English isn't difficult. _It's easy._

C. Write the question.

Ex. _Is she ugly?_ No, she isn't. She's beautiful.

1. _Is it cold_ ? No, it isn't. It's hot.
2. _Is he tall_ ? No, he isn't. He's short.
3. _Are you rich_ ? No, I'm not. I'm poor.
4. _Are they cheap_ ? No, they aren't. They're expensive.
5. _Are you married_ ? No, we aren't. We're single.

29

CHAPTER 7 OVERVIEW

TEXT PAGES 35-40

FOCUS

> 1. Prepositions:
> *around the corner from*   *next to*
> *between*   *on _____ Street*
> *across from*
>
> 2. Introduction to singular and plural nouns with:
> *There is _____.*   *There are _____.*

COMMUNICATIVE SKILLS

1. Asking about features of an apartment:
   How many rooms are there in the apartment?
   Is there a superintendent in the building?

2. Asking for and giving information about location of buildings:
   Where's the school?
   It's between the library and the park.

3. Describing one's neighborhood.

4. Getting a person's attention:
   Excuse me. Is there a laundromat in this neighborhood?

VOCABULARY

across from	department store	next to
around the corner from	doctor's office	on _____ Street
avenue	drugstore	police station
bakery	excuse me	school
barber shop	fire station	street
between	gas station	student
bus station	how many	there are
church	in this neighborhood	there is (there's)
clinic	nearby	train station

ON YOUR OWN (text page 40)

broken	elevator	mice	stove
building	fire escape	pets	superintendent
bus stop	floors	problems	tenant
closets	holes	radiator	TV antenna
cockroaches	landlord	refrigerator	walls
	mailbox	roof	

LANGUAGE NOTES

Many students have difficulty with the final *s* sound in the contraction *there's*, as in *There's a laundromat on Main Street.*

CULTURE KEY

Looking For An Apartment (text page 40)
Many people in the U.S. rent their apartments or houses.

A person who rents an apartment is called the *tenant*.

A person who owns the apartment building is called the *landlord*.

A person who the landlord hires to live in the building and take care of it is called the *superintendent*.

FOCUS

> Prepositions: *next to, across from, between, around the corner from*

GETTING READY

1. Locations in the community. Use your own visuals, SBS Picture Cards 9-17, 59, or refer to the illustrations on text pages 9 and 20.
   Review: *restaurant, bank, post office, supermarket, movie theater, park, library, hospital*
   Introduce: *school*
2. Introduce the prepositions *next to, across from* and *between*. Use your students' names and locations in the classroom and say:
   a. (Bill) is *next to* (Mary).
   b. (Mary) is *across from* (Joe).
   c. (Jane) is *between* (Ted) and (Bob).

PRESENTING THE MODEL

There are 4 model conversations. **Introduce and practice each one before going on to the next.** For each model:
1. Have students look at the model illustration in the book or on the SBS Dialog Visual Card.
2. Set the scene: "Two people are talking."
3. Present the model.
4. Full-Class Choral Repetition.
5. Ask students if they have any questions; check understanding of vocabulary.
6. Group Choral Repetition.
7. Choral Conversation.
8. Call on one or two pairs of students to present the dialog.
   (For more practice, do Choral Conversation in small groups or by rows.)
9. Give students extra pronunciation practice with the final [z] sound in *where's*.
   a. Have students repeat, "Where's the restaurant?" Then cue substitutions, such as:
      park: "Where's the park?"
      church: "Where's the church?"
   b. Practice the final [s] sound in *it's*. Have students repeat, "It's next to the bank." Cue substitutions as above.

SIDE BY SIDE EXERCISES

Examples:

1.	A. Where's the park?		2.	A. Where's the bank?
	B. It's next to the hospital.			B. It's across from the supermarket.

1. **Exercise 1:** Call on two students to present the dialog. Then do Choral Repetition and Choral Conversation Practice.
2. **Exercise 2:** Same as above.

3. **Exercises 3-8:**

> **New vocabulary:**   3. *church*   6. *police station, fire station*   7. *bus station*
> 8. *train station*
>
> Use your own visuals, SBS Picture Cards 60-64, or the illustrations in the book
> to introduce these new words.

Either Full-Class Practice or Pair Practice.

OPTIONAL WRITING PRACTICE

Have students write exercises 2, 3, 6, 7, 8 for homework.

WORKBOOK

Students can now do page 30.

EXPANSION ACTIVITIES

1. *Create a Street Scene With Your Students*
    Give visuals of the places in the community to 10 students. Use your own visuals, word
    cards, or SBS Picture Cards. Have students hold these visuals and stand in front of the class
    in 2 lines, to form 2 intersecting streets. For example,

    Call on pairs of students to ask and answer *Where* questions about the locations in this *street
    scene.* For example,
    "Where's the bank?"
    "It's across from the church."
2. *Create a Street Scene on the Board*
    Create a simple street map showing 2 intersecting streets on the board. You can tape visuals
    of locations to the board or you can write place names. For example,

    Call on pairs of students to ask and answer *Where* questions about these locations as in 2
    above.
3. *Game: What's The Building?* (Listening Activity)
    Use the illustrations for exercises 1-8 on text page 36. (Students should ignore the questions,
    and just look at the illustrations.) Have students look at these illustrations as you describe
    the location of different buildings. For example, "It's across from the library." Students
    then tell which building fits the location you described. Students can compete individually
    or in teams.

Teacher:	*Student:*
"It's around the corner from the bus station."	the fire station
"It's across from the restaurant."	the library
"It's between the library and the bank."	the church
"It's next to the post office."	the train station
	or the bus station
"It's next to the park."	the hospital
"It's around the corner from the bank."	the movie theater
"It's across from the bank."	the supermarket
"It's next to the police station."	the fire station

FOCUS

> There is/There's:
> *There's a bank on Main Street.*
> *Is there a bank on Main Street?*
> *Yes, there is.*

GETTING READY

Teach these abbreviations:

1. *St.* for Street, as in *Main St.* and *State St.*

2. *Ave.* for Avenue, as in *Central Ave.*

PRESENTING THE MODEL

1. Have students look at the model illustration in the book or on the SBS Dialog Visual Card.

2. Set the scene: "A man and a woman are talking. The man is in a new neighborhood. He's looking for a laundromat."

3. Present the model.

4. Full-Class Choral Repetition.

5. Ask students if they have questions; check understanding of new vocabulary: *excuse me, there is, there's, in this neighborhood.*

6. Group Choral Repetition.

7. Choral Conversation.

8. Call on one or two pairs of students to present the dialog.

   (For additional practice, do Choral Conversation in small groups or by rows.)

9. Point out the alternative expression *nearby*, given below the model. Have students practice the model with *nearby*.

SIDE BY SIDE EXERCISES

Examples:

> 1. A. Excuse me. Is there a post office in this neighborhood?*
>   B. Yes, there is. There's a post office on Main Street, across from the laundromat.
>
> *or *nearby*

> 2. A. Excuse me. Is there a bank in this neighborhood?*
>   B. Yes, there is. There's a bank on Central Avenue, around the corner from the post office.
>
> *or *nearby*

1. **Exercise 1**: Call on two students to present the dialog. Then do Choral Repetition and Choral Conversation Practice.

2. **Exercise 2**: Same as above.

3. **Exercises 3-8**:

> **New vocabulary**: 4. *gas station* 7. *drugstore*
>
> Use your own visuals, SBS Picture Cards 66-67 or the illustrations in the book to introduce these words.

Either Full-Class Practice or Pair Practice.

OPTIONAL WRITING PRACTICE

Have students write exercises 3, 4, 5, 6, 7 for homework.

WORKBOOK

Students can now do page 31.

EXPANSION ACTIVITIES

1. *Create a Street Scene*
   Create a simple street map on the board (as in the Expansion Activities for text page 36). Tape visuals or write names on the board to show various locations on two intersecting streets. Have pairs of students role play the model conversation. Student A pretends do be looking for an unfamiliar location; Student B tells where it is.

2. *Pronunciation Practice*
   Have students practice saying these words with [s] sounds. The [s] sound may be at the beginning, middle or end of the word.

snowing	station	school	its	what's
sleeping	state	studying	Paris	discotheque
supermarket	street	standing	fireplace	listening
address	statue	small	yes	singing
	store	sofa	sister	baseball
	Stanley's	sunny	Albert's	
	swimming		Alice	

ON YOUR OWN

In this exercise, students ask and answer questions about their own neighborhoods using the model conversation as a guide.

FOCUS

> Short answers with *there is:*
> *Yes, there is.*
> *No, there isn't.*

PRESENTING THE MODEL

1. Have students look at the model illustration in the book.
2. Set the scene: "A man and a woman are talking. The man is asking the woman about her neighborhood."
3. Present the model.
4. Ask students if they have any questions; check understanding of vocabulary.
5. Group Choral Repetition.
6. Choral Conversation.
7. Call on one or two pairs of students to present the dialog.

    (For additional practice, do Choral Conversation in small groups or by rows.)

SIDE BY SIDE EXERCISES

> **New vocabulary:**
> *bakery, barber shop, beauty parlor, clinic, department store, doctor's office*
>
> Use your own visuals or SBS Picture Cards 69-74 to introduce these new words.

Have students work independently in pairs, asking and answering questions about each other's neighborhoods. (They can draw simple maps of their neighborhoods if they wish.)

WORKBOOK

Students can now do page 32.

FOCUS

---

1. Review of: *Is there a _____?*
    Yes, there is.
    No, there isn't.

2. Introduction of: *Are there any _____s?*
    Yes, there are.
    No, there aren't.

3. Introduction of: *How many _____s are there?*
    There are _____.

ON YOUR OWN

GETTING READY

1.   Review:

   Is there a _____?
   Yes, there is.
   No, there isn't.

   a.   For an object which is in the classroom, say:
      "Is there a *(window)* in the room?"
      "Yes, there is."
      For an object which is not in the classroom, say:
      "Is there a *(TV)* in the room?"
      "No, there isn't."
      Do Choral Repetition and Choral Conversation Practice.
   b.   Ask about other objects.

2.   Briefly introduce the final s for plural nouns. (Plural nouns are taught more fully in Chapter 8.) Have students listen and repeat after you:
      "one student—two students"
      "one window—two windows"

3.   Introduce:

   Are there any _____?
   Yes, there are.
   No, there aren't.

   a.   Present these models, and then do Choral Repetition and Choral Conversation Practice:
      "Are there any *(students)* in the room?"
      "Yes, there are."

      "Are there any *(dogs)* in the room?"
      "No, there aren't."
   b.   Ask about other objects.

4. Introduce:

> How many _____s are there?
> There are _____ _____s.
> There's one _____.

    a. Present this model and then do Choral Repetition and Choral Conversation Practice:
        "How many *(windows)* are there in the room?"
        "There are *(4)* windows."

    b. Ask other questions with *how many*, using people and objects in the room. Then have students ask each other questions.

5. Introduce these new words. Use your own visuals, or have students look at the illustration in the book or on the SBS Dialog Visual Card.

building	roof	floors
stove	radiator	closets
refrigerator	every room	landlord
superintendent	mailbox	tenant
elevator	bus stop	mice
fire escape	pets	cockroaches
TV antenna		broken windows
		holes in the walls

ROLE PLAY—*LOOKING FOR AN APARTMENT*

One student pretends to be looking for an apartment. Another pretends to be the landlord of the apartment building on text page 39. (In the U.S. it's very common for a prospective tenant to ask for information about the apartment and the building.)

1. **Questions 1-15**: Call on a pair of students to ask and answer each question. The student who asks the question is the prospective *tenant*. The one who answers is the *landlord*; that student answers by looking at the illustration on text page 39 or the SBS Dialog Visual Card.

2. **Ask The Landlord Some Other Questions**
   Now you pretend to be the landlord and have the class think of additional questions to ask you about the building and the neighborhood. For example, students can ask:

   "Is there a laundromat in the neighborhood?"
   "Is there a school nearby?"
   "How many supermarkets are there?"
   "Are there any parks nearby?"

3. **Are There Any Problems In The Apartment?**
   The "prospective tenant" is looking for more information and asks various tenants in the building. Call on pairs of students to ask and answer questions 16-19. Encourage students to think of additional questions to ask the tenant.

WORKBOOK

Students can now do pages 33, 34, 35.

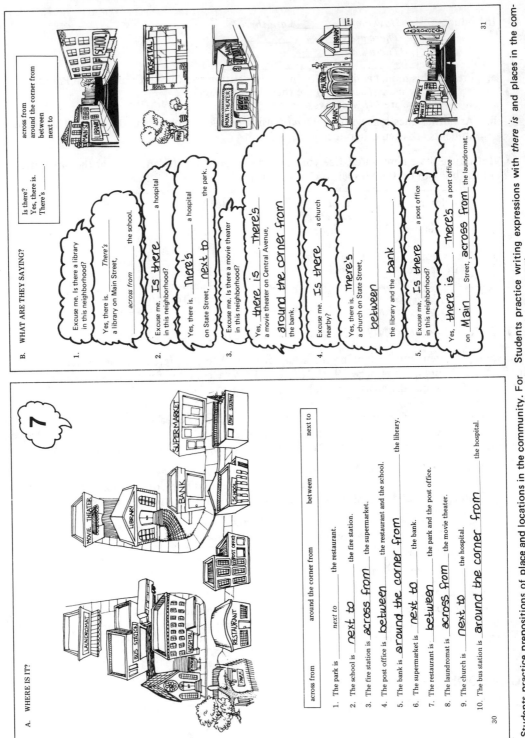

A. WHERE IS IT?

7

across from   around the corner from   between   next to

1. The park is _next to_ the restaurant.
2. The school is _next to_ the fire station.
3. The fire station is _across from_ the supermarket.
4. The post office is _between_ the restaurant and the school.
5. The bank is _around the corner from_ the library.
6. The supermarket is _next to_ the bank.
7. The restaurant is _between_ the park and the post office.
8. The laundromat is _across from_ the movie theater.
9. The church is _next to_ the hospital.
10. The bus station is _around the corner from_ the hospital.

30

B. WHAT ARE THEY SAYING?

Is there?	across from
Yes, there is.	around the corner from
There's _____.	between
	next to

1. Excuse me. Is there a library in this neighborhood?

   Yes, there is. _There's_ a library on Main Street, _across from_ the school.

2. _Is there_ a hospital in this neighborhood?

   Yes, there is. _There's_ a hospital on State Street, _next to_ the park.

3. Excuse me. Is there a movie theater in this neighborhood?

   Yes, _there is. There's_ a movie theater on Central Avenue, _around the corner from_ the bank.

4. Excuse me. _Is there_ a church nearby?

   Yes, _there's_ a church on State Street, _between_ the library and the _bank_.

5. Excuse me. _Is there_ a post office in this neighborhood?

   Yes, _there is. There's_ a post office on _Main_ Street, _across from_ the laundromat.

31

Students practice prepositions of place and locations in the community. For oral practice, have students ask and answer *where* questions about locations

Students practice writing expressions with *there is* and places in the community. (text page 37)

78   CHAPTER SEVEN

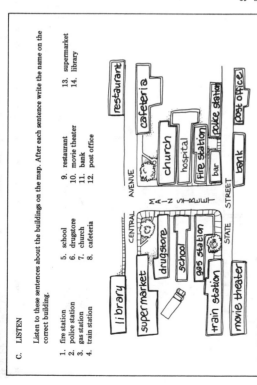

C. LISTEN

Listen to these sentences about the buildings on the map. After each sentence write the name on the correct building.

1. fire station
2. police station
3. gas station
4. train station
5. school
6. drugstore
7. church
8. cafeteria
9. restaurant
10. movie theater
11. bank
12. post office
13. supermarket
14. library

D. YES OR NO

Look at the map and answer the questions.

| Yes, there is. |
| No, there isn't. |

1. Is there a gas station on Main Street?   *Yes, there is.*
2. Is there a movie theater across from the train station? _Yes, there is._
3. Is there a supermarket around the corner from the drugstore? _Yes, there is_
4. Is there a post office across from the library? _No, there isn't_
5. Is there a school between the church and the fire station? _No, there isn't._
6. Is there a bank across from the movie theater? _No, there isn't._
7. Is there a police station next to the bar? _Yes, there is._
8. Is there a restaurant on Central Avenue? _Yes, there is._
9. Is there a hospital between the church and the fire station? _Yes, there is._
10. Is there a church next to the bank? _No, there isn't._

32

1. There's a fire station between the hospital and the bar.
2. There's a police station next to the bar.
3. There's a gas station across from the fire station.
4. There's a train station around the corner from the gas station.
5. There's a school next to the gas station.
6. There's a drugstore next to the school.
7. There's a church across from the drugstore.
8. There's a cafeteria around the corner from the church.
9. There's a restaurant across from the cafeteria.
10. There's a movie theater across from the train station.
11. There's a bank across from the bar.
12. There's a post office next to the bank.
13. There's a supermarket around the corner from the drugstore.
14. There's a library across from the supermarket.

Students practice listening comprehension with *there's*, prepositions of place and locations in the community. In Exercise D, students practice writing short answers "Yes, there is," "No, there isn't."

You can practice this exercise orally in the following ways:

1. Have students ask and answer additional yes/no questions about locations on the map. (Example: "Is there a gas station next to the school?")
2. Have students ask and answer *where* questions about locations on the map. (Example: "Where's the hospital?" "It's next to the church.") (text page 38)

CHAPTER SEVEN   79

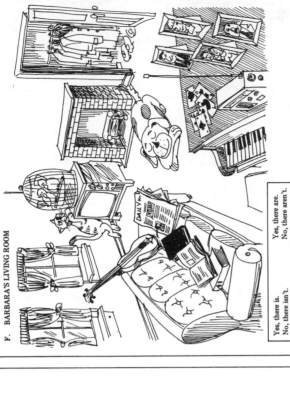

E. OUR APARTMENT BUILDING

broken	mice	roof
closet	pets	stove
fire escape	radiators	superintendent
mailbox		

1. There's a TV antenna on the _roof_.
2. There's a _stove_ in the kitchen across from the sink.
3. There are _radiators_ in the bedroom and living room. They're hot.
4. There's a _fire escape_ next to the bathroom.
5. There are two _pets_ in the building: a cat and a dog.
6. There aren't any clothes in the _closet_ in the bedroom.
7. There's a _mailbox_ between the building and the bus stop.
8. There are two _mice_ in the basement.
9. The _superintendent's_ apartment is in the basement.
10. There's a _broken_ window in the living room.

33

Students practice new vocabulary and sentences with *there is* and *there are*. (text pages 39-40)

F. BARBARA'S LIVING ROOM

Yes, there is.	Yes, there are.
No, there isn't.	No, there aren't.

1. Is there a TV in Barbara's living room? _Yes, there is._
2. Is there a fireplace in Barbara's living room? _Yes, there is._
3. Are there any windows? _Yes, there are._
4. Are there any books on the TV? _No, there aren't._
5. Are there any clothes in the closet? _Yes, there are._
6. Is there a dog in front of the fireplace? _Yes, there is._
7. Is there a cat in the closet? _No, there isn't._
8. Are there any photographs on the piano? _Yes, there are._
9. Are there any cards on the sofa? _No, there aren't._
10. Are there any pets in Barbara's living room? _Yes, there are._
11. Is there a closet next to the fireplace? _Yes, there is._

34

Students practice giving short answers to *Is there—? Are there—?* with prepositions. Students also answer questions that begin with *How many.* You can practice orally by having students look at the illustration and ask and answer questions about Barbara's Living Room. (text page 40)

12. Is there a newspaper in the closet? No, there isn't.
13. Is there a guitar on the sofa? Yes, there is.
14. How many books are there on the sofa? There are three books on the sofa.
15. How many photographs are there on the piano? There are four photographs on the piano.
16. How many pets are there in the room? There are four pets in the room.
17. How many cards are there on the piano? There are six cards on the piano.
18. How many windows are there in the room? There are two windows in the room.

G. LOOKING FOR AN APARTMENT

apt. = apartment	dinrm. = dining room	livrm. = living room
bath(s). = bathroom(s)	elev. = elevator	nr. = near
bdrm(s). = bedroom(s)	frpl(s). = fireplace(s)	rm(s). = room(s)
beaut. = beautiful	kit. = kitchen	schl. = school
bldg. = building	lge. = large	

DETROIT, quiet, sunny apt., kit., livrm., bath., 2 frpls., nr. bus , no children. $500. 492-5683.

1. The apartment is in _Detroit._
2. It's quiet and _sunny_.
3. There's a kitchen, a living room, a _bedroom_, and a _bathroom_.
4. There are two _fireplaces_ in the apartment.
5. There aren't any _children_ in the building.

BOSTON, sunny, lge. apt., kit., livrm., dinrm., 2 bdrms., bath., frpl., nr. schl., no pets. $800. 666-1700.

6. The apartment is in _Boston_.
7. It's sunny and _large_.
8. There are two _bedrooms_ in the apartment.
9. _There's_ a fireplace in the apartment.
10. There's a _school_ near the building.
11. There _aren't_ any pets in the building.

LOS ANGELES, beaut., new apt., kit., livrm., 3 bdrms., 2 baths., elev. in bldg. $600. 715-8362.

12. The apartment is in _Los Angeles_.
13. It's _beautiful_ and new.
14. _There_ _are_ three _bedrooms_ in the apartment.
15. There's an elevator in the _building_.

35

Students are introduced to some common abbreviations used in classified ads for apartments. (text page 40)

CHAPTER 8 OVERVIEW

TEXT PAGES 41-49

FOCUS

---

1. Singular and plural nouns:
   a book-books, a car-cars, a class-classes, an office-offices
2. Indefinite articles *a* and *an*.

COMMUNICATIVE SKILLS

1. Apologizing:
   I'm sorry. I think I made a mistake.

2. Excusing oneself:
   Excuse me. I think that's my jacket.

3. Identifying articles of clothing.

4. Identifying colors:
   These gloves are green.

5. Indicating possession:
   These aren't your gloves. These are my gloves.

6. Offering to help someone:
   May I help you?

VOCABULARY

black	pink	a/an		pen
blue	polka dot	a pair of		pencil
brown	purple	book		please
gold	red	but		popular
gray	silver	I'm sorry.		sure
green	striped	I think I made a mistake.		That's O.K.
orange	white	May I help you?		We all make mistakes.
	yellow			

belt	glasses	pants	stockings	child-children
blouse	gloves	pocketbook	suit	man-men
boots	hat	raincoat	sweater	mouse-mice
bracelet	jacket	shirt	tie	person-people
coat	mittens	shoes	umbrella	tooth-teeth
dress	necklace	skirt	watch	woman-women
earrings	pajamas	socks		

LANGUAGE NOTES

1. **Pronunciation of the plural ending:**

   a. When a noun ends in a voiceless consonant sound, the plural ending is pronounced [s]:

       [p] shops   [t] students   [k] books

   b. When a noun ends in a voiced consonant or a vowel sound, the plural ending is pronounced [z]:

       [b] jobs   [l] girls
       [d] yards   [r] mothers
       [g] dogs   [n] pens
       [v] gloves   [m] rooms

   c. When a noun ends in any of the following sounds, the plural ending is pronounced [iz], which forms an additional syllable on the end of the noun:

       [s] glasses   [š] dishes   [č] benches

       [z] exercises   [ž] garages   [ǰ] judges

2. **Indefinite articles** *a/an*:

   a. *a* before words beginning with consonant sounds:

       a book, a car

   b. *an* before words beginning with vowel sounds:

       an airport, an elevator

   c. *a* before *h*, when *h* is pronounced: a hole
   an before *h*, when *h* is silent: an honest man

CULTURE KEY

"Lost and Found" (text page 47)
Many restaurants, large stores, and other public buildings in the U.S. have *lost and found* departments where people may turn in and pick up lost items.

FOCUS

1. Articles of clothing.
2. Plural of regular nouns:
   a book-books, a car-cars, a class-classes
3. Irregular Plurals:
   a man-men, a woman-women
4. Indefinite articles: *a/an*

GETTING READY

Introduce the vocabulary on text page 42. Use the illustration in the book, the SBS Dialog Visual Card, your own visuals, or real articles of clothing.

1. Point to an article of clothing and say the new word several times. Whenever possible, also point to a student who is wearing that article of clothing.

2. Have students repeat the new word chorally and individually.

WORKBOOK

Students can now do pages 36 and 37 Exercise A.

SINGULAR/PLURAL (text page 43)

This exercise gives students practice saying and writing the regular plural nouns that are introduced on text page 42.

1. Give examples of singular and plural nouns by pointing out objects in the classroom. For example,
   a book- books, a window-windows

2. Introduce the 3 different pronunciations of the plural as they are shown on text page 43. Practice each final sound separately.
   a. Begin with the final [s] sound. Say the singular and plural form of each noun; then say the words again and have students repeat after you chorally and individually. Point out the articles *a* and *an*.
   b. Practice the words in the [z] column this way; then the words in the [iz] column.

3. Listening practice with books closed:
   a. Write on the board: ① ②
                           singular   plural
   Have your students listen as you read the nouns below. For each word, have students say "1" if they think the noun is singular, or "2" if they think the noun is plural:
   car, schools, banks, sock, class, classes,
   office, belts, book, umbrellas

b. Write on the board: ①   ②   ③

                                [s]   [z]   [iz]

Have students listen as you read the plural nouns at the top of text page 43 in mixed up order. For each noun have students say

"1" if they hear a final [s] sound;
"2" if they hear a final [z] sound;
"3" if they hear a final [iz] sound.

4. Practice forming plurals using the vocabulary on text page 42.

a. Make 3 columns on the board: [s] [z] [iz]

b. Say each noun on text page 42 and call on a student to give the plural form.

c. Then have the class tell you which of the 3 final sounds they hear. You write the singular and plural forms under the appropriate column on the board. Have students write these forms in the correct column on text page 43 or in their notebooks.

Answer key for text page 43

[s]	[z]	[iz]
hats	ties	glasses
shirts	shoes	watches
jackets	earrings	necklaces
belts	stockings	blouses
pants	gloves	dresses
socks	umbrellas	briefcases
bracelets	sweaters	
skirts	mittens	
coats		
pocketbooks		
suits		
raincoats		
boots		

5. Introduce irregular plurals.

Point out the irregular plural nouns at the bottom of text page 43. Say the singular and plural forms and have students repeat after you. Practice by saying the singular form and have students tell you the plural form and vice versa.

WORKBOOK

Students can now do pages 37 and 38 Exercise D.

EXPANSION ACTIVITY

Practice Singular/Plural

Point to articles of clothing that people in the class are wearing. Have one student tell you the name of that article of clothing. Have another student tell you the plural form of that word.

FOCUS

1. Singular and plural nouns (articles of clothing).
2. Colors.

GETTING READY

Teach the colors at the top of the page. Use visuals or real objects and clothing in the classroom. As you say each new word, have students listen and repeat chorally and individually.

PRESENTING THE MODEL

1. Have students look at the model illustration in the book or on the SBS Dialog Visual Card.

2. Set the scene: "A salesperson and a customer are talking in a department store."

3. Present the model.

4. Full-Class Choral Repetition.

5. Ask students if they have any questions; check understanding of new vocabulary: *May I help you? Yes, please, looking for, here's, nice, but, this, That's O.K., popular, this year.*

6. Group Choral Repetition.

7. Choral Conversation.

8. Call on one or two pairs of students to present the dialog.

   (For additional practice, do Choral Conversation in small groups or by rows.)

SIDE BY SIDE EXERCISES

   Examples:

1.	A. May I help you? B. Yes, please. I'm looking for a hat. A. Here's a nice hat. B. But this hat is GREEN! A. That's O.K. Green hats are very POPULAR this year.	2. A. May I help you? B. Yes, please. I'm looking for a blouse. A. Here's a nice blouse. B. But this blouse is ORANGE! A. That's O.K. Orange blouses are very POPULAR this year.

1. **Exercise 1:** Call on two students to present the dialog. Then do Choral Repetition and Choral Conversation Practice.

2. **Exercise 2:** Same as above.

3. **Exercises 3-8:**

> **New vocabulary:**   7. *polka dot*   8. *striped*

Either Full-Class Practice or Pair Practice.

OPTIONAL WRITING PRACTICE

Have students write exercises 2, 6, 8 for homework.

WORKBOOK

Students can now do page 38 Exercise E.

EXPANSION ACTIVITY

Role Play: "In the Department Store"
With books closed, have students role play a dialog based on the model conversation on text page 44. Put these words on the board as a guide for students:

> A. May I . . .?
> B. Yes, please. . .
> A. Here's. . .
> B. But. . .
> A. That's O.K. . . .

Speaker A is the *salesperson* and Speaker B is the *customer.* Make word cards or visuals of articles of clothing with unusual colors or patterns. Call on pairs of students to role play the dialog using one of these visuals or word cards.

FOCUS

> *A pair of* with articles of clothing.

GETTING READY

Introduce *a pair of* by pointing out examples in the classroom. For example,
> *a pair of pants*
> *a pair of shoes*
> *a pair of socks*

Have students repeat after you chorally and individually.

PRESENTING THE MODEL

1. Have students look at the model illustration in the book or on the SBS Dialog Visual Card.

2. Set the scene: "A salesperson and a customer are talking in a department store."

3. Present the model.

4. Full-Class Choral Repetition.

5. Ask students if they have any questions; check understanding of new vocabulary: *a pair of, these.*

6. Group Choral Repetition.

7. Choral Conversation.

8. Call on one or two pairs of students to present the dialog.

   (For additional practice, do Choral Conversation in small groups or by rows.)

SIDE BY SIDE EXERCISES

Examples:

1.	A. May I help you?	2.	A. May I help you?
	B. Yes, please. I'm looking for a pair of pants.		B. Yes, please. I'm looking for a pair of earrings.
	A. Here's a nice pair of pants.		A. Here's a nice pair of earrings.
	B. But these pants are PINK!		B. But these earrings are BLACK!
	A. That's O.K. Pink pants are very POPULAR this year.		A. That's O.K. Black earrings are very POPULAR this year.

1. **Exercise 1:** Call on two students to present the dialog. Then do Choral Repetition and Choral Conversation Practice.

2. **Exercise 2:** Same as above.

3. **Exercises 3-8:**

   > **New vocabulary:**   5. *pajamas*

   Either Full-Class Practice or Pair Practice.

OPTIONAL WRITING PRACTICE

Have students write exercises 1, 5, 7 for homework.

WORKBOOK

Students can now do page 39.

EXPANSION ACTIVITIES

1. *Talk About Students' Clothing*
   a. Teach the word *wearing*: tell students what you are wearing by saying, "I'm wearing _____."

      Then ask students, "What are you wearing?"

   b. Have students describe as much of their own clothing as possible by saying, "I'm wearing _____." For example,

      "I'm wearing a red shirt, brown pants, black shoes, and a silver watch."

2. Practice: *What's Your Favorite Color?*
   Ask students, "What's your favorite color?"
   Have them answer, "It's _____."
   Call on pairs of students to ask and answer.

3. *Practice Clothing With Magazine Pictures*
   Bring magazine pictures of people to class. Give the pictures to students and have them describe what the person or people are wearing. This exercise can be done orally or in writing. You can also call on pairs of students to ask and answer questions about a picture.

4. *Guessing Game*
   a. Describe the clothing of someone else in the class. Have students listen and guess who you are describing. For example,

      "She's wearing a green dress and a gold watch."
      "He's wearing yellow socks."

   b. Call on students to describe the clothing of someone in the class. Have the other students guess who it is.

5. *Chain Game*
   In this game, students practice all the vocabulary for clothing.
   a. You begin the game by saying:

      "I'm in the department store and I'm looking for a *(shirt)*."
      You can name any article of clothing you wish.

   b. Have each student take a turn in which he or she repeats what the person before has said *and* adds an article of clothing. For example,
      1) "I'm in the department store and I'm looking for a *(shirt)* and a *(pair of pants)*."
      2) "I'm in the department store and I'm looking for a *(shirt)*, *(a pair of pants)*, and *(a watch)*."

FOCUS

This – That – These – Those

GETTING READY

1. Introduce the word *this*.

   a. Hold up a book (or a pen or other object) and say, "THIS book."

   b. Give the book to several students; have each student repeat "THIS book" while holding the book.

2. Introduce the word *that*.

   a. Put the same book (used for *this*) some distance away from you and the students. Point to the book and say, "THAT book."

   b. Have students point to the book and repeat "THAT book" chorally and individually.

3. Introduce the words *these* and *those* the same way, using **several** books (or pens or other objects).

4. Put the following stick figures on the board to summarize the meanings of *this, that, these,* and *those*.

PRESENTING THE MODEL

There are 2 model conversations. **Introduce and practice each model separately.** For each model:

1. Have students look at the model illustration in the book or on the SBS Dialog Visual Card.

2. Set the scene: "Two people are talking."

3. Present the model.

4. Full-Class Choral Repetition.

5. Ask students if they have any questions; check understanding of new vocabulary: *this, that, I'm sorry. I think I made a mistake.*

6. Group Choral Repetition.

7. Choral Conversation.

8. Call on one or two pairs of students to present the dialog.

   (For additional practice, do Choral Conversation in small groups or by rows.)

SIDE BY SIDE EXERCISES

Examples:

1. A. Excuse me. I think that's my pen.
   B. This isn't YOUR pen. This is my pen.
   A. I'm sorry. I think I made a mistake.

2. A. Excuse me. I think those are my pencils.
   B. These aren't YOUR pencils. These are my pencils.
   A. I'm sorry. I think I made a mistake.

1. **Exercise 1**: Introduce the new word: *pen.* Call on two students to present the dialog. Then do Choral Repetition and Choral Conversation Practice.

2. **Exercise 2**: Introduce the new word: *book.* Same as above.

3. **Exercises 3-8**:

   New vocabulary: 3. *pencil*

   Either Full-Class Practice or Pair Practice.

OPTIONAL WRITING PRACTICE

Have students write exercises 1, 3, 7, 8 for homework.

WORKBOOK

Students can now do pages 40, 41.

EXPANSION ACTIVITY

Role Play: "I Think I Made a Mistake"
Review the model conversations; then close the books and act out the conversations using real object such as gloves, books, a handbag, or a wallet. Call on pairs of students to come to the front of the class. Give one student the object or objects; have the students act out the conversation.

ON YOUR OWN

PRESENTING THE MODEL

There are 2 model conversations. **Introduce and practice each model separately.** For each model:

1. Have students look at the model illustration in the book or on the SBS Dialog Visual Card.

2. Set the scene: "People are at the lost and found department."

3. Present the model.

4. Full-Class Choral Repetition.

5. Ask students if they have any questions; check understanding of new vocabulary:
   1st model: *sure*
   2nd model: *dirty, clean*

6. Group Choral Repetition.

7. Choral Conversation.

8. Call on one or two pairs of students to present the dialog.

   (For additional practice, do Choral Conversation in small groups or by rows.)

SIDE BY SIDE EXERCISES

In these exercises, students use colors or adjectives of their own choice.

   Examples:

1. A. Is THIS your watch?	2. A. Are THESE your glasses?
B. No, it isn't.	B. No, they aren't.
A. Are you sure?	A. Are you sure?
B. Yes, I'm sure. THAT watch is *(old)* and MY watch is *(new)*.	B. Yes, I'm sure. THOSE glasses are *(black)* and MY glasses are *(brown)*.

1. Exercises 1-5:

New vocabulary: 5. *little boy*

   Have pairs of students create dialogs based on the models. This can be done as Full-Class Practice or Pair Practice.

2. **Exercise 6**: Assign this exercise for homework. Have students create two dialogs based on the model using vocabulary of their choice, one dialog using *this* and *that* and the other using *these* and *those*. Encourage students to be creative and use the dictionary to look up new words. Have students present their dialogs orally in the next class.

WORKBOOK

Students can now do pages 42, 43.

EXPANSION ACTIVITIES

1. *Pronunciation Practice* [I] [i]
   The following groups of words have the sound [I] as in *this* and [i] as in *these*. Write some or all of these words on the board and have students practice saying these sounds.

[I] – "th<u>i</u>s"	[i] – "th<u>e</u>se"
s<u>i</u>ngle	sh<u>e</u>
s<u>i</u>t	h<u>e</u>
m<u>i</u>stake	sl<u>ee</u>ping
sw<u>i</u>m<u>i</u>ng	r<u>ea</u>ding
b<u>i</u>g	<u>ea</u>ting
<u>i</u>n	f<u>ee</u>ding
th<u>i</u>n	<u>ea</u>sy
k<u>i</u>tchen	cl<u>ea</u>ning
s<u>i</u>nk	t<u>ee</u>th
l<u>i</u>ving room	ch<u>ea</u>p
m<u>i</u>ss	b<u>ea</u>ch
b<u>u</u>sy	b<u>e</u>tw<u>ee</u>n
s<u>i</u>ster	
hosp<u>i</u>tal	
<u>i</u>t's	
Sm<u>i</u>th	

2. *Listening Practice:* [I] [i]

   Write on the board: ① ②

   it   eat

   Have students listen as you read the following words. For each word, have students say "1" if the word has the same sound as in *it*, or "2" if the word has the same sound as in *eat*.

   *big, miss, he, cheap, sister, beach, she, thin,
   sink, teeth, swimming, easy*

CLASSROOM DRAMA: *THIS/THAT*

1. Have students listen and follow along in the text as you read the classroom drama or play the tape one or more times.

2. Check understanding of new vocabulary: *Well, here. We all make mistakes.*

3. Act out the classroom drama as shown in the illustrations with a student. You read the part of *John* and have the student read the part of *Sally*. Begin by walking up to the student and taking his or her pen. Practice the drama as it is in the text. Hand the student different pens for *Arthur's pen* and *Mary's pen.*

4. Divide all the students into pairs and have the class practice the classroom drama independently. Encourage them to act out the drama as shown in the illustrations.

5. Have pairs of students role-play the classroom drama with their books closed. Students can use any classroom objects, such as pen, pencil, or book.

CLASSROOM DRAMA: *THESE/THOSE*

Introduce and practice this classroom drama the same way as on text page 48, substituting *books* for *pens.*

A.   WHAT ARE THEY WEARING?

belt	coat	jacket	raincoat	stocking
blouse	dress	mitten	shirt	suit
boot	earring	necklace	shoe	sweater
bracelet	glasses	pants	skirt	tie
briefcase	glove	pocketbook	sock	umbrella
	hat			watch

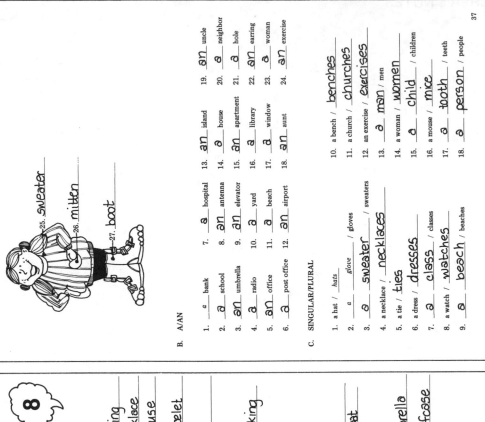

1. hat
2. glasses
3. shirt
4. tie
5. jacket
6. watch
7. belt
8. pants
9. sock
10. shoe
11. earring
12. necklace
13. blouse
14. bracelet
15. skirt
16. stocking
17. coat
18. glove
19. pocketbook
20. dress
21. suit
22. raincoat
23. umbrella
24. briefcase
25. sweater
26. mitten
27. boot

B.   A/AN

1. a bank	7. a hospital	13. an island	19. an uncle
2. a school	8. an antenna	14. a house	20. a neighbor
3. an umbrella	9. an elevator	15. an apartment	21. a hole
4. a radio	10. a yard	16. a library	22. an earring
5. an office	11. a beach	17. a window	23. a woman
6. a post office	12. an airport	18. an aunt	24. an exercise

C.   SINGULAR/PLURAL

1. a hat / hats	7. a class / classes	13. a man / men	
2. a glove / gloves	8. a watch / watches	14. a woman / women	
3. a sweater / sweaters	9. a beach / beaches	15. a child / children	
4. a necklace / necklaces	10. a bench / benches	16. a mouse / mice	
5. a tie / ties	11. a church / churches	17. a tooth / teeth	
6. a dress / dresses	12. an exercise / exercises	18. a person / people	

Students practice the indefinite articles *a* and *an* and singular and plural nouns. Note that in Exercise C the nouns in 13-18 have irregular plurals. (text page 42)

Students practice vocabulary for articles of clothing. (text page 42)

37

D. LISTEN

Listen to each word. Put a circle around the word you hear.

1. coat	(coats)	9. necklace	(necklaces)
2. car	(cars)	10. earring	(earrings)
3. (umbrella)	umbrellas	11. (belt)	belts
4. (exercise)	exercises	12. (watch)	watches
5. dog	(dogs)	13. bank	(banks)
6. (shoe)	shoes	14. house	(houses)
7. (dress)	dresses	15. jacket	(jackets)
8. restaurant	(restaurants)	16. (glove)	gloves

E. COLORS

Write sentences about yourself using colors.

red	orange	yellow	green	blue	purple
black	brown	pink	gray	white	gold
silver					

1. My house/apartment building is _____.
2. My bedroom is _____.
3. My kitchen is _____.
4. My classroom is _____.
5. My English book is _____.
6. My shoes are _____.
7. My socks/stockings are _____.
8. My coat is _____.
9. My hat is _____.
10. My teeth are _____.
11. My classroom is _____.
12. My _____ (is/are) _____.

RED
ORANGE
YELLOW
GREEN
BLUE
PURPLE

38

Key to Exercise D
Read or play the tape.

1. coats
2. cars
3. umbrella
4. exercise
5. dogs
6. shoe
7. dress
8. restaurants
9. necklaces
10. earrings
11. belt
12. watch
13. banks
14. houses
15. jackets
16. glove

In Exercise D, students practice listening for the final *s* in plural nouns. (text page 43)

In Exercise E, students practice vocabulary for colors. (text page 44)

F.   WHAT'S IN MR. AND MRS. JACKSON'S CLOSET?

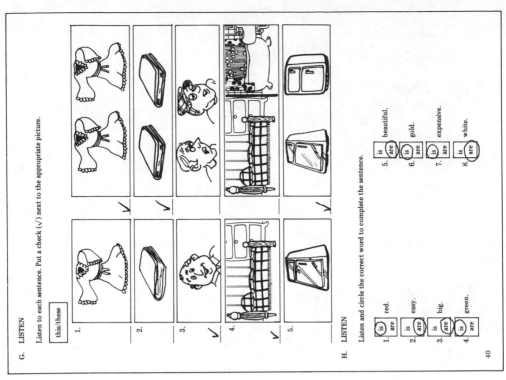

a hat
a raincoat
a briefcase
an umbrella

a pair of pajamas   two blouses
a pair of pants   two dresses
a pair of mittens   three pocketbooks
a pair of gloves   three belts
a pair of socks   four sweaters
a pair of shoes
a pair of boots

39

G.   LISTEN

Listen to each sentence. Put a check (√) next to the appropriate picture.

this/these

1.
2.
3.
4.
5.

H.   LISTEN

Listen and circle the correct word to complete the sentence.

1. is / are red.
2. is / are easy.
3. is / are big.
4. is / are green.
5. is / are beautiful.
6. is / are gold.
7. is / are expensive.
8. is / are white.

40

Students practice vocabulary for articles of clothing, the indefinite articles *a* and *an*, plural nouns, and the expression *a pair of*. (text page 45)

For Exercises G and H on page 98 above

In Exercise G, students listen for the difference between *this* and *these* and for the final *s* in plural nouns. Have students do Exercise G orally for pronunciation practice.

For additional oral practice with Exercise H, students can create their own sentences with *this* and *these.* For example, 1: *This book* is red. 2: *These questions* are easy. (text page 46)

Key to Exercise G
Read or play the tape.

1. I'm washing these dresses.
2. She's reading these books.
3. I'm looking for this man.
4. He's cleaning this room.
5. He's fixing these refrigerators.

Key to Exercise H
Read or play the tape.

1. This bicycle
2. These exercises
3. These apartments
4. This car
5. These women
6. This necklace
7. This house
8. These shirts

I. ALICE'S PHOTOGRAPH

this / these   that / those

Alice   Betty

Alice: _This_ is my favorite photograph. _This_ is my mother, and _these_ are my sisters.

Betty: _That_ 's a beautiful photograph. Is _that_ your brother?

Alice: Yes, it is, and _this_ is my uncle.

Betty: Are _those_ your cousins?

Alice: No, _these_ are my brother's friends.

Betty: Who are _those_ handsome men?

Alice: _These_ are my neighbors, and _this_ is my dog Rover.

Betty: No it isn't. _That_ 's your cat.

Alice: I'm sorry. I made a mistake. Where are my glasses?

41

Students practice *this, these, that,* and *those.* In this exercise, Alice always uses *this* and *these*; Betty always uses *that* and *those.* (text page 46)

J. THIS/THAT/THESE/THOSE

this	that
these	those

1. _This book is blue._ (blue)

2. *That book is red.* (red)

3. _These earrings are gold._ (gold)

4. _Those earrings are silver._ (silver)

5. _This bicycle is green._ (green)

6. _That bicycle is purple._ (purple)

7. _These pants are small._ (small)

8. _Those pants are big._ (big)

9. _This watch is cheap._ (cheap)

10. _That watch is expensive._ (expensive)

42

K. SINGULAR→PLURAL

Write the sentences in the plural.

1. This hat is red. _These hats are red._
2. That skirt is short. _Those skirts are short._
3. This watch is gold. _These watches are gold._
4. This necklace isn't expensive. _These necklaces aren't expensive._
5. That dress is beautiful. _Those dresses are beautiful._
6. This woman is rich. _These women are rich._
7. This is my child. _These are my children._
8. That isn't your pencil. _Those aren't your pencils._
9. Is that your glove? _Are those your gloves?_
10. This isn't my sock. _These aren't my socks._

L. PLURAL→SINGULAR

Write the sentences in the singular.

1. These bracelets are silver. *This bracelet is silver.*
2. Those exercises are easy. _That exercise is easy._
3. Are these your friends? _Is this your friend?_
4. Are those your books? _Is that your book?_
5. These are Sally's blouses. _This is Sally's blouse._
6. These men are my neighbors. _This man is my neighbor._
7. These aren't my mittens. _This isn't my mitten._
8. Those aren't my shoes. _That isn't my shoe._
9. Those churches are nearby. _That church is nearby._
10. Those are George's pets. _That's George's pet._

43

Students practice *this, these, that,* and *those* and singular and plural nouns. (text page 47)

Students practice *this, that, these,* and *those* and regular and irregular plural nouns. (text page 47)

CHECK-UP TEST: Chapters 7-8

A. Put a circle around the correct answer.

Ex. My teeth are [red / (white) / blue] .

1. Jane is wearing a pair of [dresses / blouses / (pants)] .

2. This [questions / (homework) / exercises] is easy.

3. [These / They / (There's)] a church next to the bank.

4. Is there a shirt on the bed? No, [they isn't / (there isn't) / there aren't] .

5. [What / Who / (How)] many rooms are there in the house?

6. There's a [woman / umbrella / (earring)] on the sofa.

7. There aren't any [window / pet / (children)] in the building.

B. Put a circle around the word that doesn't belong.

Ex. this, (their), those, that, these

1. green, yellow, silver, (glove), gray

2. blouse, shirt, sweater, coat, (briefcase)

3. church, drugstore, (fire escape), school, laundromat

4. sister, brother, mother, (house), father

C. Answer the questions.

Ex. Where's the post office?
It's around the corner from the hospital.

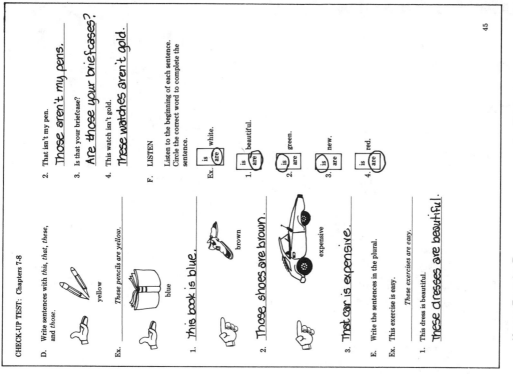

1. Where's the restaurant?
It's next to the bank.

2. Where's the school?
It's between the library and the park.

3. Where's the supermarket?
It's across from the movie theater.

44

CHECK-UP TEST: Chapters 7-8

D. Write sentences with *this, that, these,* and *those.*

Ex. *These pencils are yellow.*
yellow

1. *This book is blue.*
blue

2. *Those shoes are brown.*
brown

3. *That car is expensive.*

expensive

E. Write the sentences in the plural.

Ex. This exercise is easy.
These exercises are easy.

1. This dress is beautiful.
These dresses are beautiful.

2. That isn't my pen.
Those aren't my pens.

3. Is that your briefcase?
Are those your briefcases?

4. This watch isn't gold.
These watches aren't gold.

F. LISTEN

Listen to the beginning of each sentence. Circle the correct word to complete the sentence.

Ex. [is / (are)] white.

1. [is / (are)] beautiful.

2. [is / (are)] green.

3. [(is) / are] new.

4. [is / (are)] red.

Key to Exercise F
Read or play the tape.

Ex. My teeth

1. These gloves
2. This house
3. This bicycle
4. These stockings

45

CHAPTER 9 OVERVIEW

TEXT PAGES 51-54

FOCUS

Simple present tense:
$$\left.\begin{array}{l} \text{I} \\ \text{We} \\ \text{You} \\ \text{They} \end{array}\right\} \text{live.}$$

$$\left.\begin{array}{l} \text{He} \\ \text{She} \\ \text{It} \end{array}\right\} \text{lives.}$$

1. To express a generally known fact:
   I live in Rome.
   I speak Italian.

2. To express a habitual activity:
   Every day I eat Italian food.

COMMUNICATIVE SKILLS

1. Identifying nationalities.

2. Speaking about daily activities (with the verbs *live, speak, eat, drink, sing, read, listen to*).

VOCABULARY

Canadian	around the world	language
Chinese	beer	live
French	city	music
German	do	songs
Greek	does	speak
Italian	drink	tea
Japanese	food	think
Mexican	glad	wine
Puerto Rican	interview	wonderful
Russian		
Spanish		
Swedish		

LANGUAGE NOTES

The third person singular of verbs in the simple present tense has an *s* ending; the other persons do not (See FOCUS). Students typically need extra practice hearing and saying this *s* ending. (This ending has 3 pronunciations. These are treated in Chapter 12.)

CULTURE KEY

Many cities and nationalities are introduced in this chapter. You can bring in a world map to show where these places are. You can also bring in pictures of different countries, people, and customs. If students have visited any of the cities mentioned in this chapter, they can tell about them.

FOCUS

> 1. Simple present tense with the pronouns
>   *I, we, you, they.*
> 2. Questions with *where* and *what.*

GETTING READY

1. Introduce yourself this way. Say,
    "My name is *(your name)*."
    "I live in *(city)*."
    "I speak *(native language)*."
2. Write the following categories on the board; under each one write the correct information about yourself:

Name	City	Language
(your name)	(your city)	(native language)

3. Repeat your introduction as in 1 above, then call on students to introduce themselves the same way. Add their information to the chart. (Leave the chart on the board—you will use it again for the SIDE BY SIDE Exercises.)

PRESENTING THE MODEL

1. Have students look at the model illustration in the book or on the SBS Dialog Visual Card.
2. Set the scene: "Antonio is Italian. He's talking about his life in Rome." (Use a world map to show where Rome, Italy, is.)
3. With books closed, have students listen as you present the model or play the tape one or more times.
4. Full-Class Choral Repetition: Model each line and have students repeat.
5. Write the information about Antonio on the board, under the same 3 categories: *Name, City,* and *Language.*
6. Have students open their books and look at the model. Ask if there are any questions and check understanding of new vocabulary: *hello, Rome, speak, Italian, every day, food, wine, songs, think, wonderful, city, glad, here.*
7. Call on one or two students to present the model.
    (For additional practice, do Choral Repetition in small groups or by rows.)
8. Introduce the questions in the box; write them on the board. Say each question and have students repeat after you chorally and individually.

9. Set the scene: "Someone is interviewing Antonio." Present the following model:
   - A. What's your name?
   - B. My name is Antonio.
   - A. Where do you live?
   - B. I live in Rome.
   - A. What language do you speak?
   - B. I speak Italian.
   - A. What do you do every day?
   - B. I eat Italian food, I drink Italian wine, and I sing Italian songs.
10. Full-Class Choral Repetition.
11. Group Choral Repetition.
12. Choral Conversation.
13. Call on one or two pairs of students to present the dialog.

   (For additional practice, do Choral Conversation in small groups or by rows.)

SIDE BY SIDE EXERCISES

In these exercises students pretend to be the people in the illustrations living in various countries around the world. Other students *interview* them using the questions in the box. You can add realism by having students pretend to hold a microphone as in a radio or T V interview.

Before doing each exercise, use the chart on the board to write in the new information for that exercise. Use a world map to show where the cities are. Your chart should look like this:

Name	City	Language
(your name)	(your city)	(your native language)
Antonio	Rome	Italian
1. Marie	Paris	French
2. Carlos	Madrid	Spanish
↓	↓	↓

Introduce the vocabulary under the model: *coffee, tea,* and *beer.* Encourage students to use these words in place of wine when appropriate. For example,
3. "I drink German beer."
4. "I drink Japanese tea."

Examples:

1.	A. What's your name?	5.	A. What are your names?
	B. My name is Marie.		B. Our names are Sara and Mark.
	A. Where do you live?		A. Where do you live?
	B. I live in Paris.		B. We live in London.
	A. What language do you speak?		A. What language do you speak?
	B. I speak French.		B. We speak English.
	A. What do you do every day?		A. What do you do every day?
	B. I eat French food, I drink French wine (or tea/coffee/ beer), and I sing French songs.		B. We eat English food, we drink English tea (or wine/coffee/ beer), and we sing English songs.

1. **Exercise 1:** Introduce: *Paris, French.* Call on two students to present the interview. Then do Choral Repetition and Choral Conversation Practice.
2. **Exercise 2:** Introduce: *Madrid, Spanish.* Call on two students to present the interview. Then do Choral Repetition and Choral Conversation Practice.
3. **Exercises 3-6:**

> **New vocabulary:**   3. *Berlin, German*   4. *Tokyo, Japanese*   5. *London, English*
> 6. *Moscow, Russian*

Either Full-Class Practice or Pair Practice.

OPTIONAL WRITING PRACTICE

Have students write exercises 2, 5 for homework.

WORKBOOK

Students can now do pages 46, 47 Exercise A.

EXPANSION ACTIVITIES

1. *Practice* **I** *and* **We** *with Word Cards*
   Make up word cards with information about new people. On each card write a new name, city, and language. Have some students draw cards and pretend to be those people. Have other students interview them using the questions on text page 52. You can do this as Full-Class Practice or Pair Practice.
   Some suggestions for word cards:

1. Mr. Tonetti	2. Juanita	3. Mr. and Mrs. Schultz
Venice	Bueno Aires	Bonn
Italian	Spanish	German

2. *Practice* **They** *With Word Cards*
   Make word cards that show two or more people. Include their names, a city and a language. Have students ask and answer about the people on the cards:
   > What are their names?
   > Where do they live?
   > What language do they speak?
   > What do they do every day?

   You can do this as Full-Class Practice or Pair Practice.

   Some suggestions for word cards:

1. Sara and Mark	2. Boris and Natasha
London	Moscow
English	Russian

3. Mr. and Mrs. Ono   4. Carlos and Maria
   Tokyo   Madrid
   Japanese   Spanish

3. *Practicing* **I**: *Amnesia*

Call on two students. Have Student A pretend to be in the hospital with amnesia, a condition which causes a person to forget things. Have Student B pretend to be a friend, relative or a doctor. Have Student A ask the questions on text page 52 with *I*. For example,

    "What's my name?"

    "Where do I live?"

Have Student B answer using any information he or she wishes.

FOCUS

Simple present tense with *he* and *she*.

PRESENTING THE MODEL

1. Have students look at the model illustration in the book or on the SBS Dialog Visual Card.
2. Set the scene: "Two people are talking about Miguel."
3. With books closed, have students listen as you present the model or play the tape one or more times.
4. Full-Class Choral Repetition.
5. Put the following chart on the board and write the information about Miguel: (note that language and nationality are different)

Name	City	Language	Nationality
Miguel	Mexico City	Spanish	Mexican

6. Ask students if they have any questions; check understanding of new vocabulary: *Mexico City, Spanish, Mexican, music.*
7. Group Choral Repetition.
8. Choral Conversation.
9. Call on one or two pairs of students to present the dialog.

    (For additional practice, do Choral Conversation in small groups or by rows.)

SIDE BY SIDE EXERCISES

Before doing each exercise, use the chart on the board to write in the new information for that exercise. Use a world map to show where the cities are. Your chart should look like this:

Name	City	Language	Nationality
Miguel	Mexico	Spanish	Mexican
1. Anna	Athens	Greek	Greek
2. Lee	Hong Kong	Chinese	Chinese
3. Margarita	San Juan	Spanish	Puerto Rican
↓	↓	↓	↓

Examples:

1. A. What's her name?
   B. Her name is Anna.
   A. Where does she live?
   B. She lives in Athens.
   A. What language does she speak?
   B. She speaks Greek.
   A. What does she do every day?
   B. She eats Greek food, she reads Greek newspapers, and she listens to Greek music.

3. A. What's her name?
   B. Her name is Margarita.
   A. Where does she live?
   B. She lives in San Juan.
   A. What language does she speak?
   B. She speaks Spanish.
   A. What does she do every day?
   B. She eats Puerto Rican food, she reads Puerto Rican newspapers, and she listens to Puerto Rican music.

1. Model the questions in the box and have students repeat chorally and individually.
2. **Exercise 1:** Introduce: *Athens, Greek.* Call on two students to present the dialog. Then do Choral Repetition and Choral Conversation Practice.
3. **Exercise 3:** Introduce: *Hong Kong, Chinese.* Same as above.
4. **Exercises 3-6:**

> **New vocabulary:** 3. *San Juan, Puerto Rican* 4. *Toronto, Canadian*
> 6. *Stockholm, Swedish*

Either Full-Class Practice or Pair Practice.

OPTIONAL WRITING PRACTICE

Have students write exercises 1, 3, 4 for homework.

WORKBOOK

Students can now do pages 47 Exercise B, 48.

EXPANSION ACTIVITIES

1. *Pronunciation Practice*
   Practice the final *s* sound. Write on the board and have students repeat chorally and individually: (Read from left to right)

I live	he lives	she lives		I drink	he drinks	she drinks
I speak	he speaks	she speaks		I read	he reads	she reads
I eat	he eats	she eats				

2. *Practice With Word Cards*
   Make up word cards with information about new men and women from different countries. Include the person's name, city, language, and nationality. Have students draw cards; then ask and answer questions about the person. Suggestions for word cards:

1. Olaf	2. Raquel	3. Rosa	4. Mrs. Yen
Stockholm	Rome	Cancun	Hong Kong
Swedish	Italian	Spanish	Chinese
Swedish	Italian	Mexican	Chinese

3. *Listening Practice: I or He?*
   Have students listen as you read each of the words below. Have students say "he" (for 3rd person) if they hear a final *s* sound. Have students say "I" (for non-3rd person) if they do not hear a final *s* sound.

1. eat		6. read	
2. lives		7. does	
3. drinks		8. do	
4. listen		9. thinks	
5. listens		10. eats	

4. *Dictation*
   Read these sentences slowly and have students write them on a separate piece of paper. When you have finished you can collect them and correct them later; or write the sentences on the board and have students correct their own papers.

1. He speaks English.	4. She lives in Rome.
2. She eats Italian food.	5. He listens to music.
3. He drinks coffee.	6. She sings songs.

5. *Talk About Students In The Class*
   Use the questions in the box on text page 53 to answer questions about students in the class. You can begin by asking about one student; then call on pairs of students to ask and answer questions about someone in the class. Encourage students to use any vocabulary they wish to answer the last question, *"What does he/she do every day?"*

FOCUS

Review of the simple present tense.

GETTING READY

Read the forms in the grammar boxes at the top of the page. Form sentences by reading from left to right. Have students repeat after you. For example,

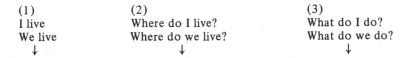

(1)	(2)	(3)
I live	Where do I live?	What do I do?
We live	Where do we live?	What do we do?
↓	↓	↓

ON YOUR OWN

In this role play exercise students pretend to be famous celebrities who are being interviewed on television. One student is the interviewer and asks the questions; another pretends to be the famous person and answers using any information he or she wishes.

1. For homework, have students choose a famous person and make up information about that person. Encourage students to use dictionaries to find new vocabulary. For example,

    1. Pélé
       Brazil
       Portuguese
       play soccer

    2. Princess Anne
       England
       English
       ride horses

2. In class the next day, call pairs of students to the front of the class; have one role play the famous person (using the information prepared at home) and another ask the questions. For example,

    A. What's your name?
    B. My name is Princess Anne.
    A. Where do you live?
    B. I live in England.
    A. What language do you speak?
    B. I speak English.
    A. What do you do every day?
    B. I ride horses.

3. After each interview, ask someone who watched it to *report* or tell about the famous person. For example,

> "Her name is Princess Anne.
> She lives in England.
> She speaks English.
> Every day she rides horses."

WORKBOOK

Students can now do pages 49, 50, 51.

9

A.   INTERVIEWS AROUND THE WORLD

what	language	we	our	is	drink	read
what's	name	you	your	are	eat	sing
where	names	they	their	do	live	speak

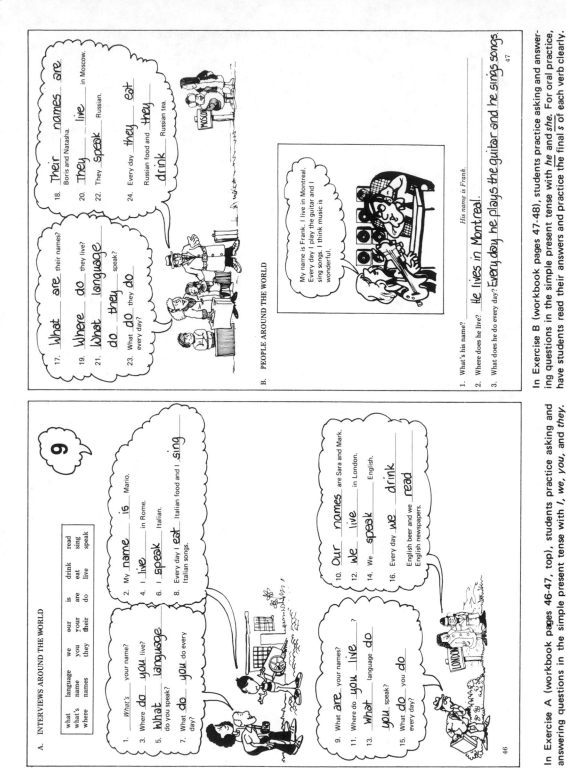

1. _What's_ your name?
2. My _name_ _is_ Mario.
3. Where _do_ _you_ live?
4. I _live_ in Rome.
5. _What_ _language_ do you speak?
6. I _speak_ Italian.
7. What _do_ _you_ do every day?
8. Every day I _eat_ Italian food and I _sing_ Italian songs.

9. What _are_ your names?
10. _Our_ _names_ are Sara and Mark.
11. Where do _you_ _live_ ?
12. We _live_ in London.
13. _What_ language _do_ _you_ _do_ speak?
14. We _speak_ English.
15. What _do_ you _do_ every day?
16. Every day _we_ _drink_ English beer and we _read_ English newspapers.

17. _What_ _are_ their names?
18. Their _names_ _are_ Boris and Natasha.
19. _Where_ _do_ they live?
20. _They_ _live_ in Moscow.
21. _What_ _language_ do they speak?
22. They _speak_ Russian.
23. What _do_ they do every day?
24. Every day _they_ _eat_ Russian food and _they_ _drink_ Russian tea.

B.   PEOPLE AROUND THE WORLD

My name is Frank. I live in Montreal. Every day I play the guitar and I sing songs. I think music is wonderful.

His name is Frank.

1. What's his name? _He lives in Montreal._ *His name is Frank.*
2. Where does he live? _He lives in Montreal._
3. What does he do every day? _Every day he plays the guitar and he sings songs._

47

In Exercise A (workbook pages 46-47, top), students practice asking and answering questions in the simple present tense with *I, we, you,* and *they.* (text page 52)

In Exercise B (workbook pages 47-48), students practice asking and answering questions in the simple present tense with *he* and *she.* For oral practice, have students read their answers and practice the final *s* of each verb clearly. (text page 53)

46

My name is Robert. I live in Paris. I speak French. Every day I read French books and I listen to French music. I think French is a wonderful language.

4. What's his name? _____ ? His name is Robert.

5. Where does he live ? _____ ? He lives in Paris.

6. What language does he speak? He speaks French.

7. What does he do every day? He reads French books and he listens to French music.

My name is Inga. I live in Stockholm. I speak Swedish. Every day I do exercises and I play soccer. I think sports are wonderful.

8. What's her name? Her name is Inga.

9. Where does she live? She lives in Stockholm.

10. What language does she speak? She speaks Swedish

11. What does she do every day? She does exercises and she plays soccer

C. WRITE ABOUT YOURSELF

1. What's your name? _____

2. Where do you live? _____

3. What language do you speak? _____

4. What do you do every day? _____

48

D. MARIA'S FAMILY

Put a circle around the correct word.

(1) My name is Maria. (2) I [live / lives] in London. (3) I [speak / speaks] English and Spanish. (4) My husband's name is John. (5) He [speak / speaks] English. (6) Our children Fred and Sara [speak / speaks] English and Spanish. (7) At school they [sing / sings] English and Spanish songs.

(8) We [live / lives] in a big house. (9) Every day I [cook / cooks] lunch and dinner, and I [clean / cleans] the house. (10) Every day my husband [cook / cooks] breakfast, and he [clean / cleans] the yard. (11) We [eat / eats] big English breakfasts and big Spanish dinners.

(12) Every day my husband and I [read / reads] the newspaper. (13) We [drink / drinks] tea and we [listen / listens] to the radio. (14) I [read / reads] Spanish newspapers and my husband [read / reads] English newspapers. (15) What do you [do / does] every day? (16) What languages [do / does] you speak?

49

Students practice the simple present tense with all pronouns. For oral practice, have students read the story aloud, pronouncing the final *s* clearly when it is used. (text page 54)

In Exercise C, students answer questions about themselves. Encourage them to use different verbs when answering question C-4. (Example: *What do you do every day? I clean the house.*) (text page 53)

In Exercise E, students answer questions about the story in Exercise D. Exercise F is a dictation. Read the dictation or play the tape several times so that the students can listen, write, and make any corrections. (text page 54)

Key to Exercise F
Read or play the tape.

(1) Every day I sit in the park. (2) I *read* the newspaper, I *play* cards, I *eat* my lunch, and I *listen* to the radio. (3) *I'm* not a busy person. (4) My friend Harry *lives* around the corner from my house. (5) Every day Harry *cleans* his apartment, he *plays* the piano, he *reads* books, he *does* exercises, and he *cooks*. (6) My friend Harry *is* a very busy person.

E.   WRITE ABOUT MARIA'S FAMILY

She lives in London.

1.   Where does Maria live?

2.   What languages does she speak? She speaks English and Spanish.

3.   What language does Maria's husband speak? He speaks English.

4.   What languages do Fred and Sara speak? They speak English and Spanish.

5.   What do they do at school? They sing English and Spanish songs.

6.   What does Maria do every day? She cooks lunch and dinner, and she cleans the house.

7.   What does John do every day? He cooks breakfast, and he cleans the yard.

F.   LISTEN

Listen to the story. Write the missing words.

(1) Every day I sit in the park. (2) I read the newspaper, I play cards, I eat my lunch, and I listen to the radio. (3) I'm not a busy person. (4) My friend Harry lives around the corner from my house. (5) Every day Harry cleans his apartment, he plays the piano, he reads books, he does exercises, and he cooks. (6) My friend Harry is a very busy person.

50

These pronunciation exercises should be done as an oral activity. Students practice saying the sounds č as in children and ž as in shirt. In Exercise G, have students repeat each word chorally and individually. Make sure that they hear the difference between the č sound and the š sound. Have many students read the sentences in Exercise H aloud. For additional oral practice students can ask and answer questions about the pictures. (Example: 1. What's Charlie doing? Charlie is eating Chinese food.) (text page 54)

G. LOUD AND CLEAR   Listen to each word and then say it.

1. beach   7. kitchen   13. she's
2. bench   8. teacher   14. shirt
3. Charlie   9. watching   15. shoes
4. children   10. English   16. station
5. Chinese   11. Natasha   17. washing
6. church   12. Sharp   18. Washington

ch! sh!

H. Fill in the words, then read the sentences aloud.

| beach | Charlie | Chinese |

1. *Charlie* is eating *Chinese* food at the *beach*.

| Natasha | station | Washington |

2. *Natasha* is at the train *station* in *Washington* D.C.

| children | kitchen | watching |

3. The *children* are *watching* TV in the *kitchen*.

| Sharp | shirt | washing |

4. Mr. *Sharp* is *washing* a *shirt*.

| bench | church | teacher |

5. Our *teacher* is sitting on a *bench* in front of the *church*.

| English | she's | shoes |

6. *She's* wearing an *English* coat and English *shoes*.

51

CHAPTER 10 OVERVIEW

TEXT PAGES 55-60

FOCUS

Simple Present Tense:

1. Yes/No questions with *do/does* and short answers:

Does he cook?	*Do they like American food?*
Yes, he does.	*Yes, they do.*
No, he doesn't.	*No, they don't.*

2. Negatives:

He doesn't cook.	*They don't like American food.*

3. Questions with *When* and *What kind of:*

   When does he cook Italian food?
   What kind of food do they like?

COMMUNICATIVE SKILLS

1. Asking for and giving information about likes and dislikes: *food, movies, books, school subjects, TV programs, music, sports.*

2. Identifying days of the week.

3. Identifying nationalities.

VOCABULARY

American	don't	like	to
Arabic	go	place	very well
because	goes	smoke	what kind of
different	Hungarian	special	when
doesn't	international	there	why

ON YOUR OWN (text page 59)

athlete	golf	popular music	sports
author	history	rock and roll	tennis
cartoons	hockey	school subjects	TV programs
classical music	jazz	science	TV star
comedies (comedy)	movies	science fiction	war movies
dramas	novels	short stories (story)	westerns
football	poetry	singer	

LANGUAGE NOTES

Students may have difficulty distinguishing the *t* sound in *Tuesday* from the *th* sound in *Thursday*.

CULTURE KEY

This chapter, like Chapter 9, has an international theme. Talk with your students about ethnic foods, customs, and clothing they know. They might also sing songs they know from different countries.

FOCUS

Simple present tense with *he*.
1. Days of the week: *on Monday*
2. Yes/No questions with *does* and short answers: *Yes, he does. No, he doesn't.*
3. Questions with *When* and *What kind of.*

GETTING READY

1. Introduce the days of the week. Write them on the board or use word cards or a calendar. Say each word and have students repeat after you chorally and individually.
2. Review the nationalities: *Italian, Greek, Chinese, Puerto Rican, Japanese, Mexican.* Introduce *American*.

STANLEY'S INTERNATIONAL RESTAURANT

Text page 56 and all of Chapter 10 are about a chef named Stanley and his restaurant, called Stanley's International Restaurant. For the SIDE BY SIDE Exercises on this page and throughout the chapter, students will need to look at the picture of Stanley's *menu*, which shows each day of the week with the type of food served on that day. You can have students look at the illustration on text page 56 or on the SBS Dialog Visual Card, or you can draw a simple version of Stanley's menu on the board.

There are 3 model conversations on text page 56, each followed by SIDE BY SIDE Exercises.

PRESENTING THE 1ST MODEL

1. Have students look at Stanley's *menu*.
2. Set the scene: "Stanley's International Restaurant is a very special place. Every day Stanley cooks a different kind of food."
3. Present the model:

   A. What kind of food does Stanley cook on Monday?
   B. On Monday he cooks Italian food.

4. Full-Class Choral Repetition.
5. Have students open their books; check understanding of new vocabulary: *special, place, cook, different kind of, what kind of, does, on Monday.*

6. Group Choral Repetition.
7. Choral Conversation.
8. Call on one or two pairs of students to present the model.
   (For additional practice, do Choral Conversation in small groups or by rows.)

SIDE BY SIDE EXERCISES

Examples:

> A. What kind of food does Stanley cook on Tuesday?
> B. On Tuesday he cooks Greek food.
> A. What kind of food does Stanley cook on Wednesday?
> B. On Wednesday he cooks Chinese food.

1. **Tuesday**: Call on two students to ask and answer about Tuesday. Then do Choral Repetition and Choral Conversation Practice.
2. **Wednesday**: Same as above.
3. **Thursday–Sunday**: Either Full-Class Practice or Pair Practice.

PRESENTING THE 2ND MODEL

1. Have students look at Stanley's menu.
2. Set the scene: "People are talking about Stanley's International Restaurant."
3. Present the model:

> A. Does Stanley cook Greek food on Tuesday?
> B. Yes, he does.

4. Full-Class Choral Repetition.
5. Have students open their books and look at the dialog. Ask if there are any questions.
6. Group Choral Repetition.
7. Choral Conversation.
8. Call on one or two pairs of students to present the dialog.
   (For additional practice, do Choral Conversation in small groups or by rows.)

SIDE BY SIDE EXERCISES

Examples:

> A. Does Stanley cook Chinese food on Wednesday?
> B. Yes, he does.
> A. Does Stanley cook Puerto Rican food on Thursday?
> B. Yes, he does.

1. **Wednesday**: Call on two students to ask and answer about Wednesday. Then do Choral Repetition and Choral Conversation Practice.
2. **Thursday**: Same as above.
3. **Friday–Monday**: Either Full-Class Practice or Pair Practice.

PRESENTING THE 3RD MODEL

Same as above. Check understanding of *doesn't, when.*

SIDE BY SIDE EXERCISES

Students can ask about any food and any day. For example,

> A. Does Stanley cook Mexican food on Tuesday?
> B. No, he doesn't.
> A. When does he cook Mexican food?
> B. He cooks Mexican food on Saturday.
>
> A. Does Stanley cook Puerto Rican food on Sunday?
> B. No, he doesn't.
> A. When does he cook Puerto Rican food?
> B. He cooks Puerto Rican food on Thursday.

1. Call on two students to create a dialog. Then do Choral Repetition and Choral Conversation Practice.
2. Call on two other students to create a dialog. Then do Choral Repetition and Choral Conversation Practice.
3. Have pairs of students create 5 more dialogs. This can be Full-Class Practice or Pair Practice.

OPTIONAL WRITING PRACTICE

For the 1st model, have students write questions and answers about Wednesday, Thursday, Saturday, Sunday.

For the 2nd and 3rd models, have students write 3 dialogs based on each model for homework.

WORKBOOK

Students can now do pages 52 and 53.

EXPANSION ACTIVITY

Role Play: "Calling Stanley's International Restaurant on the Telephone"

The questions and answers on text page 56 can be reviewed through a *telephone conversation* in which students pretend to call the restaurant for information about Stanley's menu. Use the illustration of Stanley's menu on text page 56, the SBS Dialog Visual Card, or a simplified version on the board. Have one student pretend to work at the restaurant; have another student *call* for information.

Write this skeletal dialog on the board for students to use as a guide:

> *(ring, ring)*
>
> A. Hello, Stanley's International Restaurant.
>   May I help you?
> B. Yes, please. _____?
> A. _____ .
> B. Thank you very much.
> A. You're welcome.

In the blank lines, students can ask and answer questions such as:
"What kind of food does Stanley cook on *(Monday)*?"
"Does Stanley cook *(Greek)* food on *(Tuesday)*?"

FOCUS

> Simple present tense with *I, you,* and *we.* (non-3rd person singular)
> 1. Yes/No questions with *do* and short answers: *Yes, I do. No, I don't.*
> 2. Questions with *When* and *What kind of?*

GETTING READY

Briefly review Stanley's menu.

PRESENTING THE 1ST MODEL

1. Have students look at Stanley's *menu.*
2. Set the scene: "People are talking about Stanley's International Restaurant."
3. Present the model.
4. Full-Class Choral Repetition.
5. Ask students if they have any questions; check understanding of new vocabulary: *do, go, to, why, because.*
6. Group Choral Repetition.
7. Choral Conversation.
8. Call on one or two pairs of students to present the dialog.
   (For additional practice, do Choral Conversation in small groups or by rows.)

SIDE BY SIDE EXERCISES

Examples:

> 1. A. Do you go to Stanley's International Restaurant on Friday?
>   B. Yes, I do.
>   A. Why?
>   B. Because I like Japanese food.
> 2. A. Do you go to Stanley's International Restaurant on Saturday?
>   B. Yes, we do.
>   A. Why?
>   B. Because we like Mexican food.

1. **Exercise 1**: Call on two students to present the dialog. Then do Choral Repetition and Choral Conversation Practice.
2. **Exercise 2**: Same as above.
3. **Exercises 3-4**: Either Full-Class Practice or Pair Practice.

PRESENTING THE 2ND MODEL

Same as above. Check understanding of *don't, why not.*

SIDE BY SIDE EXERCISES

Examples:

> 5. A. Do you go to Stanley's International Restaurant on Monday?
>   B. No, I don't.
>   A. Why not?
>   B. Because I don't like Italian food.
> 7. A. Do you go to Stanley's International Restaurant on Wednesday?
>   B. No, we don't.
>   A. Why not?.
>   B. Because we don't like Chinese food.

1. **Exercise 5**: Call on two students to present the dialog. Then do Choral Repetition and Choral Conversation Practice.
2. **Exercise 6**: Same as above.
3. **Exercises 7-8**: Either Full-Class Practice or Pair Practice.

PRESENTING THE 3RD MODEL

Same as above.

SIDE BY SIDE EXERCISES

Examples:

> 9. A. What kind of food do you like?
>   B. I like French food.
>   A. When do you go to Stanley's International Restaurant?
>   B. I don't go to Stanley's International Restaurant.
>   A. Why not?
>   B. Because Stanley doesn't cook French food.
> 10. A. What kind of food do you like?
>   B. We like German food.
>   A. When do you go to Stanley's International Restaurant?
>   B. We don't go to Stanley's International Restaurant.
>   A. Why not?
>   B. Because Stanley doesn't cook German food.

1. **Exercise 9:** Call on two students to present the dialog. Then do Choral Repetition and Choral Conversation Practice.
2. **Exercise 10:** Same as above.
3. **Exercises 11-12:**

> **New vocabulary:** 11. *Arabic*   12. *Hungarian*

Either Full-Class Practice or Pair Practice.

OPTIONAL WRITING PRACTICE

Have students write exercises 1, 4, 6, 8, 11, 12 for homework.

WORKBOOK

Students can now do page 54.

EXPANSION ACTIVITY

Students Talk About Themselves
Have students create conversations about themselves. Write the conversation cues below on the board as a guide. Call on pairs of students to ask and answer questions according to their own likes and dislikes.
Conversation cues:

    A. Do you go to Stanley's International Restaurant on _____?
    B. _____.
    A. Why/Why not?
    B. Because _____.

    A. What kind of food do you like?
    B. _____.
    A. When do you go _____?
    B. I go _____./ I don't go because _____.

You can do this as Full-Class Practice or Pair Practice.

TEACHER'S NOTES

FOCUS

Simple present tense:
1. Practice with all pronouns.
2. Questions with *What, When, Why.*

GETTING READY

Write the following verb forms on the board:

I, we, you, they   he, she

I, we, you, they	he, she
speak	speaks
eat	eats
drink	drinks
smoke	smokes
listen	listens

Make sentences with the *non-s* and *s* forms of each verb and have students repeat. For example,
"They speak"   "He speaks"
"I eat"   "She eats"

PRESENTING THE MODEL

1. Have students look at the model illustration in the book or on the SBS Dialog Visual Card.

2. Set the scene: "People are talking about Stanley's International Restaurant."

3. Present the model:

   A. What do people do at Stanley's International Restaurant?
   B. On Monday they speak Italian, eat Italian food, drink Italian wine, smoke Italian cigarettes, and listen to Italian music.

4. Full-Class Choral Repetition.

5. Ask students if they have any questions; check understanding of new vocabulary: *smoke, cigarettes.*

6. Group Choral Repetition.

7. Choral Conversation.

8. Call on one or two pairs of students to present the model.

9. Give further practice with the model by calling on pairs of students to ask and answer about Friday and Sunday.

SIDE BY SIDE EXERCISES

Examples:

1. A. Henry likes Greek food.
      When does he go to Stanley's International Restaurant?
   B. He goes to Stanley's International Restaurant on Tuesday.
   A. What does he do there?
   B. He speaks Greek, eats Greek food, drinks Greek wine, smokes Greek cigarettes, and listens to Greek music.

2. A. Mr. and Mrs. Wilson go to Stanley's International Restaurant on Wednesday.
      What kind of food do they like?
   B. They like Chinese food.
   A. What do they do there?
   B. They speak Chinese, eat Chinese food, drink Chinese wine, smoke Chinese cigarettes, and listen to Chinese music.

1. **Exercise 1:** Introduce the new word: *there.* Call on two students to present the dialog. Then do Choral Repetition and Choral Conversation Practice.

2. **Exercise 2:** Same as above.

3. **"Ask Another Student In Your Class":** Either Full-Class Practice or Pair Practice.

OPTIONAL WRITING PRACTICE

Have students write exercise 1 and the last exercise for homework.

WORKBOOK

Students can now do page 55.

EXPANSION ACTIVITY

Talk About Local Restaurants
Have students ask each other about restaurants they go to. Write these question cues on the board as a guide:

(Do/Does) _____ go to _____ Restaurant?
When (do/does) _____ go there?
What (do/does) _____ do there?

FOCUS

Use of the simple present tense to talk about personal likes and dislikes.

> Do you like _____?
> Yes, I do.
> No, I don't.
>
> Who ⎱
> What ⎰ is your favorite _____?
>
> My favorite _____ is _____.
>
> What kind of _____ do you like?
> Which _____ do you like?
>
> I like _____.
> I don't like _____.

1. Go over the questions. Introduce new vocabulary:

    1. movies, comedies (comedy), dramas, westerns, war movies, science fiction, cartoons
    2. novels, poetry, short stories (story), author
    3. school subjects, science, history
    4. TV programs, TV star
    6. classical music, popular music, jazz, rock and roll, singer
    7. sports, football, golf, hockey, tennis

2. For homework, have students write answers to these questions. In the next class, have students ask and answer the questions. (They should not refer to their written homework when practicing.)

    This can be Full-Class Practice or Pair Practice.

WORKBOOK

Students can now do page 56.

CLASSROOM DRAMA: *YOU SPEAK ENGLISH VERY WELL*

In this exercise students practice short answers in a playful context—one in which a teacher and two students are disagreeing.

1. Review the short answers in the boxes at the top of the page. Have students repeat after you. For example, "Yes, I do," "Yes, we do," "Yes, you do."

2. Have students listen and follow along in the text as you read the dialog or play the tape one or more times.

3. Check understanding of the new words: *very well.*

4. Act out the drama with two of your most outgoing and playful students. You take the part of the teacher.

5. Have several groups of students act it out.

   You can activate this dialog at any future time by complimenting a student with, "You speak English very well!"

A. FRANKLIN'S INTERNATIONAL DISCOTHEQUE

Students practice asking and answering questions in the simple present tense with *he* and *she*. Students ask and answer questions with *What kind of* and *When* and practice *yes/no* questions and answers. You can practice this exercise orally by covering up the questions and having students ask and answer about Franklin's International Discotheque based on the illustration. (text page 56)

In Exercise B, students practice using *do* and *does* in simple present tense questions.

In Exercise C, students practice listening comprehension with *wh-* questions in the simple present tense. (text page 57)

Key to Exercise C
Read or play the tape.

1. What kind of music does Mrs. Harris like?
2. Where do Gloria and Barbara study English?
3. Do Frank and Martha go to school?
4. Why do you go to Wilson's Department Store?
5. What does Mr. Larson do in the park?
6. Why do your aunt and uncle eat at Lee's Chinese Restaurant?
7. When does Mrs. Williams go to the bank?
8. What do the children do at the beach?
9. Does your sister do her homework?
10. When do you and your husband go to the supermarket?

B.   WHAT'S THE WORD?

[do/does]

1. What kind of books _do_ you read?
2. _Does_ Margarita like American TV?
3. Why _does_ Marie live in Tokyo?
4. Where _do_ Mr. and Mrs. Smith play cards?
5. Why _does_ Mrs. Wilson clean her house every day?
6. What _does_ Mr. Wilson do every day?
7. _Do_ you like your new school? Yes, we do.
8. When _does_ Henry do his homework?
9. What kind of music _do_ your mother and father listen to?
10. How many languages _do_ you speak?
11. What kind of songs _do_ you and your friends sing?
12. _Does_ Tommy cry at the doctor's office?   Yes, he _does_ .

C.   LISTEN

Listen to each question. Put a circle around the correct answer.

1. **a.** Mexican music.
   b. American food.
   c. Every day.

2. a. On Monday, Wednesday and Friday.
   b. At school.
   c. Because they live in London.

3. a. Yes, he does.
   b. No, we don't.
   c. Yes, they do.

4. a. On Tuesday.
   b. We don't go there on Sunday.
   c. Because we like the clothes there.

5. **a.** He reads the newspaper.
   b. She plays cards.
   c. They feed the birds.

6. a. On Sunday.
   b. In Hong Kong.
   c. Because they like Chinese food.

7. **a.** On Friday.
   b. Across the street from the supermarket.
   c. Because she's rich.

8. a. He eats lunch.
   b. They play.
   c. Because it's hot.

9. **a.** No, she doesn't.
   b. No, we don't.
   c. Yes, they do.

10. **a.** He goes to the supermarket on Monday.
    b. We go to the supermarket on Tuesday.
    c. On Main Street.

54

D.   YES AND NO

YES!

1. My grandfather drinks tea.
2. David and Tommy play baseball.
3. David's sister plays the guitar.
4. Albert and Walter drink lemonade.
5. Walter's father cleans the yard.
6. On Sunday we *go* to church.
7. Mr. and Mrs. Johnson *read* the newspaper.
8. Their children *like* _____ TV.
9. The dog sleeps in the yard.
10. Peter's cat *likes* mice.
11. I wear mittens to school.
12. My mother *wears* stockings.
13. My sister feeds the dog.
14. On Saturday Mr. Johnson *goes* to the beach.
15. Toshi speaks Japanese.
16. Margarita's cousin *lives* in New York.

NO!

1. He *doesn't* *drink* beer.
2. They *don't* *play* soccer.
3. She *doesn't* *play* the piano.
4. They *don't* *drink* the coffee.
5. He *doesn't* *clean* the apartment.
6. We don't go to school.
7. They don't read books.
8. They don't like homework.
9. It *doesn't* *sleep* in the house.
10. It doesn't like children.
11. I *don't* *wear* gloves.
12. She doesn't wear socks.
13. She *doesn't* *feed* the cat.
14. He doesn't go to the library.
15. He *doesn't* *speak* Greek.
16. He doesn't live in San Juan.

E.   WRITE ABOUT YOURSELF

YES!

1. I like _____.
2. I play _____.
3. I speak _____.
4. I eat _____.
5. I drink _____.

NO!

1. I don't like _____.
2. I don't play _____.
3. I don't speak _____.
4. I don't eat _____.
5. I don't drink _____.

55

F.   A LETTER TO A PEN PAL   Read and practice.

Dear Paul,

My family and I live in Athens. We speak Greek. My mother is a music teacher. She plays the piano and sings. My father cooks at a restaurant.

My sister Helen and I go to a school near our house. We study history, Greek, science, mathematics, and English. My favorite school subject is history. I don't like mathematics and science, but I like languages.

Do you like sports? Every day at school I play soccer. On Saturday I play tennis. Which sports do you play?

What kind of music do you like? I think classical music is beautiful. I like jazz, but I don't like rock and roll.

What kind of movies do you like? I like American westerns and Italian comedies. I think war movies are terrible.

Tell me about your family and your school.

Your friend,
Anna

Friday

G.   YOUR LETTER TO A PEN PAL

Dear _____,

My family and I live in _____. We speak _____.

At school I study _____, and _____. My favorite subject is _____. I don't like _____.

Which sports do you like? I play _____ and _____. I think _____ is wonderful. I don't like _____.

What kind of movies do you like? I like _____, and _____ very much, but I don't like _____. My favorite kind of music is _____. I don't listen to _____.

Tell me about your school and your city.

Your friend,
_____.

English	
history	
mathematics	
music	
science	

baseball	
football	
golf	
hockey	
soccer	
tennis	

cartoons	
comedies	
dramas	
science fiction	
war movies	
westerns	

classical music	
jazz	
popular music	
rock and roll	

56

Students practice positive and negative sentences in the simple present tense. For oral practice have students read their answers, pronouncing the final *s* clearly when it is used.
In Exercise E students write about themselves using the same structures and format as in Exercise D. (text page 58)

Students practice the new vocabulary of school subjects, sports, movies, and music. Exercise F is a reading exercise that serves as a model for the pen pal letter in Exercise G. Have several students read Exercise F aloud. Encourage students to look up new words in the dictionary when writing about themselves in Exercise G. (text page 59)

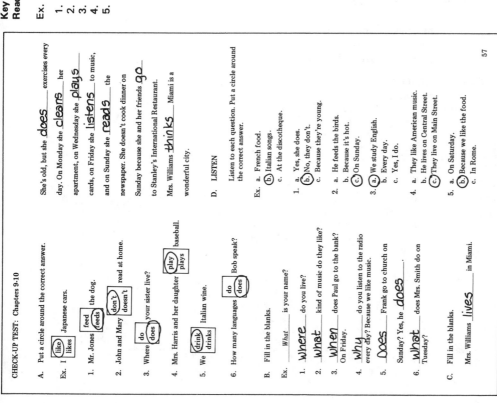

CHAPTER TEN 133

CHECK-UP TEST: Chapters 9-10

A. Put a circle around the correct answer.

Ex. I (like) / likes Japanese cars.

1. Mr. Jones feed / (feeds) the dog.

2. John and Mary (don't) / doesn't read at home.

3. Where do / (does) your sister live?

4. Mrs. Harris and her daughter (play) / plays baseball.

5. We (drink) / drinks Italian wine.

6. How many languages do / (does) Bob speak?

B. Fill in the blanks.

Ex. _What_ is your name?

1. _Where_ do you live?

2. _What_ kind of music do they like?

3. _When_ does Paul go to the bank? On Friday.

4. _Why_ do you listen to the radio every day? Because we like music.

5. _Does_ Frank go to church on Sunday? Yes, he does.

6. _What_ does Mrs. Smith do on Tuesday?

C. Fill in the blanks.

Mrs. Williams _lives_ in Miami. She's old, but she _does_ exercises every day. On Monday she _cleans_ her apartment, on Wednesday she _plays_ cards, on Friday she _listens_ to music, and on Sunday she _reads_ the newspaper. She doesn't cook dinner on Sunday because she and her friends _go_ to Stanley's International Restaurant.

Mrs. Williams _thinks_ Miami is a wonderful city.

D. LISTEN

Listen to each question. Put a circle around the correct answer.

Ex. a. French food.
(b.) Italian songs.
c. At the discotheque.

1. a. Yes, she does.
(b.) No, they don't.
c. Because they're young.

2. a. He feeds the birds.
b. Because it's hot.
(c.) On Sunday.

3. (a.) We study English.
b. Every day.
c. Yes, I do.

4. a. They like American music.
b. He lives on Central Street.
(c.) They live on Main Street.

5. a. On Saturday.
(b.) Because we like the food.
c. In Rome.

57

Key to Exercise D
Read or play the tape.

Ex. What kind of songs does Carmen Jones sing?

1. Do Bob and Judy go to school?
2. When does Mr. Johnson go to the park?
3. What do you do at school?
4. Where do John's cousins live?
5. Why do you go to Mario's Italian Restaurant?

CHAPTER 11 OVERVIEW

TEXT PAGES 61-65

FOCUS

1. Object pronouns: *me, him, her, it, us, you, them*
2. Adverbs of frequency: *always, usually, sometimes, rarely, never*
3. Simple present tense—contrast of *s* and *non-s* endings:
   he reads—I read
   she thinks—they think
4. Irregular verb *have*:

   I
   we } *have*
   you
   they

   he
   she } *has*
   it

COMMUNICATIVE SKILLS

1. Describing oneself in comparison to others:
   My brother and I look very different.
   I'm tall and thin. He's short and heavy.

2. Expressing frequency:
   *You **never** help me.*
   *I **usually** watch TV and **rarely** go out.*

VOCABULARY

always	him	musical instrument	talk
both	hungry	never	tennis
curly	I'm really upset.	occupation	them
different	it	of course	together
divorced	journalist	on the weekend	upset
eyes	lazy	parties (party)	us
golf	long	rarely	usually
go out	look at	really	with
hair	look like	sometimes	you
help	love	straight	
her	me	suburbs	

LANGUAGE NOTES

1. **Pronunciation**
   The $\underline{s}$ ending of the 3rd person singular in the simple present tense has 3 pronunciations.

   a. When a verb ends in a voiceless consonant sound, the ending is pronounced [s] :

   > [p] hel<u>ps</u>
   > [t] si<u>ts</u>
   > [k] thin<u>ks</u>

   b. When a verb ends in a voiced consonant or vowel sound, the ending is pronounced [z] :

   > [d] rea<u>ds</u>   [l] cal<u>ls</u>
   > [v] lo<u>ves</u>   [o] g<u>oes</u>
   > [n] liste<u>ns</u>

   c. When a verb ends in [s] , [z] , [š] , [ž] , [č] , or [ǰ] , the ending is pronounced [iz] , which forms an additional syllable on the end of the word. For example,

   > [s] dan<u>ces</u>
   > [č] wat<u>ches</u>
   > [š] wa<u>shes</u>

2. **Spelling Rules**

   a. When a verb ends in the letters $\underline{s}$, $\underline{sh}$, $\underline{ch}$, or $\underline{x}$, add $\underline{es}$. For example,

   > watch—watch<u>es</u>
   > wash—wash<u>es</u>
   > miss—miss<u>es</u>

   b. When a verb ends in a $\underline{y}$ which is preceded by a consonant, the y changes to i and $\underline{es}$ is added. For example,

   > stud<u>y</u>—stud<u>ies</u>

   c. The verb *go* is spelled *goes* in the 3rd person singular. The verb *do* is spelled *does* in the 3rd person singular.

CULTURE KEY

1. **Friend** (text page 62)
   The notion of what a *friend* is varies from culture to culture. In the U.S. people may know each other only casually and yet think of each other as *friends*.

2. **The Suburbs** (text page 65)
   The suburbs are the residential areas (either towns or small cities) which are located near a large city. In the U.S. people who work in the city often live in the suburbs and commute to work.

FOCUS

---

1. Introduction of object pronouns.
2. Review of possessive adjectives:
   my, his, her, our, your, their.

GETTING READY

Introduce the object pronouns:

1. Read the words in the grammar box and have students repeat after you chorally and individually.

2. Draw a face on the board and say, "This is George."
   Then say these sentences and have students repeat:
   (Point to yourself.) "George is *my* friend." "George likes *me*."
   (Point to a female student.) "George is *her* friend." "George likes *her*."
   (Point to a male student.) "George is *his* friend." "George likes *him*."
   (Gesture to everyone) "George is *our* friend." "George likes *us*."
   (Point to one student and say to *that* student.) "George is *your* friend." "George likes *you*."
   (Point to 2 students.) "George is *their* friend." "George likes *them*."

PRESENTING THE MODEL

1. Have students look at the model illustration in the book.

2. Set the scene: "Two people are talking."

3. Present the model.

4. Full-Class Choral Repetition.

5. Ask students if they have any questions; check understanding of new vocabulary: *of course.*

6. Group Choral Repetition.

7. Choral Conversation.

8. Call on one or two pairs of students to present the dialog.

   (For additional practice, do Choral Conversation in small groups or by rows.)

SIDE BY SIDE EXERCISES

1. **Exercise 1:** Call on two students to present the dialog. Then do Choral Repetition and Choral Conversation Practice.

2. **Exercise 2**: Same as above.

3. Call on pairs of students to do exercises 1 and 2 using names of male students in the class.

4. **Exercise 3**: Call on two students to present the dialog. Then do Choral Repetition and Choral Conversation Practice.

5. **Exercise 4**: Same as above.

6. Call on pairs of students to do exercises 3 and 4 using names of female students in the class.

7. **Exercise 5**: Call on two students to present the dialog. Then do Choral Repetition and Choral Conversation Practice.

8. **Exercise 6**: Same as above.

9. Call on pairs of students to do exercises 5 and 6 using names of other students in the class.

10. **Exercise 7**: Call on two students to present the dialog. Then do Choral Repetition and Choral Conversation Practice.

11. **Exercise 8**: Same as above.

12. Call on pairs of students to do exercises 7 and 8 using names of other students in the class.

WORKBOOK

Students can now do pages 58 and 59 Exercise A.

EXPANSION ACTIVITY

Famous People
Make up word cards with the names of famous people. Have students use them as cues to make up conversations like those on text page 62.

FOCUS

1. Simple present tense: contrast of *s* and *non-s* endings.
   (See CHAPTER OVERVIEW for pronunciation of these endings.)
2. Adverbs of frequency.
   (Percentage figures in the box at the top of the page refer to amounts of time.)

GETTING READY

1. Form sentences using the *s* and *non-s* endings for each verb in the grammar boxes. For example,
   Have students listen and repeat:
   "I sit—He sits."
   "I help—He helps."
   "I look—He looks."

2. Listening Exercise. Write on the board: (I)   (He)
   a. Have students listen as you read these *s* and *non-s* verbs:
        looks   love   watches   feeds   talk
   b. For each verb, have students say "I" if they don't hear a final *s* sound; have students say "He" if they hear a final *s* sound.

3. Introduce the adverbs *always, usually, sometimes, rarely, never*.
   a. Have students read these words in the box at the top of the page.
   b. Say each word and have students repeat chorally and individually.
   c. Make a sentence with each word to show the meaning. Describe yourself. For example, describe your clothing habits:
   "I *always* wear shoes."
   "I *usually* wear a watch."
   "I *sometimes* wear gloves."
   "I *rarely* wear a hat."
   "I *never* wear a tie."
   d. For each adverb, call on a student to make a sentence describing himself or herself.

PRESENTING THE MODEL: *HARRY! I'M REALLY UPSET!*

1. Have students look at the model illustration in the book or on the SBS Dialog Visual Card.
2. Set the scene: "Harry's wife is talking. She's very upset."
3. Present the model.
4. Full-Class Choral Repetition.
5. Have students open their books and look at the model. Ask if there are any questions and check understanding of new vocabulary: *really, upset, always, never, look at, together, talk to, parties (party), usually, with, rarely, lazy, help, hungry, sometimes, love.*
   (For additional practice, do Choral Repetition in small groups or by rows.)
6. Appoint a male student to be *Harry*. Call on female students to say the lines in the model to him. (Remind them they're supposed to be upset.)
7. Change *Harry* to *Harriet* and have the husband complain about his wife. Appoint a female student to be *Harriet*. Call on male students to say the lines in the model to her.

8. Practice with key words on the board. Write on the board:

1. sit/living room	always/watch TV	never/look at
2. eat/breakfast	always/read	never/talk to˙
3. go to/parties	usually/sit	rarely/dance
4. lazy	never/help	
5. windows/dirty	never/wash	
6. car/broken	never/fix	
7. cats/hungry	never/feed	
8.	sometimes/think	

With books closed, call on students to say each line of the model using these key words as cues.

WHY IS SHE UPSET WITH HARRY?

Answer Key:

1. When they sit in the living room, he always watches TV and never looks at her.
2. When they eat breakfast together, he always reads the newspaper and never talks to her.
3. When they go to parties, he usually sits with his friends and rarely dances with her.
4. And he's lazy! He never helps her.
5. When their windows are dirty, he never washes them.
6. When their car is broken, he never fixes it.
7. And when their cats are hungry, he never feeds them.
8. Sometimes she thinks he doesn't love her.

1. **Writing Practice:** Have students write these sentences.
    and/or
2. **Oral Practice:** Have students say these sentences using key words on the board as cues (see 8 above).

WORKBOOK

Students can now do pages 59, 60.

EXPANSION ACTIVITY

Correct the Statement
Ask Student A to make a statement about Student B using *always, usually, sometimes, rarely,* or *never.* For example,

"Bill always cooks dinner."
"Mary never studies English."

Student B must respond:

"That's true," or "That's not true."

If Student B responds, "That's not true," then he or she must correct the statement. For example,

"Mary never studies English."
"That's not true. I always study English."

If students need ideas, write key words on the board. For example,

wears _____	works _____
eats _____	watches TV _____
reads _____	dances _____
studies _____	drinks _____
sings _____	

FOCUS

> The irregular verb *have.*

GETTING READY

Introduce the forms of the verb *have.* Read the forms in the box at the top of the page and have students repeat chorally and individually. For example,

"I have."
"We have."

PRESENTING THE MODEL

1. Have students look at the model illustration in the book or on the SBS Dialog Visual Card.

2. Set the scene: "A man is comparing himself to his brother."

3. Present the model.

4. Full-Class Choral Repetition.

5. Ask students if they have any questions; check understanding of new vocabulary: *look like, look different, eyes, both, hair, short, long, curly, straight.*

6. Call on one or two students to present the model.

   (For additional practice, do Choral Repetition in small groups or by rows.)

ON YOUR OWN

In this exercise students complete sentences in which they compare themselves to two people: someone they look like (1) and someone they don't look like (2). Students can compare themselves to family members, friends, other students in the class, or famous people.

1. Give some examples.
   Make sentences about yourself or read these:

   1. A. Who do you look like?
      B. I look like my father.
         We're both tall and thin.
         We both have brown eyes and black hair.

   2. A. Who *don't* you look like?
      B. I don't look like my mother.
         I have brown eyes and she has gray eyes.
         I'm tall and she's short.

2. Have students write similar sentences for homework and then present them in class the next day.

WORKBOOK

Students can now do page 61.

EXPANSION ACTIVITIES

1. *Picture-Story*
   Practice the verb *have* and new vocabulary by telling this story.

   a. Draw two people on the board:

   Carol Jane

   Say: "Carol and Jane are sisters."
   "Carol has short curly brown hair."
   "She has brown eyes."

   "Jane has long straight brown hair."
   "She has brown eyes."

   b. Point to Carol and ask students, "Tell me about Carol." Students answer using the picture as a cue.

   c. Next, point to Jane and ask students, "Tell me about Jane."

   d. Ask students, "Does Jane look like her sister?"/"Does Carol look like her sister?"
      Students answer "Yes" or "No" and explain why. For example,

      "Carol has short hair and Jane has long hair."
      "They both have brown eyes and brown hair."

2. *Practice with Pictures*
   Bring magazine pictures of people to class. Have students describe the people in the pictures.

3. *Guessing Game*
   Take turns describing someone in the class. Others have to guess the student you are describing. For example,

      A. She has long black curly hair. She has brown eyes.
      B. It's *(name)*!

FOCUS

Simple present tense: contrast of *s* and *non-s* endings.

PRESENTING THE MODEL

1. Have students look at the illustration in the book.

2. Set the scene: "A woman is comparing herself to her sister."

3. Present the model.

4. Full-Class Choral Repetition.

5. Ask students if they have any questions; check understanding of new vocabulary: *journalist, Chicago, the suburbs, golf, tennis, musical instrument, on the weekend, go out.*

6. Call on one or two students to present the model.

   (For additional practice, do Choral Repetition in small groups or by rows.)

7. Talk about the two sisters.

   a. Name them **Jane** and **Sally**; have students label them in the book. Indicate that **Jane** is the *speaker* in the text.

   b. Make true and false statements about the sisters. Have students respond, "That's true," or "That's not true." If students respond, "That's not true," they must correct the statement. For example,

Teacher:	Students:
1. "Jane lives in Chicago."	"That's true."
2. "She's a journalist."	"That's not true. She's a teacher."
3. "Sally has a large house."	"That's not true. She has a large apartment."
4. "She plays tennis."	"That's true."

   c. Have students make true and false statements. Have other students answer as before.

ON YOUR OWN

In this exercise students again compare themselves to someone else. The letter cues *a* through *g* in the text are suggested topics for writing these sentences. Introduce the new words: *occupation, divorced.*

1. For homework, have students choose a person to compare themselves with, and then write at least 5 sentences. They can use all or some of the suggested topics.
2. Have students present their comparisons in the next class.

WORKBOOK

Students can now do pages 62, 63.

A. WHAT ARE THEY SAYING?

me	us
him	you
her	them
it	

1. Do you like me? — Of course I like *you*.
2. Do you like Bob? — Of course I like *him*.
3. Do you like my new tie? — Of course I like *it*.
4. Do you like Fred and Martha? — Of course I like *them*.
5. Do you like Mary? — Of course I like *her*.
6. Does Mary like you? — Of course she likes *me*.
7. Does the teacher like you? — Of course he likes *us*.
8. Do you like discotheques? — Of course I like *them*.
9. Do you like your new apartment? — Of course I like *it*.
10. Do you like your new neighbors? — Of course I like *them*.

58

B. WRITE ABOUT YOURSELF

always	usually	sometimes	rarely	never

1. I *always* read the newspaper.
2. I _____ eat breakfast.
3. I _____ cook dinner.
4. I _____ dance at parties.
5. I _____ watch TV.
6. I _____ do my homework.
7. I _____ listen to American music.
8. I _____ go to Italian restaurants.
9. I _____ drink champagne at parties.
10. I always _____
11. I usually _____
12. I sometimes _____
13. I rarely _____
14. I never _____

C. WRITE AND SAY IT

Correct the word in parentheses and then say the sentence.

1. John never (feed) *feeds* his cat.
2. Nancy rarely (help) *helps* her brother.
3. Judy always (fix) *fixes* her car.
4. Mrs. Smith rarely (talk) *talks* to her husband.
5. Mary usually (brush) *brushes* her teeth.
6. My father sometimes (wash) *washes* the clothes.
7. Linda never (go) *goes* to school.
8. Tommy sometimes (dance) *dances* with his sister.
9. When Jane (do) *does* her homework, she usually (eat) *eats*
10. When my grandfather (watch) *watches* TV, he always (sit) *sits* on the sofa.

59

Students practice writing object pronouns. (text page 62)

In Exercise B, students practice using adverbs of frequency while writing about themselves. Encourage students to look up new words in the dictionary when answering 10-14. (text page 63)
In Exercise C, have several students read each sentence aloud pronouncing clearly the final [s], [z], or [iz] of each verb. (text page 63)

Students practice the object pronouns *it*, *her*, *him*, and *them*. Exercise E is a listening comprehension. (text page 63)

Key to Exercise E
Read or play the tape.

1. I usually listen to her.
2. I never read it.
3. I help him when I'm at school.
4. I always sit with them.
5. I play with him every day.
6. I don't like them.

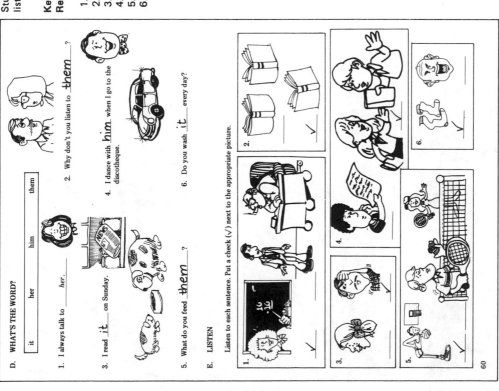

D. WHAT'S THE WORD?

it	her	him	them

1. I always talk to ___her___.

2. Why don't you listen to ___them___?

3. I read ___it___ on Sunday.

4. I dance with ___him___ when I go to the discotheque.

5. What do you feed ___them___?

6. Do you wash ___it___ every day?

E. LISTEN

Listen to each sentence. Put a check (✓) next to the appropriate picture.

60

F. WHAT ARE THEY SAYING?

have	don't
has	doesn't
do	
does	

1. **Does** Johnny **have** any brothers?
   No. He **doesn't have** any brothers, but he **has** a big sister.

2. Do you have any French wine?
   No. We **don't have** any French wine, but we **have** Italian wine.

3. We're looking for our child.
   What color eyes does she **have**?
   She **has** long brown hair.

4. Do your children have a good teacher?
   Yes. They **have** a wonderful teacher.

5. What kind of car **does** your brother **have**?
   He **has** a Toyota.

6. **Do** they **have** any shirts?
   No. They **don't have** any shirts, but they **have** beautiful ties.

7. **Does** your new apartment **have** a dining room?
   Yes. It **has** a dining room and a big kitchen.

Students practice using the verb *have* in positive and negative sentences and in questions. (text page 64)

61

G. LISTEN

MY GRANDMOTHER

Listen to the story. Write the missing words.

(1) My grandmother *has* brown eyes and gray curly *hair* . (2) She's short and heavy. (3) She **lives** with **us** , and I'm very glad. (4) Here's why I **think** she's wonderful.

(5) When we **go** to parties, my grandmother always **dances** with me. (6) When I **talk** to her, she always **listens** to me, and when my friends talk to her, she listens to **them** . (7) When I have difficult homework, my grandmother usually **helps** me. (8) When I'm hungry, she always **feeds** **me** to me, and when I'm upset, she always **sits** with **me** together, she **eat** . (9) When we **eat** **talks** **fixes** it. (13) When my little sisters are noisy, she **plays** with **them** .

(10) My grandmother is rarely upset. (11) When our clothes are dirty, she **washes** them. (12) When the sink is broken, she **fixes** it. (13) When my little sisters are noisy, she **plays** with **them** .

(14) My grandmother is really wonderful.

H. YES OR NO

| Yes, she is. | No, she isn't. |
| Yes, she does. | No, she doesn't. |

1. Does my grandmother have brown eyes?   *Yes, she does.*
2. Does she have brown hair?   **No, she doesn't.**
3. Is she tall?   **No, she isn't.**
4. Is she heavy?   **Yes, she is.**
5. Does she dance with me when we go to parties?   **Yes, she does.**
6. Does she watch TV when we eat together?   **No, she doesn't.**
7. Is she usually upset?   **No, she isn't.**
8. Does she listen to my friends when they talk to her?   **Yes, she does.**
9. Is she lazy?   **No, she isn't.**
10. Is she wonderful?   **Yes, she is.**

62

Exercise G is a dictation that reviews the vocabulary and structures taught in the lesson. Read the dictation or play the tape several times so that the students can listen, write, and make any corrections.

In Exercise H, students use short answers to answer questions about the dictation. (text page 65)

Key for Exercise G (above)
Read or play the tape.

My grandmother has brown eyes and gray curly hair. She's short and heavy. She lives with us, and I'm very glad. Here's why I think she's wonderful.

When we go to parties, my grandmother always dances with me. When I talk to her, she always listens to me, and when my friends talk to her, she listens to them.

When I have difficult homework, my grandmother usually helps me. When I'm hungry, she always feeds me. When we eat together, she always talks to me, and when I'm upset, she always sits with me.

My grandmother is rarely upset. When our clothes are dirty, she washes them. When the sink is broken, she fixes it. When my little sisters are noisy, she plays with them.

My grandmother is really wonderful.

I. A WONDERFUL PERSON

Write sentences about a person you think is wonderful. Tell why.

1. _____
2. _____
3. _____
4. _____
5. _____

J. WHAT'S THE WORD?

Put a circle around the correct word.

1. Maria is listening ⟨to / at / with⟩ the radio.

2. My uncle always dances ⟨to / at / (with)⟩ me.

3. John is playing soccer ⟨to / at / (with) / to⟩ us.

4. My children never talk ⟨at / at / on⟩ me.

5. Do you live ⟨(in) / on / at⟩ Tokyo?

6. Tell me ⟨to / at / (about)⟩ your city.

7. The post office is ⟨in / (on) / between⟩ Main Street.

8. I always listen ⟨at / (to) / on⟩ the radio when I eat breakfast.

9. I'm having a wonderful time ⟨in / on / (at)⟩ my party.

10. Is there a refrigerator ⟨(in) / on / at⟩ the kitchen?

11. Do Paul and Robert go ⟨(to) / at / in⟩ school?

12. We're looking ⟨from / (for) / to⟩ a yellow umbrella.

13. The children are ⟨to / (at) / in⟩ the beach.

14. Natasha is wearing a pair ⟨(of) / from / for⟩ boots.

15. Alice is sitting ⟨in / (on) / with⟩ a bench ⟨in / on / with⟩ the park.

16. Martha goes ⟨(to) / at / in⟩ church ⟨in / (on) / at⟩ Sunday.

63

In Exercise I, students write sentences about someone they know, using Exercise G as a model. Have students present their answers in class.
In Exercise J, students practice with the prepositions that have been used throughout the book. (text pages 64-65)

CHAPTER 12 OVERVIEW

TEXT PAGES 67-71

FOCUS

Contrast of simple present and present continuous tenses:
I'm smoking.	*I'm washing the dishes.*
I always smoke.	*I always wash the dishes.*

COMMUNICATIVE SKILLS

1. Describing emotional states:
     I'm sad.   *I'm nervous.*

2. Expressing regret:
     I'm sorry to hear that.

VOCABULARY

across the street	embarrassed	perspire	telephone
angry	floor	sad	That's strange!
bathtub	go to the doctor	shiver	thirsty
bite—nails	happy	shout	tired
blush	hitchhike	sick	work (n)
broken	lamp	sink	yawn
by candlelight	nervous	smile	

LANGUAGE NOTES

In this chapter there are several new words with the <u>sh</u> sound: <u>sh</u>out, <u>sh</u>iver, di<u>sh</u>es. Have students practice with this sound in contrast with the *s* sound. (See Expansion Activity for text pages 70-71.)

CULTURE KEY

In the exercises on text page 69, students tell how they personally react to different emotional and physical states. You may want to discuss cultural differences in these reactions. For example, a common reaction to angry feelings in one culture may be shouting; in another it may be silence. You may also want to discuss differences in male and female expression of emotion. For example, in one culture, men and women may often cry when they are sad; in another culture men may not usually cry.

FOCUS

1. Contrast of simple present and present continuous tenses.
2. *Why* questions with the present continuous tense.
3. Adjectives describing emotional and physical states.

GETTING READY

1. Introduce these new words; use your own visuals, SBS Picture Cards 75-85, or the illustrations on text page 69:

nervous	sick	thirsty
sad	cold	angry
happy	hot	embarrassed
tired	hungry	

    a. For each word, point to the visual and say the word one or more times. Act out the meaning whenever possible.
    b. Have students repeat chorally and individually.
    c. After introducing all the words, point to each visual and have students tell you the word.

2. Review and contrast present continuous and simple present tense forms.
    a. Write on the board:

    > I'm
    > He's
    > She's
    > We're ⎱ drinking.
    > You're
    > They're

    > He
    > She ⎱ always drinks.

    > I
    > We
    > You ⎱ always drink.
    > They

    b. Make sentences using these forms. Have students repeat chorally. For example,
    "He's drinking."   "He always drinks."
    c. Do the same with the verbs *go* and *study.*

PRESENTING THE MODEL

1. Have students look at the illustration in the book.
2. Set the scene: "Two people are talking."
3. Present the model.
4. Full-Class Choral Repetition.
5. Ask students if they have any questions.
6. Group Choral Repetition.
7. Choral Conversation.
8. Call on one or two pairs of students to present the dialog.
    (For additional practice, do Choral Conversation in small groups or by rows.)
9. Practice the model with other pronouns. Substitute *she, he,* and *they.* Put on the board:

    > she   he   they

    For each pronoun, have students listen, repeat, and practice as usual.

Examples:

"she"	"Why is she crying?" "She's crying because she's sad." "She always cries when she's sad."
"he"	"Why is he crying?" "He's crying because he's sad." "He always cries when he's sad."
"they"	"Why are they crying?" "They're crying because they're sad." "They always cry when they're sad."

SIDE BY SIDE EXERCISES

Examples:

> 1. A. Why are you smiling?
>   B. I'm smiling because I'm happy.
>   I always smile when I'm happy.
> 2. A. Why is he shouting?
>   B. He's shouting because he's angry.
>   He always shouts when he's angry.

In the following exercises, use the illustrations in the text or SBS Picture Cards 86-93 to introduce the new vocabulary.

1. **Exercise 1:** Introduce the new word: *smiling*. Call on two students to present the dialog. Then do Choral Repetition and Choral Conversation Practice.
2. **Exercise 2:** Introduce the new word: *shouting*. Same as above.
3. **Exercises 3-10:**

> **New vocabulary:** 6. *go to the doctor* 7. *shiver* 8. *perspire*
> 9. *yawn* 10. *blush*

Either Full-Class Practice or Pair Practice.

OPTIONAL WRITING PRACTICE

Have students write exercises 2, 5, 8, 9, 10 for homework.

WORKBOOK

Students can now do pages 64, 65.

EXPANSION ACTIVITY

Act It Out!
1. Make word cards for the following actions:
   cry   eat   smoke   perspire
   smile   yawn   drink   blush
2. Have students take a word card *without showing it to anyone.*
3. Have each student act out the action on his or her word card.
4. Then call on pairs of students to create conversations like the ones on text page 68.

FOCUS

Students describe how they usually react to emotional states. For example,
When I'm nervous I bite my nails.
When I'm thirsty I drink tea.

GETTING READY

1. Present the following model:

   A. What do you do when you're nervous?
   B. When I'm nervous I *smoke*.

2. Full-Class Choral Repetition.

3. Group Choral Repetition.

4. Choral Conversation.

5. Call on one or two pairs of students to practice the dialog.

6. Substitute the word *perspire* for *smoke*, and practice as above.

7. Next substitute *bite my nails*, and practice as above.

8. Then ask students,
   "What do *you* do when you're nervous?"
   Have students answer using any vocabulary they wish.

SIDE BY SIDE EXERCISES

1. For homework, have students write exercises 2-11, using exercise 1 as a guide. Encourage students to use dictionaries to find new words they need to describe themselves.

2. The next day in class, call on pairs of students to ask and answer:
   A. What do you do when you're _____?
   B. When I'm _____ I _____.

   Students shouldn't refer to their written homework when practicing.

   Examples:

   2. A. What do you do when you're sad?
      B. When I'm sad I cry.
         (or "When I'm sad I go to my room.")
   3. A. What do you do when you're happy?
      B. When I'm happy I smile.
         (or "When I'm happy I sing Irish songs.")

EXPANSION ACTIVITIES

1. *Review Vocabulary With Visuals*

   Use your own visuals or SBS Picture Cards 75-93 to review the vocabulary on text pages 68 and 69.

   a. Point to a visual; ask a *Yes/No* question.

   b. Have students answer "Yes" or "No." If the answer is "No," have them give the correct information.

   c. Examples:

   > "Is he happy?"
   > "Yes."
   > "Is he smiling?"
   > "Yes."
   >
   > "Is she smiling?"
   > "No. She's crying."
   > "Is she happy?"
   > "No. She's sad."

2. *Sentence Game*

   Write answers for exercises 1-11 on cards. You can use your students' homework answers or write new ones. Cut each card in half. For example:

When I'm happy	I tell jokes.

   Mix up all these cards and have students put them back together to make meaningful sentences. Have students try new combinations to see how many sentences are possible.

ON YOUR OWN

FOCUS

> Contrast of simple present and present continuous tenses:
> *I NEVER wash the dishes in the bathtub, but I'm washing the dishes in the bathtub TODAY.*

PRESENTING THE MODEL

1. Have students look at the model illustration in the book or on the SBS Dialog Visual Card.

2. Set the scene: "Two women are talking. One woman is surprised because the other woman is doing something very strange."

3. Present the model.

4. Full-Class Choral Repetition.

5. Ask students if they have any questions; check understanding of new vocabulary: *dishes, bathtub, sink, broken, That's strange!*

6. Group Choral Repetition.

7. Choral Conversation.

8. Call on one or two pairs of students to present the dialog.

   (For additional practice, do Choral Conversation in small groups or by rows.)

SIDE BY SIDE EXERCISES

Examples:

1. A. What are you doing?!
   B. I'm sleeping on the floor.
   A. That's strange! Do you USUALLY sleep on the floor?
   B. No. I NEVER sleep on the floor, but I'm sleeping on the floor TODAY.
   A. Why are you sleeping on the floor?
   B. Because my BED is broken.
   A. I'm sorry to hear that.

2. A. What are you doing?!
   B. I'm cooking on the radiator.
   A. That's strange! Do you USUALLY cook on the radiator?
   B. No! I NEVER cook on the radiator, but I'm cooking on the radiator TODAY.
   A. Why are you cooking on the radiator?
   B. Because my STOVE is broken.
   A. I'm sorry to hear that.

1. **Exercise 1:** Introduce the new word: *floor.* Call on two students to present the dialog.

2. **Exercise 2:** Introduce the new word: *radiator.* Same as above.

3. **Exercises 3-5:**

   > **New vocabulary:**   3. *by candlelight, lamp*   4. *across the street*
   >   5. *hitchhike, work*

   Either Full-Class Practice or Pair Practice.

4. **Exercise 6:** For homework, have students use the model as a guide to create 2 new conversations about people doing things they don't usually do. Have students present their conversations in class the next day. (Students can bring in *props* if they wish.)

WORKBOOK

Students can now do pages 66, 67, 68, 69.

EXPANSION ACTIVITY

Practice *sh* and *s* sounds

1. Have students practice saying these words with *sh* sounds. Write some or all of them on the board; have students repeat after you.

1.	shout	6.	blush	11.	station
2.	shiver	7.	wash	12.	Swedish
3.	shirt	8.	dishes	13.	fiction
4.	short	9.	international		
5.	sure	10.	Russian		

2. Have students practice saying these words with *s* sounds. Write some or all of them on the board; have students repeat after you.

1.	sing	6.	baseball	11.	smoke
2.	sad	7.	office	12.	sports
3.	listen	8.	Miss	13.	study
4.	hospital	9.	fix	14.	sleeps
5.	discotheque	10.	what's		

A. WHAT'S THE WORD?

angry	hot	sad
embarrassed	hungry	sick
happy	nervous	thirsty
		tired

12

1. Henry is wearing a suit at the beach.
   He's _hot._

2. Alice is yawning. She's _tired_ .

3. Mr. Smith's students never do their homework. Mr. Smith is _angry_ .

4. Robert made a mistake in class.
   He's _embarrassed_ .

5. Gloria likes her new apartment.
   She's _happy_ .

6. Edward is drinking lemonade.
   He's _thirsty_ .

7. Walter's new car is broken.
   He's _sad_ .

8. Jane has an English test on Monday.
   She's _nervous_ .

9. Paul is eating a big breakfast.
   He's _hungry_ .

10. Peter is in the hospital.
    He's _sick_ .

Students practice new adjectives. (text page 68)

64

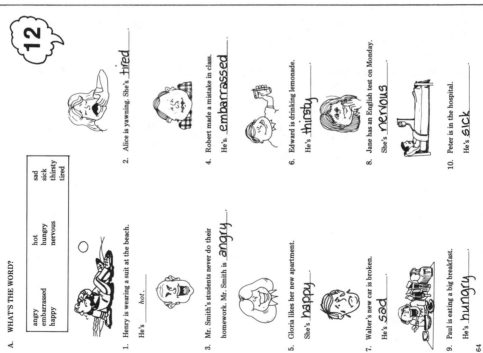

B. TELL ME WHY

1. Why is he smoking?
   He's smoking because he's nervous.
   He always _smokes when he's nervous._

2. Why are you yawning?
   I'm yawning because I'm tired.
   I always _yawn when I'm tired._

3. Why are they shouting?
   They're shouting because they're angry.
   They always _shout when they're angry._

4. Why are you shivering?
   We're shivering because we're cold.
   We always _shiver when we're cold._

5. Why is he perspiring?
   He's perspiring because he's hot.
   He always _perspires when he's hot._

6. Why are they crying?
   They're crying because they're sad.
   They always _cry when they're sad._

7. Why is he going to a restaurant?
   He's going to a restaurant because he's hungry.
   He always _goes to a restaurant when he's hungry._

8. Why is she smiling?
   She's smiling because she's happy.
   She always _smiles when she's happy._

9. Why are you blushing?
   I'm blushing because I'm embarrassed.
   I always _blush when I'm embarrassed._

Exercise B is a review of the present continuous and the simple present. (text page 68)

65

Students practice using the present continuous and the simple present. Note that the pairs of sentences always use the same verb. You can also do this exercise orally. For each exercise, call on a pair of students, one to read the sentence on the left, the other to read the sentence on the right. (text pages 70-71)

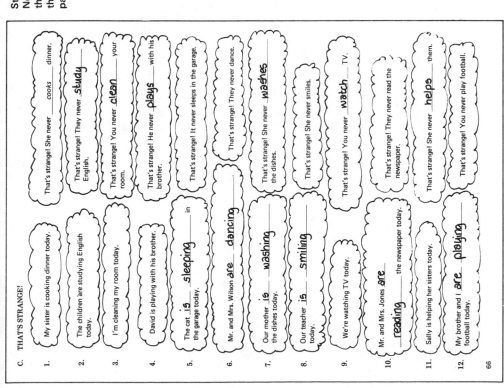

C. THAT'S STRANGE!

1. My sister is cooking dinner today. — That's strange! She never _cooks_ dinner.

2. The children are studying English today. — That's strange! They never _study_ English.

3. I'm cleaning my room today. — That's strange! You never _clean_ your room.

4. David is playing with his brother. — That's strange! He never _plays_ with his brother.

5. The cat _is_ _sleeping_ in the garage today. — That's strange! It never sleeps in the garage.

6. Mr. and Mrs. Wilson _are_ _dancing_. — That's strange! They never dance.

7. Our mother _is_ _washing_ the dishes today. — That's strange! She never _washes_ the dishes.

8. Our teacher _is_ _smiling_ today. — That's strange! She never smiles.

9. We're watching TV today. — That's strange! You never _watch_ TV.

10. Mr. and Mrs. Jones _are_ _reading_ the newspaper today. — That's strange! They never read the newspaper.

11. Sally is helping her sisters today. — That's strange! She never _helps_ them.

12. My brother and I _are_ _playing_ football today. — That's strange! You never play football.

66

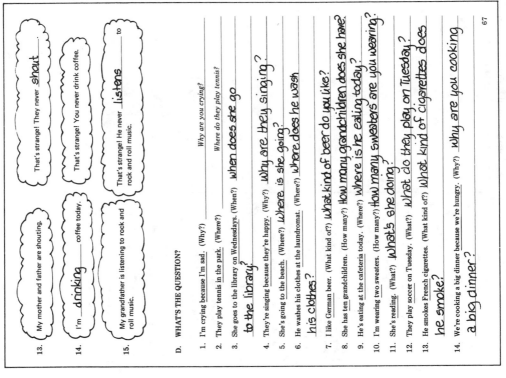

13. My mother and father are shouting.

That's strange! They never **shout** .

14. I'm **drinking** coffee today.

That's strange! You never drink coffee.

15. My grandfather is listening to rock and roll music.

That's strange! He never **listens** to rock and roll music.

D. WHAT'S THE QUESTION?

1. I'm crying because I'm sad. (Why?) _____ *Why are you crying?*

2. They play tennis in the park. (Where?) _____ *Where do they play tennis?*

3. She goes to the library on Wednesdays. (When?) **when does she go to the library?**

4. They're singing because they're happy. (Why?) **why are they singing?**

5. She's going to the beach. (Where?) **where is she going?**

6. He washes his clothes at the laundromat. (Where?) **where does he wash his clothes?**

7. I like German beer. (What kind of?) **what kind of beer do you like?**

8. She has ten grandchildren. (How many?) **How many grandchildren does she have?**

9. He's eating at the cafeteria today. (Where?) **Where is he eating today?**

10. I'm wearing two sweaters. (How many?) **How many sweaters are you wearing?**

11. She's reading. (What?) **what is she doing?**

12. They play soccer on Tuesday. (What?) **what do they play on Tuesday?**

13. He smokes French cigarettes. (What kind of?) **what kind of cigarettes does he smoke?**

14. We're cooking a big dinner because we're hungry. (Why?) **why are you cooking a big dinner?**

67

In Exercise D, students practice writing information questions in the present continuous and the simple present. (text page 70-71)

158 CHAPTER TWELVE

In Exercise E, students listen to four short stories and answer *yes* or *no* to statements about the stories.

Key to Exercise E

For each story, read or play the tape twice. Have students look at the sentences in their workbooks as they listen.

JANE AND BETTY
1. Jane and Betty are looking for a restaurant. They're very hungry. They usually eat dinner at home, but their mother isn't cooking today.

AM I LAZY?
2. My teacher thinks I'm lazy because I never do my homework, but my mother isn't angry at me. She's happy because I always help her in the kitchen, and I always wash the dishes. I'm glad my mother doesn't think I'm lazy.

TOM
3. Tom is usually very happy. He loves his friends and his family, and he usually smiles at them. But today Tom isn't smiling. He's shouting at his little sister because she isn't studying.

VACATION
4. When my family and I are on vacation, I always have a wonderful time. I usually go to the beach, but when it's cold, I read books and listen to music. Today is a beautiful vacation day, and I'm playing tennis with my sister in the park.

Exercise F is a pronunciation exercise which gives practice with the [s] sound. Have students read the sentences aloud. For additional practice, students can ask and answer questions about the pictures. (Ex. Why is Stanley smiling? Stanley is smiling because he likes his new suit.) (text pages 70-71)

E. LISTEN

As you listen to each story, read the following sentences and check yes or no. You will hear each story twice.

Jane and Betty
1. yes ☐ no ☑   Jane and Betty are looking for a discotheque.
2. yes ☐ no ☑   Jane and Betty are very angry.
3. yes ☐ no ☑   Their mother isn't cooking dinner today.

Am I Lazy?
4. yes ☑ no ☐   I always do my homework.
5. yes ☑ no ☐   I always help my mother in the kitchen.
6. yes ☐ no ☑   My mother thinks I'm lazy.

Tom
7. yes ☑ no ☐   Tom is usually happy.
8. yes ☐ no ☑   Tom is smiling today.
9. yes ☐ no ☑   Tom's sister is studying.

Vacation
10. yes ☑ no ☐   I like vacations.
11. yes ☐ no ☑   When it's hot, I read books and listen to music.
12. yes ☑ no ☐   My sister and I are playing tennis in the park.

F. LOUD AND CLEAR

Fill in the words, then read the sentences aloud.

| Spanish | Steven | studying | what's | likes | smiling | Stanley | suit |

1. _What's_ _Steven_ doing?
   He's _studying_ _Spanish_.

2. _Stanley_ is _smiling_ because he _likes_ his new _suit_.

68

3.

Alice	boss	nervous	talks

Alice is nervous when she talks to her boss.

4.

bicycle	Stuart	school	sunny

When it's sunny, Stuart goes to school on his bicycle.

5.

Sam	sister	singing	sleeping	song

Sam isn't sleeping because his sister is singing a loud song.

6.

hospital	Mrs.	sick	sorry	Wilson

Mr. Wilson is in the hospital. Mrs. Wilson is sorry he's sick.

7.

Boris	bus	next	school

Boris always sits next to the bus driver on the school bus.

8.

asks	listen	science	students	question

When the science teacher asks a question, her students always listen.

69

160   CHAPTER TWELVE

Ex. What are Fred and Jane doing today?
1. What do you usually do when you go to parties?
2. Where are you going today?
3. What does Robert usually do when he's nervous?
4. What kind of food does Mrs. Jones usually cook?
5. Is Henry fixing the car?

CHECKUP TEST: Chapters 11-12

A. Fill in the blanks.

| me | him | her | it | us | you | them |

Ex. Do you like Mr. Wilson?
Of course I like _him_.

1. Does John listen to his mother?
Of course he listens to _her_.

2. When the windows are dirty, I always wash _them_.

3. I don't like TV, but I'm watching _it_ today.

4. Bob rarely plays with his brother, but he's playing with _him_ today.

5. When my sister and I are hungry my mother always feeds _us_.

B. Fill in the blanks.
Ex. I never eat breakfast, but I'm _eating_ breakfast today.

1. Mary never shouts, but she's _shouting_ today.

2. We never _go_ to the library, but we're going to the library today.

3. Mr. and Mrs. Jones never dance, but they're _dancing_ today.

4. John never _fixes_ his car, but he's fixing his car today.

5. Tommy never _washes_ the dishes, but he's washing the dishes today.

C. Fill in the blanks.

| do | does | is | are |

Ex. What _does_ Walter usually do on Sunday?
b. Where _is_ Bobby studying?

1. When _do_ Mary and Walter usually go to the bank?

2. Why _is_ Barbara shivering?

70

---

3. _Does_ Bill usually wash the dishes?
4. _Are_ Jack and Judy cooking dinner today? Yes, they _are_.
5. Do they have any pets? Yes, they _do_.

D. Write the question.
Ex. I'm crying because I'm sad. (Why?)
   Why are you crying?

They play tennis in the park. (Where?)
   Where do they play tennis?

1. She goes to the supermarket on Wednesdays. (When?)
   When does she go to the supermarket?

2. He's yawning because he's tired. (Why?)
   Why is he yawning?

3. They're sleeping on the floor. (Where?)
   Where are they sleeping?

4. She has three children. (How many?)
   How many children does she have?

5. I'm drinking coffee. (What?)
   What are you drinking?

E. LISTEN
Listen to each question. Put a circle around the correct answer.

Ex. (a.) They're playing baseball.
    b. They play tennis.

1. a. We're dancing.
   (b.) We drink champagne.

2. (a.) I'm going to the beach.
   b. I go to school.

3. (a.) He's smoking.
   b. He eats.

4. a. She's cooking Italian food.
   (b.) She cooks French food.

5. (a.) Yes, he is.
   b. Yes, he does.

CHAPTER 13 OVERVIEW

TEXT PAGES 73-77

FOCUS

1. *Can/Can't:*	*Can you sing?* *Yes, I can.* *No, I can't.*
2. *Have to/Has to:*	*I have to work.* *She has to go to the doctor.*

COMMUNICATIVE SKILLS

1. Expressing ability:
    I can speak English.

2. Expressing obligation:
    I have to work.

3. Extending and declining an invitation:
    Can you go to a movie with me on Wednesday?
    I'm sorry. I can't.

4. Identifying professions:
    He's a mechanic.
    She's a baker.

VOCABULARY

act	checkers	go jogging	mechanic
actor	chef	go sailing	singer
actress	chess	go shopping	skate
apple pies	dancer	go skating	ski
bake	dentist	go skiing	teach
baker	depressed	go swimming	truck
baseball game	do my laundry	have a party	truck driver
bus	drive	have dinner	violin
bus driver	go bowling	have lunch	violinist
can	go dancing	have to	visit
can't			work (v)

LANGUAGE NOTES

1. When *can* is used with another verb (as in *I can skate.*) it is unstressed and pronounced [kun]. In other cases, *can* is pronounced [kæn]. *(Yes, I can.)*

2. In informal speech,
    have to is usually pronounced [hafta].
    "I have to go."

    has to is usually pronounced [hasta].
    "He has to go."

CULTURE KEY

1. **Chess** and **checkers** (see text page 74) are popular board games in the U.S.

2. **Jogging** (see text page 77), or running at a slow pace for exercise, is very popular in the U.S. Many people jog early in the morning before going to work or school, or late in the day.

FOCUS

> Introduction of *can* and *can't*.

GETTING READY

1. Introduce *can* and *can't*. Have students look at the right hand box at the top of the page, or write on the board:

   > Can you _____?   Yes, I can.
   >   No, I can't.

   a. Have students repeat, "Yes, I can," chorally and individually.
   b. Have several students answer, "Yes, I can," as you ask about their ability to speak their native language:
      "Can you speak _____?"
      "Yes, I can."
   c. Call on a few pairs of students to ask and answer the same question.
   d. Have students repeat, "No, I can't," chorally and individually.
   e. Have several students answer, "No, I can't," as you ask about a language they don't know:
      "Can you speak _____?"
      "No, I can't."
   f. Call on a few pairs of students to ask the same or a similar question and answer, "No, I can't."

2. Make sentences using the forms in the box at the top of the page; have students repeat chorally and individually. For example,
      "I can sing."   "I can't sing."
      "He can sing."   "He can't sing."

PRESENTING THE MODEL

1. Have students look at the model illustration in the book or on the SBS Dialog Visual Card.
2. Set the scene: "Two diplomats are talking in front of the United Nations Building in New York City."
3. Present the model.
4. Full-Class Choral Repetition.
5. Ask students if they have any questions; check understanding of *can* and *can't*.
6. Group Choral Repetition.
7. Choral Conversation.
8. Call on one or two pairs of students to present the dialog.
   (For additional practice, do Choral Conversation in small groups or by rows.)

SIDE BY SIDE EXERCISES

Examples:

1. A. Can Mary ski?
    B. No, she can't. But she can swim.
2. A. Can Sam cook Chinese food?
    B. No, he can't. But he can cook French food.
3. A. Can they play the violin?
    B. No, they can't. But they can play the piano.

1. **Exercise 1:** Introduce the new word: *ski.* Call on two students to present the dialog. Then do Choral Repetition and Choral Conversation Practice.
2. **Exercise 2:** Same as above.
3. **Exercises 3-8:**

> **New vocabulary:**   3. *violin*   5. *chess, checkers*   7. *football*   8. *skate*

Either Full-Class Practice or Pair Practice.

4. **Exercise 9:** Here students talk about themselves. Have pairs of students ask and answer using any vocabulary they wish.

OPTIONAL WRITING PRACTICE

Have students write exercises 4, 5, 6, 7, 8 for homework.

WORKBOOK

Students can now do pages 71, 72 Exercise B.

EXPANSION ACTIVITY

Students Talk About Themselves

1. Put some or all of these words on the board or on word cards. You can also use visuals for these activities:

    play *(football)*   ski
    play the *(piano)*   cook
    speak *(French)*   dance
    fix *(cars)*   sing
                           swim

2. Point to each activity and call on pairs of students to ask about and describe their *own* abilities. For example,

    "Can you ski?"   "Can you speak French?"
    "No, I can't.   "Yes, I can."

    "Can you dance?"
    "No, I can't. But I can sing."

3. You can practice *he* or *she* by talking about the student who has just answered.
    "Can he/she _____?"

FOCUS

1. Professions and related activities:
   He's a mechanic. He fixes cars every day.
   She's a truck driver. She drives a truck every day.

2. Emphatic short answers with *can*:
   "Of course he can."

GETTING READY

1. Practice *Of Course* _____ *can,* using *I, he, she, you, they.*
   a. Ask questions about students' ability to speak their native language(s). Encourage students to answer emphatically,
      "OF COURSE, _____ CAN!"
   b. Ask, "Can I speak _____?"
      "Can *(name of male student)* speak _____?"
      "Can *(name of a female student)* speak _____?"
      "Can *(names of students)* speak _____?"
      "Can we speak _____?"

PRESENTING THE MODEL

1. Have students look at the model illustration in the book or on the SBS Dialog Visual Card.
2. Set the scene: "Two people are talking about Jack."
3. Present the model.
4. Full-Class Choral Repetition.
5. Ask students if they have any questions; check understanding of new vocabulary: *mechanic.*
6. Group Choral Repetition.
7. Choral Conversation.
8. Call on one or two pairs of students to present the dialog.
   (For additional practice, do Choral Conversation in small groups or by rows.)

SIDE BY SIDE EXERCISES

Examples:

1. A. Can Arthur play the violin?
   B. Of course he can. He plays the violin every day. He's a violinist.
2. A. Can Fred and Ginger dance?
   B. Of course they can. They dance every day. They're dancers.

Use the illustrations in the text or SBS Picture Cards 94-104 to introduce the new vocabulary.

1. **Exercise 1:** Introduce the new word: *violinist.* Call on two students to present the dialog. Then do Choral Repetition and Choral Conversation Practice.
2. **Exercise 2:** Introduce the new word: *singer.* Same as above.

3. Exercises 3-10:

> **New vocabulary:** 3. *dancer* 4. *chef* 5. *baker, apple pies* 6. *act, actor*
> 7. *actress* 8. *teach* 9. *drive, truck, truck driver* 10. *bus, bus driver*

Either Full-Class Practice or Pair Practice.

OPTIONAL WRITING PRACTICE

Have students write exercises 1, 3, 6, 7, 9 for homework.

WORKBOOK

Students can now do pages 72 Exercises C, D, 73.

EXPANSION ACTIVITIES

1. *Practice Professions With Visuals*
   a. Review the professions on text page 75 using your own visuals or SBS Picture Cards 94-104. For example,

      > Point to a visual and ask: "What does he/she do?"
      > Have students answer: "He's/She's a *(teacher)*."

   b. Teach additional names of professions according to your students' interests. Use your own visuals or SBS Picture Cards 105-120:

doctor	secretary
nurse	factory worker
dentist	businessman/businesswoman
carpenter	salesman/saleswoman
plumber	computer programmer
scientist	mailman
policeman	painter

      Point to each visual and say: "He's/She's a _____."
      Have students repeat chorally and individually.
      Point to each visual; have students ask and answer:

      > "What does he/she do?"
      > "He's/She's a _____."

2. *Role Play Professions*
   Use visuals or word cards of professions to assign imaginary professions to students in the class. Have students create conversations based on the models on text pages 74 and 75.
   a. Students can talk about themselves and their imaginary professions.
      A. Can you fix cars?
      B. Of course I can. I fix cars every day. I'm a mechanic. Can YOU fix cars?
      A. No, I can't. But I can cook. I cook every day. I'm a cook.
   b. Students can talk about other people in the class and their imaginary professions:
      A. Can *(Henry)* drive a bus?
      B. Of course he can. He drives a bus every day. He's a bus driver.
      A. Can *(Jane)* bake apple pies?
      B. No, she can't. But she can dance. She dances every day. She's a dancer.

3. *Guessing Game*
   Give one student a card with a profession on it. Have other students ask Yes/No questions with *Do* in order to guess the profession. For example, students can ask,

   > "Do you cook every day?"
   > "Do you drive a bus every day?"

FOCUS

> Introduction of *have to* to express obligation.
> *I have to work.*
> *He has to go to the doctor.*

GETTING READY

1. Write *have to* and *has to* on the board. Introduce *have to* by describing typical obligations. For example,

   "You *have to* go to school on Monday, but
      you *don't have to* go to school on Sunday."

   "In this class you *have to* speak English."
   "You *have to* eat every day."

2. Form sentences using the words in the grammar box. Have students repeat chorally after you. For example,

   "I have to work."
   "We have to work."
   "She has to work."

PRESENTING THE MODEL

1. Have students look at the model illustration in the book or on the SBS Dialog Visual Card.
2. Set the scene: "Herbert is depressed. He's having a party today, but his friends can't go to his party. They're all busy."
3. Present the model.
4. Full-Class Choral Repetition.
5. Ask students if they have any questions; check understanding of new vocabulary: *depressed, having a party, has to.*
6. Group Choral Repetition.
7. Choral Conversation.
8. Call on one or two pairs of students to present the dialog.

   (For additional practice, do Choral Conversation in small groups or by rows.)

SIDE BY SIDE EXERCISES

Examples:

> 1. A. Can Peggy go to Herbert's party?
>   B. No, she can't. She has to fix her car.
> 2. A. Can George and Martha go to Herbert's party?
>   B. No, they can't. They have to go to the supermarket.

1. **Exercise 1:** Call on two students to present the dialog. Then do Choral Repetition and Choral Conversation Practice.

2. **Exercise 2:** Same as above.

3. **Exercises 3-7:**

   > **New vocabulary:**   3. *dentist*

   Either Full-Class Practice or Pair Practice.

4. **Exercise 8:** Here students pretend they are Herbert's friends and tell why they can't go to his party.

OPTIONAL WRITING PRACTICE

Have students write exercises 2, 3, 4, 5, 8 for homework.

WORKBOOK

Students can now do pages 74, 75.

EXPANSION ACTIVITY

Role Play: Having a Party

1. Have each student write a simple schedule showing *Monday* through *Friday* and one thing he or she has to do on those days. Students can use the vocabulary on text page 76 or any vocabulary they wish. For example,

   > Monday—wash my car
   > Tuesday—go to the dentist
   > Wednesday—fix my TV
   > Thursday—study English
   > Friday—go to the bank

2. Call on pairs of students to create conversations using the following framework:

   > A.   What do you have to do on _____?
   > B.   On _____ I have to _____.

3. Pretend you are having a party. Create conversations with your students where you *invite* them and they either accept or decline, depending upon their *schedules* from above. For example,

   > You: I'm having a party on Monday. (Gesture to a student)
   >   Can you go to my party?
   > Student: No, I can't. I have to go to the doctor.
   >
   > You: (pointing to Student B) Can you go to my party?
   > Student: No, I can't. I have to wash my car.

   Keeping changing the day of your party to expand the practice.

ON YOUR OWN

FOCUS

> Using *can* and *have to* to extend and decline an invitation.

PRESENTING THE MODEL

There are two model conversations. Introduce and practice each one separately. For each model:

1. Have students look at the model illustration in the book.
2. Set the scene: "Two friends are talking."
3. Present the model.
4. Full-Class Choral Repetition.
5. Ask students if they have any questions; check understanding of new vocabulary: *do my laundry, go skating.*
6. Group Choral Repetition.
7. Choral Conversation.
8. Call on one or two pairs of students to present the dialog.

SIDE BY SIDE EXERCISES

Examples:

> 1. A. Mary. Can you go sailing with me on Tuesday?
>   B. I'm sorry. I can't. I have to visit a friend in the hospital.
> 2. A. Jack. Can you have dinner with me on Saturday?
>   B. I'm sorry. I can't. I have to study.

1. Have students look at the two columns at the bottom of the page. The expressions on the left are activities someone might do with a friend. The expressions on the right are reasons someone might use to decline an invitation.
2. Introduce new vocabulary. Use your own visuals or SBS Picture Cards 121-134.

    > *go to a movie, baseball game, have lunch, go swimming, go dancing, go skating, go skiing, go shopping, go bowling, go sailing, go jogging, visit, work*

3. Have students think of other reasons for declining an invitation. Add them to the list.
4. Have students create dialogs based on the model. Either Full-Class Practice or Pair Practice.
5. **Writing Practice**
    For homework, have students write out 5 conversations based on the model. Encourage students to use dictionaries to find new words.

WORKBOOK

Students can now do page 76.

A. CAN OR CAN'T

cook	skate	speak
dance	sing	swim
play		

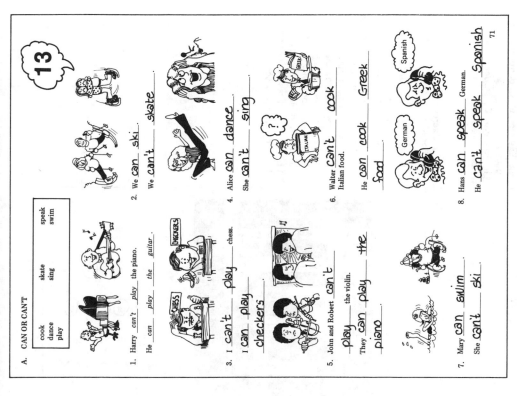

1. Harry *can't* play the piano.
   He *can play the guitar*.

2. We *can ski*.
   We *can't skate*.

3. I *can't play* chess.
   I *can play checkers*.

4. Alice *can dance*.
   She *can't sing*.

5. John and Robert *can't play* the violin.
   They *can play the piano*.

6. Walter *can't cook* Italian food.
   He *can cook Greek food*.

7. Mary *can swim*.
   She *can't ski*.

8. Hans *can speak* German.
   He *can't speak Spanish*.

71

Students practice *can* and *can't*. Note that some sentence pairs have *can't* in the first sentence and others have *can*. (text page 74)

CHAPTER THIRTEEN   171

In Exercise B, students write about what they *can* and *can't* do. Encourage students to use dictionaries. (text page 74)

In Exercise C, students practice the new vocabulary of professions. (text page 75)

In Exercise D, students listen for the difference between *can* and *can't*. (text page 75)

Key to Exercise D
Read or play the tape.

1. My grandmother can speak Russian.
2. My sister can't sing.
3. My sister can't bake.
4. John and his brother can play checkers.
5. We can't fix the car.
6. My father can't play football.
7. Tommy can play the violin.
8. I can't drive a bus.
9. Can you cook Mexican food?
10. Mr. and Mrs. Johnson can ski.
11. They can't read Greek newspapers.
12. They can play soccer.

B. WRITE ABOUT YOURSELF

What can you do?

1. I can _____
2. _____
3. _____
4. _____
5. _____

What can't you do?

1. I can't _____
2. _____
3. _____
4. _____
5. _____

C. PUZZLE

What do they do for a living?

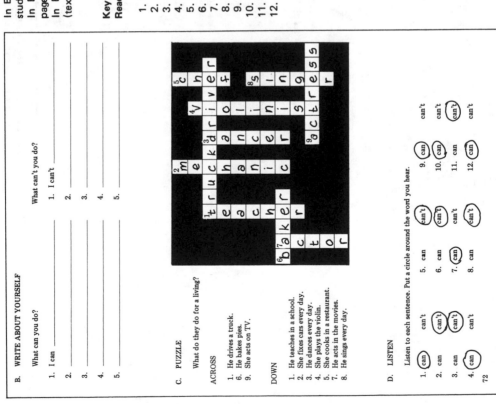

ACROSS

1. He drives a truck.
6. He bakes pies.
9. She acts on TV.

DOWN

1. He teaches in a school.
2. She fixes cars every day.
3. He dances every day.
4. She plays the violin.
5. She cooks in a restaurant.
7. He acts in the movies.
8. He sings every day.

D. LISTEN

Listen to each sentence. Put a circle around the word you hear.

1. (can)   can't
2. can   (can't)
3. can   (can't)
4. (can)   can't
5. can   (can't)
6. can   (can't)
7. (can)   can't
8. can   (can't)
9. (can)   can't
10. (can't)
11. can   can't
12. (can't)   can't

72

In Exercise E, students practice forming questions with *can*.

In Exercise F, students fill in the blanks with the most appropriate word. For more practice you can have the students read the story aloud, and then ask and answer questions with *can*. (Ex. Can Bob speak Russian? No, he can't./Can Sally play golf? Yes, she can./Can Sally speak Spanish? We don't know.)(text page 75)

Key to Exercise F

Sally Nelson *is* an actress. She's young and pretty, but when she acts, she can look young or old, beautiful or *ugly*, happy or *sad*.

Her husband Bob *is* an English *teacher*. He teaches students from cities around the world. His students speak Spanish, French, Russian, and Arabic. Bob sometimes *speaks* Spanish and French with them, but he can't *speak* Russian or Arabic.

Sally is a good athlete. She *plays* tennis and golf very well. When it's cold she skis, and when it's *hot* she swims *every* day.

Bob doesn't like sports. He can't *play* tennis or golf, but he *can* ski. When he isn't busy, he usually *reads* the newspaper or *plays* checkers. He likes chess because he *can* play very well.

Sally and Bob both love music. Sally sings popular *songs* and *plays* the piano. Bob can't play the piano, but he *can* sing and he can *play* the violin.

E. WHAT'S THE QUESTION?

1. _Can she bake ?_
Yes, she can.

2. _Can he play baseball_?
No, he can't.

3. _Can they play the violin_?
Yes, they can.

4. _Can you drive_?
Yes, I can.

5. _Can they skate_ ?
No, they can't.

6. _Can he swim_ ?
Yes, he can.

F. THE NELSON FAMILY

Fill in the blanks.

Sally Nelson _is_ an actress. She's young and pretty, but when she acts, she can look young or old, beautiful or _ugly_, happy or _sad_.

Her husband Bob _is_ an English _teacher_. He teaches students from cities around the world. His students speak Spanish, French, Russian and Arabic. Bob sometimes _speaks_ Russian or Arabic.

Sally is a good athlete. She _plays_ tennis and golf very well. When it's cold she skis, and when it's _hot_ she swims _every_ day.

Bob doesn't like sports. He can't _play_ tennis or golf, but he _can_ ski. When he isn't busy, he usually _reads_ the newspaper or _plays_ chess. He likes chess because he _can_ play very well.

Sally and Bob both love music. Sally sings popular _songs_ and _plays_ the piano. Bob can't play the piano, but he _can_ sing and he can _play_ the violin.

73

CHAPTER THIRTEEN   173

174 CHAPTER THIRTEEN

G. WHAT ARE THEY SAYING?

have to	do	don't
has to	does	doesn't

1. Why are you upset? — I _have_ _to_ go to the dentist.

2. Why is Johnny angry? — He _has_ _to_ clean his room.

3. Do we _have_ _to_ go to the supermarket?

4. Do you _have_ _to_ work today? — No, I _don't_ . I'm on vacation.

5. Do I _have_ _to_ wear a sweater? — Of course you _do_ . It's very cold today.

6. Why is Mr. Jones smiling? — He _doesn't_ _have_ _to_ work on Friday.

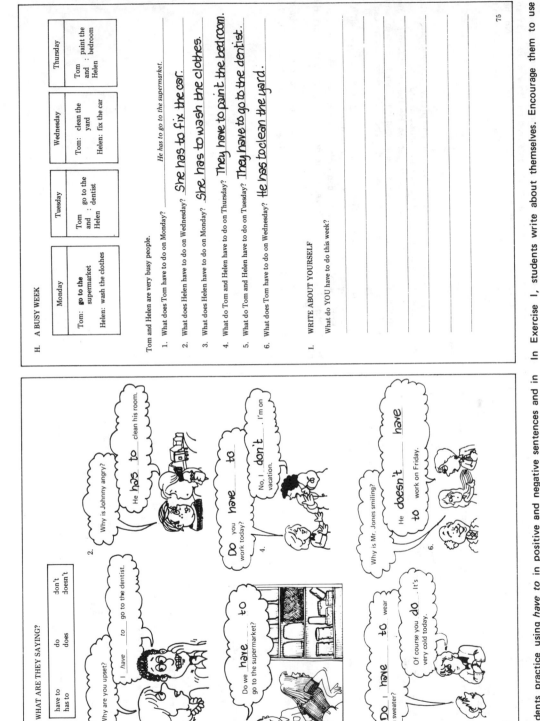

74

H. A BUSY WEEK

Monday	Tuesday	Wednesday	Thursday
Tom: **go to the supermarket**	Tom and Helen: go to the dentist	Tom: clean the yard	Tom and Helen: paint the bedroom
Helen: wash the clothes		Helen: fix car	

Tom and Helen are very busy people.

1. What does Tom have to do on Monday? _He has to go to the supermarket._

2. What does Helen have to do on Wednesday? _She has to fix the car._

3. What does Helen have to do on Monday? _She has to wash the clothes._

4. What do Tom and Helen have to do on Thursday? _They have to paint the bedroom._

5. What do Tom and Helen have to do on Tuesday? _They have to go to the dentist._

6. What does Tom have to do on Wednesday? _He has to clean the yard._

I. WRITE ABOUT YOURSELF

What do YOU have to do this week?

75

Students practice using *have to* in positive and negative sentences and in questions. (text page 76)

In Exercise I, students write about themselves. Encourage them to use dictionaries. (text page 76)

J. WE'RE BUSY

can't	do the laundry	go skiing	play cards
have to	fix the TV	go swimming	play tennis
has to	go dancing	go to the dentist	study
	go jogging	go to the doctor	teach
	go sailing	go to the zoo	wash the kitchen floor
			work

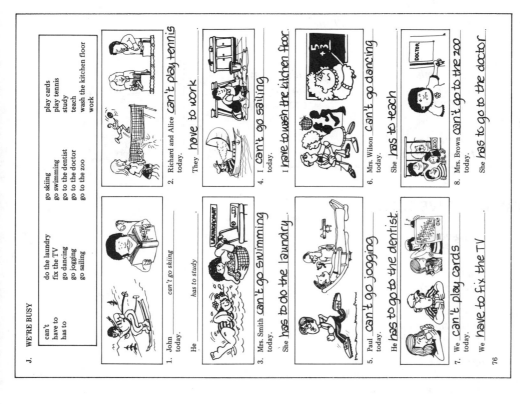

1. John _can't go skiing_ today.

   He _has to study_.

2. Richard and Alice _can't play tennis_ today.

   They _have to work_.

3. Mrs. Smith _can't go swimming_ today.

   She _has to do the laundry_.

4. I _can't go sailing_ today.

   I _have to wash the kitchen floor_.

5. Paul _can't go jogging_ today.

   He _has to go to the dentist_.

6. Mrs. Wilson _can't go dancing_ today.

   She _has to teach_.

7. We _can't play cards_ today.

   We _have to fix the TV_.

8. Mrs. Brown _can't go to the zoo_ today.

   She _has to go to the doctor_.

76

Students practice using *have to, can't* and the new vocabulary of Chapter 13. (text page 77)

TEXT PAGES 79-86

FOCUS

1. Future tense with going to:
   What's Fred going to do today?
   He's going to fix his car.

   When are you going to call the plumber?
   I'm going to call him right now.

2. Time expressions:
   this morning　　　　　*this Friday*
   tomorrow afternoon　　*this April*
   next year　　　　　　*next spring*

3. Want to:
   I want to study.
   He wants to study.

COMMUNICATIVE SKILLS

1. Expressing concern:
   Oh no!

2. Expressing desire:
   I want to go swimming.

3. Indicating time:
   What time is it?
   It's twelve o'clock.

4. Talking about future activities:
   What's Tom going to do tomorrow afternoon?
   He's going to play baseball.

VOCABULARY

according to	have a picnic	right away	January
afternoon	I don't know.	right now	February
at once	I hope you're right	shave	March
autumn	immediately	spring	April
bad	iron	suitcase	May
begin	late for class	summer	June
call	leave	take a bath	July
concert	month	take a shower	August
cut	morning	the radio says	September
evening	Oh no!	today	October
fall	pack	tomorrow	November
flowers	plane	tonight	December
football game	plant	visit	
forecast	play (n)	want to	
garden	Please try to hurry!	week	
get up	plumber	winter	
going to	put on	write to	
		year	

LANGUAGE NOTES

In informal speech, many speakers often pronounce *going to* as *gonna*, *want to* as *wanna*, and *wants to* as *wansta*. Tell your students they may hear these pronunciations.

CULTURE KEY

Weather forecasts (text page 84) are a regular part of TV and radio news programs in the U.S. Daily newspapers also publish weather forecasts.

FOCUS

Introduction of the future tense with *going to:*	am is are	⎱ ⎰ + *going to* + Verb

What's Fred going to do today?
He's going to fix his car.

GETTING READY

1. Introduce the word *tomorrow*; use a calendar to indicate *tomorrow*.

2. Introduce *going to*. For example,

   Every day I read the newspaper.
   *Tomorrow I'm **going to read** the newspaper.*

   I'm wearing my glasses.
   I always wear my glasses.
   *Tomorrow I'm **going to wear** my glasses.*

3. Form sentences with *going to* and the words in the boxes at the top of text page 80. Have students repeat chorally. (When you read from the box on the left, form contractions.) For example,

   I'm going to read.
   He's going to read.

PRESENTING THE MODEL

There are 2 model conversations. Introduce and practice each separately. For each model:

1. Have students look at the model illustration in the book or on the SBS Dialog Visual Card.

2. Set the scene: "Two people are talking."

3. Present the model.

4. Full-Class Choral Repetition.

5. Ask students if they have any questions; check understanding of new vocabulary.

   1st model: *going to*
   2nd model: *tomorrow*

6. Group Choral Repetition.

7. Choral Conversation.

8. Call on one or two pairs of students to present the dialog.

   (For additional practice, do Choral Conversation in small groups or by rows.)

9. Introduce the time expressions for *today* at the bottom of the page. Practice the 1st model again, substituting these time expressions. For example,

   A.   What's Fred going to do this morning?
   B.   He's going to fix his car.

   Do Choral Repetition, Choral Conversation, and call on pairs of students.

10. Introduce the time expressions for *tomorrow*. Practice the 2nd model again, substituting these time expressions. For example,

    A.   What are Mr. and Mrs. Brown going to do tomorrow morning?
    B.   They're going to go to the beach.

SIDE BY SIDE EXERCISES

Examples:

> 1. A. What's Mary going to do this morning?
>   B. She's going to clean her apartment (or clean her house/living room).
> 2. A. What are Carol and Dan going to do tomorrow morning?
>   B. They're going to wash their clothes (or do their laundry).
>
> *Answer Key:*
>   3. We're going to play cards.
>   4. He's going to play baseball.
>   5. They're going to go to a movie.
>   6. She's going to go to a concert.
>   7. I'm going to read a book.
>   8. He's going to listen to music.

1. **Exercise 1:** Call on two students to present the dialog. Then do Choral Repetition and Choral Conversation Practice.
2. **Exercise 2:** Same as above.
3. **Exercises 3-8:** Either Full-Class Practice or Pair Practice.
4. **Exercise 9:** Students talk about themselves. Have pairs of students create dialogs using any of the time expressions on text page 80.

OPTIONAL WRITING PRACTICE

Have students write exercises 4, 5, 6, 7, 8, and 3 questions and answers for exercise 9.

WORKBOOK

Students can now do page 77.

EXPANSION ACTIVITIES

1. ***Practice Going To On The Board***
   a. Put the following on the board:

S	M	T	W	T	F	S
sleep	play cards	go to the beach	go to a restaurant	go to a concert		

   b. Tell a story about George.
      "George is going on vacation."
      "On Sunday George is going to sleep."
      "On Monday he's going to play cards."
      (Continue for Tuesday, Wednesday, Thursday.)
   c. Ask students *What* and *When* questions about George's plans. Students can answer by looking at the schedule on the board. For example,
      A. What's George going to do on Monday?
      B. On Monday he's going to play cards.

      A. When is George going to go to a concert?
      B. He's going to go to a concert on Thursday.
   d. Call on pairs of students to ask and answer questions about George's vacation schedule. Leave Friday and Saturday *open*. Have students decide what George is going to do.
2. ***Students Talk About Themselves***
   Ask students and have students ask each other:
      "What are you going to do this weekend?"
      "What are you going to do on your vacation?"

FOCUS

> Practice *going to* with time expressions.

GETTING READY

1. Introduce these new words:

The months of the year:		The seasons:
January	*July*	*spring*
February	*August*	*summer*
March	*September*	*fall (autumn)*
April	*October*	*winter*
May	*November*	
June	*December*	

   a. Practice the months by asking students about their birthdays or other important holi-days. For example,
   "When is your birthday?"
   "It's in (March)."

   b. Practice the season by asking about the typical weather. For example,

   A. How's the weather in the $\begin{cases} \text{spring} \\ \text{summer} \\ \text{fall} \\ \text{winter} \end{cases}$?

   B. It's usually $\begin{cases} \text{warm} \\ \text{hot} \\ \text{cool} \\ \text{cold} \\ \text{sunny} \\ \text{cloudy} \end{cases}$

2. Review object pronouns.
   a. Have students listen as you say each of the sentences below.
   b. Call on students to substitute the object pronoun and say the sentence.

Teacher	Student
Ex. I'm going to wash *my car.*	I'm going to wash *it.*
1. I'm going to wash *my windows.*	(I'm going to wash *them.*)
2. I'm going to clean *my apartment.*	(I'm going to clean *it.*)
3. I'm going to visit *my friends.*	(I'm going to visit *them.*)
4. I'm going to visit *Mary.*	(I'm going to visit *her.*)
5. I'm going to visit *John.*	(I'm going to visit *him.*)
6. I'm going to visit *Mr. and Mrs. Jones.*	(I'm going to visit *them.*)

PRESENTING THE MODEL

There are 2 model conversations. Introduce and practice each separately. For each model:

1. Have students look at the model illustration in the book or on the SBS Dialog Visual Card.
2. Set the scene:
   1st model: "Two roommates are talking."
   2nd model: "A wife and husband are talking. The wife is very upset."

3. Present the model.
4. Full-Class Choral Repetition.
5. Ask students if they have any questions; check understanding of new vocabulary.
      1st model: *this week*
      2nd model: *plumber, right now.*
6. Group Choral Repetition.
7. Choral Conversation.
8. Call on one or two pairs of students to present the dialog.

   (For additional practice, do Choral Conversation in small groups or by rows.)

9. Introduce the time expressions under the 1st model. Have pairs of students practice the model again, substituting some of these time expressions. For example,
      A. When are you going to wash your clothes?
      B. I'm going to wash them next month.
10. Introduce the time expressions under the 2nd model. Have pairs of students practice the model again, substituting these time expressions.

SIDE BY SIDE EXERCISES

In these exercises, students answer the questions using any of the time expressions on text page 82.

> **Examples:**
>
> | | | |
> |---|---|---|
> | 1. | A. | When are you going to wash your car? |
> | | B. | I'm going to wash it next week. |
> | 2. | A. | When are you going to call your grandmother? |
> | | B. | I'm going to call her this Sunday. |

1. **Exercise 1:** Call on two students to present the dialog. Then do Choral Repetition and Choral Conversation Practice.
2. **Exercise 2:** Same as above.
3. **Exercises 3-8:**

> **New vocabulary:**   *2. call   4. cut   5. plant flowers   7. write to   8. iron*

   Either Full-Class Practice or Pair Practice.
4. **Exercise 9:** Students talk about themselves. Have pairs of students create dialogs using any of the time expressions on text page 82.

OPTIONAL WRITING PRACTICE

Have students write exercises 2, 4, 5, 7, 8 and 3 questions and answers for exercise 9.

WORKBOOK

Students can now do pages 78, 79 Exercise C.

EXPANSION ACTIVITIES

1. *Practice Going to With Word Cards or Visuals*
   Make word cards for a variety of activities. You can also use your own visuals or SBS Picture Cards. Suggested activities:

go to Paris	write to _____
do _____ homework	call _____
go to the dentist	visit _____
go to the beach	go to the supermarket
plant flowers	go to a movie
do your laundry	play _____
cut your hair	

   a. Have each student draw a card or visual and ask another student:
   > A. When are you going to *(go to Paris)?*

   b. The other student can answer using any time expression. For example,
   > B. I'm going to *(go to Paris)* { tonight / tomorrow / this Sunday / next month / next year / on Monday }

   c. Practice *he* and *she*:
   Give cards or visuals to pairs of students. Have them create conversations about other students in the class. For example,
   > A. When is Hector going to go to Paris?
   > B. He's going to go to Paris next month.

2. *Scrambled Sentences: The Smiths Are Going On Vacation*
   Here is the Smith family's vacation schedule:

   > On Sunday the Smiths are going to go to Acapulco, Mexico.
   >
   > On Monday they're going to go swimming.
   >
   > On Tuesday they're going to eat in a Mexican restaurant and they're going to go to a concert.
   >
   > On Wednesday they're going to visit friends in a nearby city.
   >
   > On Thursday they're going to write letters to their friends.
   >
   > On Friday they're going to go shopping and they're going to go dancing at a discotheque.
   >
   > On Saturday they are going to have a party.

   a. Write each sentence on a strip of paper; then cut the words apart. Mix up the words in each sentence and clip them together.

   b. Divide the class into small groups of 2-5 students. Give each group 1 or 2 sentences to unscramble.

   c. When everyone has put the words in correct order, have one student from each group write the sentence(s) on the board (in order of the days of the week). Now you have the Smiths' schedule on the board.

   d. Call on several pairs of students to ask and answer questions about the Smiths. For example,
   > "When are they going to have a party?"
   > "What are they going to do on Monday?"

TEACHER'S NOTES

FOCUS

Introduction of *want to + verb*.

GETTING READY

1. Introduce *want to* by telling about something you want to do. For example,
   "I want to watch TV tonight, but I can't.
   I have to work."

2. Introduce *want to* by telling what someone else wants to do.
   "Joe wants to buy a car, but he can't. He doesn't have $4,000."

3. Form sentences with the words in the box at the top of the page. Have students repeat chorally and individually. For example,
   "I want to study."
   "We want to study."

PRESENTING THE MODEL

1. Have students look at the model illustration in the book or on the SBS Dialog Visual Card.
2. Set the scene: "Two friends are talking."
3. Present the model.
4. Full-Class Choral Repetition.
5. Ask students if they have any questions; check understanding of new vocabulary: *I don't know, want to, be, bad, really, forecast, the radio says, according to, I hope you're right.*
6. Group Choral Repetition.
7. Choral Conversation.
8. Call on one or two pairs of students to present the dialog.

   (For additional practice, do Choral Conversation in small groups or by rows.)

SIDE BY SIDE EXERCISES

Examples:

1. A. What are you going to do tomorrow?
   B. I don't know. I want to have a picnic, but I think the weather is going to be bad.
   A. Really? What's the forecast?
   B. The radio says it's going to rain.
   A. That's strange! According to the newspaper, it's going to be nice.
   B. I hope you're right.
      I REALLY want to have a picnic.

2. A. What are you going to do tomorrow?
    B. I don't know. I want to go skiing, but I think the weather is going to be bad.
    A. Really? What's the forecast?
    B. The radio says it's going to be warm.
    A. That's strange! According to the newspaper, it's going to snow.
    B. I hope you're right.
        I REALLY want to go skiing.

1. **Exercise 1**: Introduce the new expression: *have a picnic*. Call on two students to present the dialog. Then do Choral Repetition and Choral Conversation.

2. **Exercise 2**: Same as above.

3. **Exercises 3-6**:

    > **New vocabulary:**   4. *garden*   5. *foggy, clear*

    Either Full-Class Practice or Pair Practice.

OPTIONAL WRITING PRACTICE

Have students write exercises 3, 4 for homework.

WORKBOOK

Students can now do pages 79 Exercise D, 80, 81, 82.

EXPANSION ACTIVITIES

1. *Students Talk About Themselves*
    a. For homework, have each student make a list of several things he or she wants to do next year. Encourage students to use dictionaries to find new words to express their real-life goals.
    b. In the next class, have students present their ideas conversationally. Call on pairs of students to ask and answer:
        A. What do you want to do next year?
        B. Next year I want to *(learn German, visit my aunt in Mexico, and buy a bicycle)*.
    c. Practice "He/She wants to _____."
        After a few students have presented their ideas, talk about them:
        A. What does (Bob) want to do next year?
        B. He wants to _____.

2. *Discuss the Weather*
    See the suggestions at the bottom of text page 84. Ask students questions about the weather today and tomorrow. For homework, you can have students listen to the local forecast and present the forecast in English during the next class. Have students point to a map showing the regions in your country as they tell the forecast.

FOCUS

Telling time.

WHAT TIME IS IT?

Practice time expressions using a large clock or clock face with movable hands to display the time.

1.   Review the numbers 1-12.

2.   Introduce the time expressions for each hour, as you point to the hands of the clock.

"It's one o'clock."   "It's twelve o'clock."
"It's two o'clock."   "It's (twelve o'clock) noon."
"It's three o'clock."   "It's (twelve o'clock) midnight."
        •
        •
        •

   a.   Say each new expression one or more times.

   b.   Have students repeat chorally and individually.

   c.   Practice conversationally. Ask students, "What time is it?" as you point to the clock.

3.   Review numbers 1-60.

4.   Using the same approach as above, introduce time expressions for the quarter and half hours.

It's one fifteen.   *It's one thirty.*   *It's one forty-five.*
It's two fifteen.   *It's two thirty.*   *It's two forty-five.*

5.   Review the time expressions:

   a.   Set the clock hands at various times, such as 11:00, 1:15, 3:30, 8:45 and ask "What time is it?"

   b.   Give the clock to a student and call out a time; have the student set the clock.

6.   Introduce and practice these alternate expressions in the same way:

> 11:15—"It's a quarter after eleven."
> 11:30—"It's half past eleven."
> 11:45—"It's a quarter to twelve."

WORKBOOK

Students can now do page 83.

ON YOUR OWN

FOCUS

> 1. Time expressions: *The plane leaves at 2:00.*
> 2. Review of *going to, have to, want to.*

PRESENTING THE MODEL

1. Have students look at the model illustration in the book or on the SBS Dialog Visual Card.

2. Set the scene: "A husband and wife are talking. They're going to a concert, and she's upset because he isn't ready."

3. Present the model.

4. Full-Class Choral Repetition.

5. Ask students if they have any questions; check understanding of new vocabulary: *begin, at (8:00), late (for), leave, shave, Please try to hurry! Oh no!*

6. Group Choral Repetition.

7. Choral Conversation.

8. Call on one or two pairs of students to present the dialog.

   (For additional practice, do Choral Conversation in small groups or by rows.)

SIDE BY SIDE EXERCISES

Examples:

---

1. A. What time does the football game begin?
   B. It begins at 2:00.
   A. Oh no! I think we're going to be late!
   B. Why? What time is it?
   A. It's 1:30. And we have to leave RIGHT NOW!
   B. I can't leave now. I'm taking a bath!
   A. Please try to hurry! I don't want to be late for the football game.

2. A. What time does the plane leave?
   B. It leaves at 4:15.
   A. Oh no! I think we're going to be late!
   B. Why? What time is it?
   A. It's 3:45. And we have to leave RIGHT NOW!
   B. I can't leave now. I'm putting on my clothes.
   A. Please try to hurry! I don't want to be late for the plane.

---

1. **Exercise 1**: Introduce the new vocabulary: *football game, take a bath.* Call on two students to present the dialog. Then do Choral Repetition and Choral Conversation.

2. **Exercise 2**: Introduce the new vocabulary: *plane, put on.*

3. **Exercises 3-6**:

New vocabulary:	3. *class, get up*	4. *pack, suitcase*	5. *take a shower*
	6. *play (n)*		

   Either Full-Class Practice or Pair Practice.

4. **Exercise 7**: For homework, have students write an original dialog based on the model. Have students present their dialogs in the next class.

WORKBOOK

Students can now do page 84.

EXPANSION ACTIVITIES

1. *Role Play:* "I Think We're Going To Be Late!"
   Have students role play new situations using the same conversational framework at the top of text page 86.

   a. Make up situation cues like the ones below and write them on cards.

   b. Give cards to pairs of students and allow some time for preparation.

   c. Have students present their conversations to the class (with books closed).

   d. Sample situation cues:

1. a parent and child a baseball game 2:00/1:30 parent/taking/bath

2. husband and wife a party 8:00/7:45 one is talking to the boss on the phone

3. 2 roommates a movie 4:15/3:45 1 roommate/doing/homework

2. *Talk About Daily Schedules*

Put your own morning schedule on the board or have one student in the class volunteer to tell what he or she does every morning before going to work or school.

a.   Put times and key words on the board (or use stick figure drawings). For example,

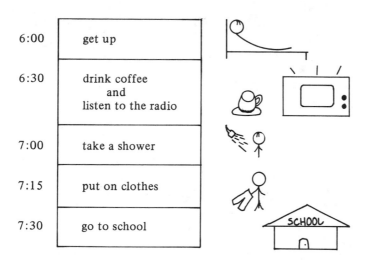

6:00	get up
6:30	drink coffee and listen to the radio
7:00	take a shower
7:15	put on clothes
7:30	go to school

b.   Talk about *every day*.

Ask questions about the schedule; then call on pairs of students to ask and answer. For example,

    A.   What time does Mary get up every day?
    B.   She gets up at 6:00.

c.   Talk about *tomorrow*.

Again, you ask a few questions; then call on pairs of students to ask and answer. For example,

    A.   What's Mary going to do at 7:30 tomorrow?
    B.   She's going to go to school.

d.   Talk about other students' daily schedules by asking or having students ask each other questions such as:

    "What time do you usually get up in the morning?"
    "What do you usually do in the morning?"
    "What time do you usually leave your apartment?"
    "What time do you usually have lunch?"

3. *Talk About Other Schedules*

Bring bus, train, plane, and/or TV schedules to class. Have students ask and answer questions about them.

A. WHAT ARE THEY GOING TO DO?

14

1. What's Sally going to do this afternoon?

She's going to study English.

2. What are Mr. and Mrs. Green going to do tomorrow morning?

They're going to play tennis.

3. What's Helen going to do tomorrow afternoon?

She's going to wash her car.

4. What are you and George going to do this morning?

We're going to do our exercises.

5. What's your grandfather going to do this evening?

He's going to read the newspaper.

6. What are Jane and her mother going to do today?

They're going to go to the dentist.

7. What's Linda going to do tonight?

She's going to watch TV.

8. What are you going to do this morning?

I'm going to go to the bank.

77

B. AN INTERNATIONAL MOVIE ACTOR

JANUARY- Rome
FEBRUARY- Geneva
APRIL - London
JUNE - Honolulu
SEPTEMBER - TOKYO

George Dupont is a famous international movie actor. He lives in Paris, but he always works in cities around the world.

Next January George is going to act in Rome. He's glad he's going to work there because he loves Italian music. In the evening when he isn't busy, he's going to go to concerts.

Next February George is going to go skiing in Geneva with his wife and son. George always goes skiing on his winter vacation, and he always has a wonderful time.

Next April George is going to go to work in London. His wife and son are going to go to visit him every weekend. When they're together, they're going to go shopping in expensive London stores, and his son is going to go to the London Zoo.

Next June George and his family are going to go to Honolulu on their summer vacation. They love the beautiful beaches there, and they're going to go swimming and sailing every day.

Next September George is going to go to Tokyo. He's going to act in a Japanese movie. His family can't go with him, but he isn't upset because his son and wife are going to write to him from Paris. When he isn't working, he's going to go to Japanese restaurants and baseball games with his friends.

1. When is George going to go to Rome?   *He's going to go to Rome next January.*

2. What's he going to do in Rome in the evening? He's going to go to concerts.

3. When are George and his family going to go to Geneva? They're going to go to Geneva next February.

4. What are they going to do there? They're going to go skiing.

5. Where is George going to work next April? He's going to go to work in London.

6. What are George and his family going to do in London? They're going to go shopping in expensive stores, and his son is going to go to the London Zoo.

7. When are George and his family going to go to Honolulu? They're going to go to Honolulu next June.

8. What are they going to do there? They're going to go swimming and sailing.

9. When is George going to go to Tokyo? He's going to go to Tokyo next September.

10. Why is George going to go to Tokyo? He's going to act in a Japanese movie.

11. What's he going to do there when he isn't working? He's going to go to Japanese restaurants and baseball games with his friends.

78

Students practice asking and answering questions with *going to.* (text pages 80-81)

Exercise B is a reading comprehension passage. Students answer questions with *going to.* For additional practice, have students read the story aloud. (text pages 82-83)

Key to Exercise D

For each forecast, read or play the tape twice. Have students look at the questions in their workbooks as they listen.

TODAY'S WEATHER FORECAST

This is Tom Jones with today's weather forecast. This afternoon it's going to be warm and sunny with temperatures from 70° to 75°. This evening it's going to be cool and very cloudy, but it isn't going to rain.

THE WEEKEND'S FORECAST

This is Nancy Peters with your weekend weather forecast. Tonight it's going to be foggy and cool with 50° temperatures, but on Saturday it's going to be clear and sunny. On Sunday wear your heavy clothes. It's going to be very cold.

MONDAY'S WEATHER FORECAST

This is Dan Richards with Monday's weather forecast. Monday morning it's going to be cool and cloudy, but wear your snow boots when you go to work because in the afternoon and evening it's going to snow. Tuesday's skiing is going to be wonderful. It's going to be sunny and cold.

C. WHAT'S THE QUESTION?

1. I'm going to fix my car this afternoon. (What?) *What are you going to do this afternoon?*
2. He's going to cut his hair next week. (When?) *When is he going to cut his hair?*
3. They're going to go to Madrid next summer. (Where?) *Where are they going to go next summer?*
4. She's going to plant flowers this spring. (When?) *When is she going to plant flowers?*
5. He's going to visit his grandmother because she's sick. (Why?) *Why is he going to visit his grandmother?*
6. They're going to write to their brother this morning. (What?) *What are they going to do this morning?*
7. I'm going to call the plumber right away. (When?) *When are you going to call the plumber?*
8. He's going to eat at a restaurant tonight. (Where?) *Where is he going to eat tonight?*

D. LISTEN

Listen to the following weather forecasts. Put a circle around the correct answer. You will hear each forecast twice.

TODAY'S WEATHER FORECAST
1. This afternoon: warm cool (sunny) cloudy rain
2. This evening: warm (cool) sunny (cloudy) rain

THIS WEEKEND'S FORECAST
3. Tonight: (cool) cold sunny clear (foggy)
4. Saturday: cool cold (sunny) (clear) foggy
5. Sunday: cool (cold) sunny clear foggy

MONDAY'S WEATHER FORECAST
6. Monday morning: (cool) cold sunny (cloudy) snow
7. Monday afternoon and evening: cool cold sunny cloudy (snow)
8. Tuesday: cool (cold) (sunny) cloudy snow

79

In Exercise C, students practice *wh-* questions with *going* to. (text pages 82-83)

In Exercise D, students practice listening to weather forecasts. (text page 84)

CHAPTER FOURTEEN 191

E. BAD WEATHER

go skating	paint the house
go to a baseball game	wash the car
go to the park	
have a picnic	

be cloudy
be cold
be warm
rain
snow

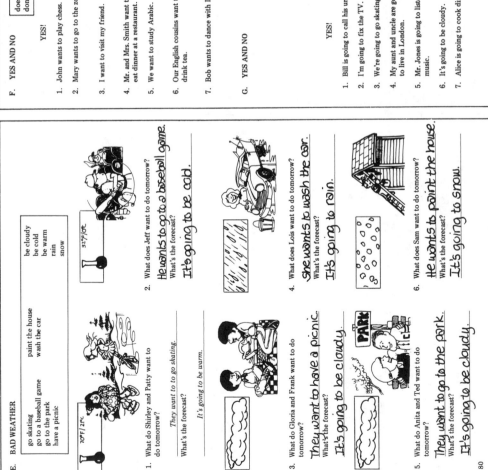

1. What do Shirley and Patty want to do tomorrow?
They want to go skating.
What's the forecast?
It's going to be warm.
[70°F / 21°C]

2. What does Jeff want to do tomorrow?
He wants to go to a baseball game.
What's the forecast?
It's going to be cold.
[32°F / 0°C]

3. What do Gloria and Frank want to do tomorrow?
They want to have a picnic.
What's the forecast?
It's going to be cloudy.

4. What does Lois want to do tomorrow?
She wants to wash the car.
What's the forecast?
It's going to rain.

5. What do Anita and Ted want to do tomorrow?
They want to go to the park.
What's the forecast?
It's going to be cloudy.

6. What does Sam want to do tomorrow?
He wants to paint the house.
What's the forecast?
It's going to snow.

80

Students practice using *want to*, *going to*, and *weather* vocabulary. (text page 84)

F. YES AND NO

	doesn't want to
	don't want to

YES	NO!
1. John wants to play chess.	*He doesn't want to play checkers.*
2. Mary wants to go to the zoo.	*She doesn't want to go* to a concert.
3. I want to visit my friend.	*I don't want to visit* my grandmother.
4. Mr. and Mrs. Smith want to eat dinner at a restaurant.	*They don't want to eat* dinner at home.
5. We want to study Arabic.	*We don't want to study* mathematics.
6. Our English cousins want to drink tea.	*They don't want to drink* coffee.
7. Bob wants to dance with Lois.	*He doesn't want to dance* with his sister.

G. YES AND NO

I'm not	
He	
She } isn't	going to
It	
We	
You } aren't	
They	

YES!	NO!
1. Bill is going to call his uncle.	*He isn't going to call* his mother.
2. I'm going to fix the TV.	*I'm not going to fix* the sink.
3. We're going to go skating.	*We aren't going to go* skiing.
4. My aunt and uncle are going to live in London.	*They aren't going to live* in Berlin.
5. Mr. Jones is going to listen to music.	*He isn't going to listen* to the forecast.
6. It's going to be cloudy.	*It isn't going to be* sunny.
7. Alice is going to cook dinner.	*She isn't going to cook* lunch.

81

Students practice negative sentences with *want to* and *going to*. (text page 84)

H. FUTURE HOPES

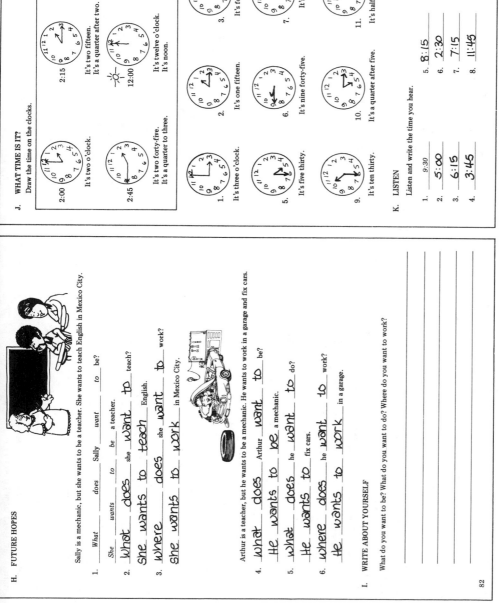

Sally is a mechanic, but she wants to be a teacher. She wants to teach English in Mexico City.

1. *What* ___*does*___ Sally ___*want*___ ___*to*___ be?
   She __want__ __does__ she __want__ __to__ a teacher.

2. __what__ __does__ __want__ __to__ teach?
   __She wants to teach__ English.

3. __where__ __does__ she __want__ __to__ work?
   __She wants to work__ in Mexico City.

Arthur is a teacher, but he wants to be a mechanic. He wants to work in a garage and fix cars.

4. __what__ __does__ Arthur __want__ __to__ be?
   __He wants to be__ a mechanic.

5. __what__ __does__ he __want__ __to__ do?
   __He wants to__ fix cars.

6. __where__ __does__ he __want__ __to__ work?
   __He wants to work__ in a garage.

I. WRITE ABOUT YOURSELF

What do you want to be? What do you want to do? Where do you want to work?

_____

_____

_____

_____

_____

J. WHAT TIME IS IT?

Draw the time on the clocks.

2:00   It's two o'clock.
2:15   It's two fifteen. It's a quarter after two.
2:30   It's two thirty. It's half past two.
2:45   It's two forty-five. It's a quarter to three.
12:00 It's twelve o'clock. It's noon.
12:00 It's twelve o'clock. It's midnight.

1. It's three o'clock.
2. It's one fifteen.
3. It's four thirty.
4. It's seven forty-five.
5. It's five thirty.
6. It's nine forty-five.
7. It's noon.
8. It's six fifteen.
9. It's ten thirty.
10. It's a quarter after five.
11. It's half past eleven.
12. It's a quarter to eight.

K. LISTEN

Listen and write the time you hear.

1. _9:30_
2. _5:00_
3. _6:15_
4. _3:45_
5. _8:15_
6. _2:30_
7. _7:15_
8. _11:45_
9. _12:00_
10. _1:30_
11. _3:15_
12. _4:45_

In Exercise H, students practice writing questions and answers with *want to*. In Exercise I, students write about themselves. Encourage them to use dictionaries. (text page 84)

In Exercise J, students practice reading time expressions. In Exercise K, students practice listening to time expressions. (text page 85)

CHAPTER FOURTEEN   193

L. PAUL SMITH'S DAY

Paul Smith gets up every day at 8:00. He takes a bath and reads the newspaper. At 8:30 he eats breakfast and at 8:45 he leaves the house.

School begins at 9:00 and Paul is usually late. When he gets there at 9:15, his friends are busy at work.

At 12:00 Paul is tired and hungry, and he and his friends go to the school cafeteria for lunch. They sit and talk and do their homework.

At 12:30 Paul's mathematics class begins, and at 2:00 he studies science. Mathematics and science are Paul's favorite subjects, but he's glad when it's 3:00 and he can go home.

1. What time does Paul get up every day?   *He gets up at 8:00.*

2. What does he do at 8:30?   He eats breakfast.

3. What time does he leave the house?   He leaves the house at 8:45.

4. What time does school begin?   School begins at 9:00.

5. What time does he eat lunch?   He eats lunch at 12:00.

6. What time does his mathematics class begin?   His mathematics class begins at 12:30.

7. What does he do at 2:00?   He studies science.

8. What does he do at 3:00?   He goes home.

M. YOUR DAY

Answer in complete sentences.

1. What time do you usually get up? _____

2. What do you do after you get up? _____

3. What time do you usually leave for school/work? _____

4. What time do you usually have lunch? _____

5. What time do you get home from school/work? _____

6. What time do you usually have dinner? _____

7. What do you usually do after dinner? _____

_____

8. What time do you usually go to bed? _____

84

Read or play the tape.

1. nine thirty
2. five o'clock
3. six fifteen
4. three forty-five
5. eight fifteen
6. half past two
7. seven fifteen
8. eleven forty-five
9. twelve o'clock
10. half past one
11. a quarter after three
12. four forty-five

Students practice using time expressions as they read and write about daily schedules. (text pages 85-86)

CHECK-UP TEST : Chapters 13-14

A.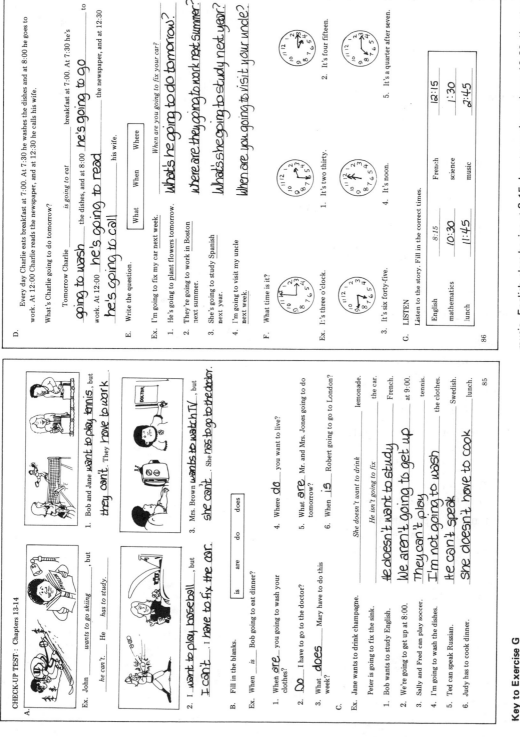

Ex. John _wants to go skiing_, but he can't. He _has to study._

1. Bob and Jane _want to play tennis_, but _they can't._ They have to work

2. I _want to play baseball_, but _I can't. I have to fix the car._

3. Mrs. Brown _wants to watch TV_, but _she can't. She has to go to the doctor._

B. Fill in the blanks.

is	are	do	does

Ex. When _is_ Bob going to eat dinner?

1. When _are_ you going to wash your clothes?

2. _Do_ I have to go to the doctor?

3. What _does_ Mary have to do this week?

4. Where _do_ you want to live?

5. What _are_ Mr. and Mrs. Jones going to do tomorrow?

6. When _is_ Robert going to go to London?

C.

Ex. Jane wants to drink champagne. _She doesn't want to drink_ lemonade.
    Peter is going to fix the sink. _He isn't going to fix_ the car.

1. Bob wants to study English. _He doesn't want to study_ French.
2. We're going to get up at 8:00. _We aren't going to get up_ at 9:00.
3. Sally and Fred can play soccer. _They can't play_ tennis.
4. I'm going to wash the dishes. _I'm not going to wash_ the clothes.
5. Ted can speak Russian. _He can't speak_ Swedish.
6. Judy has to cook dinner. _She doesn't have to cook_ lunch.

85

D. Every day Charlie eats breakfast at 7:00. At 7:30 he washes the dishes and at 8:00 he goes to work. At 12:00 Charlie reads the newspaper, and at 12:30 he calls his wife.

What's Charlie going to do tomorrow?

Tomorrow Charlie _is going to eat_ breakfast at 7:00. At 7:30 he's _going to wash_ the dishes, and at 8:00 _he's going to go_ to work. At 12:00 _he's going to read_ the newspaper, and at 12:30 _he's going to call_ his wife.

E. Write the question.

What	When	Where

Ex. I'm going to fix my car next week. _When are you going to fix your car?_

1. He's going to plant flowers tomorrow. _What's he going to do tomorrow?_
2. They're going to work in Boston next summer. _Where are they going to work next summer?_
3. She's going to study Spanish next year. _What's she going to study next year?_
4. I'm going to visit my uncle next week. _When are you going to visit your uncle?_

F. What time is it?

Ex. It's three o'clock.
1. It's two thirty.
2. It's four fifteen.
3. It's six forty-five.
4. It's noon.
5. It's a quarter after seven.

G. LISTEN
Listen to the story. Fill in the correct times.

English	_8:15_	French	_12:15_
mathematics	_10:30_	science	_1:30_
lunch	_11:45_	music	_2:45_

86

Key to Exercise G
Read or play the tape twice.
Every day at school I study English, mathematics, French, science, and music. English class begins at 8:15. I go to mathematics at 10:30. I'm always happy at 11:45 because we have lunch. We go to French class at 12:15. We have science at 1:30 and we go to music at 2:45.

CHAPTER 15 OVERVIEW

TEXT PAGES 87-91

FOCUS

Past tense
1. Regular verbs: *ed* ending for all persons.

I worked.	*We cooked.*
He played.	*You danced.*
She talked.	*They smoked.*

2. Irregular verbs: *eat—ate*
    sing—sang
    drink—drank
    sit—sat

COMMUNICATIVE SKILLS

1. Asking for and giving information about how one feels:
    How do you feel today?
    I feel great.

2. Describing common physical ailments:
    I have a headache.

3. Expressing happiness/regret:
    I'm glad to hear that.
    I'm sorry to hear that.

4. Expressing past activity:
    Yesterday I worked.

5. Making an appointment with the doctor.
    (See text page 91.)

VOCABULARY

all afternoon	fine	rest
all day	good-bye	See you tomorrow.
all evening	great	soda
all morning	headache	sore throat
all night	hello	so-so
baby	How about _____?	stomachache
backache	How are you?	That's fine.
bark	How do you feel?	toothache
basketball	I'm glad to hear	vodka
candy	that.	wait for
cold	make an appointment	What seems to be the
cookies	not so good	problem?
Do you have any	O.K.	What's the matter?
idea why?	probably	When can you see me?
earache		yesterday

LANGUAGE NOTES

1. **Pronunciation of the *ed* ending**

   The *ed* ending of regular verbs in the past tense is pronounced as follows:

   a. When a verb ends in a voiceless consonant sound other than [t], the ending is pronounced [t].

[k]	work<u>ed</u>	[č]	watch<u>ed</u>
[s]	danc<u>ed</u>	[š]	wash<u>ed</u>

   b. When a verb ends in a voiced consonant sound or a vowel sound, the ending is pronounced [d]:

[v]	shav<u>ed</u>	[i]	stud<u>ied</u>
[l]	smil<u>ed</u>	[e]	play<u>ed</u>
[n]	clean<u>ed</u>		

   c. When a verb ends in a [t] or a [d] sound, the ending is pronounced [id] and forms an additional syllable:

[t]	shout<u>ed</u>	wait<u>ed</u>
	paint<u>ed</u>	plant<u>ed</u>

2. **Spelling Rules**

   a. When a verb ends in a *y* which is preceded by a consonant, the *y* changes to *i* when *ed* is added. For example,

   study—stud<u>ied</u>

   b. When a verb ends in *e*, add only *d*. For example,

   smile—smil<u>ed</u>

FOCUS

> 1. Talking about how one feels.
> 2. Describing common physical ailments.

PRESENTING THE 1ST MODEL

People are telling how they feel, using expressions which range from very positive *(I feel great)* to very negative *(I feel terrible)*. (Note that their facial expressions reflect the difference in how they feel.)

There are 6 model conversations. Introduce and practice each before going on to the next.

A. How do you feel today? B. I feel great! A. I'm glad to hear that.	A. How do you feel today? B. So-so. A. I'm sorry to hear that.
A. How do you feel today? B. I feel fine. A. I'm glad to hear that.	A. How do you feel today? B. Not so good. A. I'm sorry to hear that.
A. How do you feel today? B. I feel O.K. A. I'm glad to hear that.	A. How do you feel today? B. I feel terrible. A. I'm sorry to hear that.

1. Have students look at the illustration at the top of the page.
2. Set the scene: "People are talking about how they feel."
3. Present the model.
4. Full-Class Choral Repetition.
5. Ask students if they have any questions; check understanding of new vocabulary: *How do you feel? great, fine, O.K., so-so, not so good, terrible, I'm glad to hear that, I'm sorry to hear that.*
6. Group Choral Repetition.
7. Choral Conversation.
8. Call on one or two pairs of students to present the dialog.
   (For additional practice, do Choral Conversation in small groups or by rows.)

PRESENTING THE 2ND MODEL

1. Have students look at the model illustration in the book or on the SBS Dialog Visual Card.
2. Set the scene: "Two people are talking."
3. Present the model.
4. Full-Class Choral Repetition.
5. Ask students if they have any questions; check understanding of new vocabulary: *What's the matter with—? headache.*
6. Group Choral Repetition.
7. Choral Conversation.
8. Call on one or two pairs of students to present the dialog.
   (For additional practice, do Choral Conversation in small groups or by rows.)

SIDE BY SIDE EXERCISES

Examples:

1. A. What's the matter with her?
      B. She has a stomachache.
	2. A. What's the matter with him?
	      B. He has a toothache.

3. A. What's the matter with you? B. I have a backache.	

Use the illustrations in the text or on the SBS Dialog Visual Card, SBS Picture Cards 140-146, or your own visuals to introduce the new vocabulary for *ailments*.

1. **Exercise 1:** Introduce the word: *stomachache.* Call on two students to present the dialog. Then do Choral Repetition and Choral Conversation Practice.
2. **Exercise 2:** Introduce the word: *toothache.* Same as above.
3. **Exercises 3-6:**

> **New vocabulary:**   3. *backache*   4. *earache*   5. *sore throat*   6. *cold*

Either Full-Class Practice or Pair Practice.

Ask Another Student in Your Class   ·

In this exercise students choose one of the 2 conversations to talk about how they feel today. Have pairs of students create conversations using the vocabulary they have learned on this page. This can be either Full-Class Practice or Pair Practice.

OPTIONAL WRITING PRACTICE

Have students write exercises 1-6 and one conversation for each of the models at the bottom of the page.

WORKBOOK

Students can now do page 87.

EXPANSION ACTIVITY

Picture Story: "My Friends Are Sick"
Practice talking about how people feel by telling this story and having students ask and answer questions about it.

1. Draw 7 stick figures and write names under them. (To help students remember the vocablary, the first letter of each name is also the first letter of the ailment that person has.)

  Sally   Stanley   Harry   Tommy   Edward   Carol   Barbara

2. Tell this story, pointing to each person as you tell about him or her: "All my friends are sick today. They all feel TERRIBLE! What's the matter with them?"
> *Sally* has a *sore throat.*   *Tommy* has a *toothache.*   *Carol* has a *cold.*
> *Stanley* has a *stomachache.* *Edward* has an *earache.*   *Barbara* has a *backache.*
> *Harry* has a *headache.*

3. Create conversations about the story. First you ask questions; then have students ask and answer. For example,
>   A. How does Sally feel today?
>   B. She feels terrible!
>   A. What's the matter with her?
>   B. She has a sore throat.
>   A. I'm sorry to hear that.

FOCUS

> Past tense of regular verbs.
> Pronunciations of *ed* ending: [t] , [d] , or [id]

GETTING READY

1. Introduce the new word *yesterday.*
2. Introduce the past tense:
   a. Read the pairs of sentences in the box at the top of the page.
   b. Have students repeat each sentence chorally and individually.
   c. Practice the 3 pronunciations of the *ed* ending (See CHAPTER OVERVIEW, Pronunciation).
      1) In the smaller box near the top of the page, read the simple forms and the past tense forms of the verbs *work, play,* and *rest.*
      2) Have students repeat each form chorally and individually.
      3) Point out the pronunciation cues for the final sounds: [t] , [d] , [id] .
      4) Say the simple form and have a student tell you the past tense form.

WHAT DID YOU DO YESTERDAY?

In these exercises students use past tense verbs to answer the question, *What did you do yesterday?* The exercises are presented in 3 groups: verbs with final [t] , [d] , and [id] sounds.

PRESENTING THE MODEL

> A. What did you do yesterday?
> B. I worked.

1. Have students look at the illustration for exercise 1 in the book.
2. Set the scene: "People are talking about yesterday."
3. Present the model.
4. Full-Class Choral Repetition.
5. Ask students if they have any questions.
6. Group Choral Repetition.
7. Choral Conversation.
8. Call on one or two pairs of students to present the dialog.
   (For additional practice, do Choral Conversation in small groups or by rows.)

SIDE BY SIDE EXERCISES

In these exercises students can add objects to the verbs when appropriate.

Examples:

2. A. What did you do yesterday? B. I cooked breakfast (lunch/dinner).	3. A. What did you do yesterday? B. I talked on the telephone.
4. A. What did you do yesterday? B. I fixed my car.	5. A. What did you do yesterday? B. I brushed my teeth.

1. **Exercise 2:** Call on two students to present the dialog. Then do Choral Repetition and Choral Conversation.
2. **Exercise 3:** Introduce new vocabulary: *talk on the telephone.* Same as above.
3. **Exercises 4-20:**

> | **New vocabulary:** 19. *wait for* |

Either Full-Class Practice or Pair Practice.

OPTIONAL WRITING PRACTICE

Have students write exercises 2-5, 9-12, 17-20 for homework.

WORKBOOK

Students can now do pages 88, 89.

EXPANSION ACTIVITIES

1. *Practice With Visuals*
    Use your own visuals for the verbs on text page 89 or SBS Picture Cards 147-167. Give these visuals to students.
    a. Ask students holding visuals: "What did you do yesterday?" Have students answer using the past tense of the verb shown in the visual.
    b. Call on pairs of students holding visuals. Have them ask and answer, "What did you do yesterday?"

2. *Pronunciation Practice:* Pete, Ted, and David Stories
    Tell the following stories to provide additional practice with the final [t] [d] and [id] pronunciations of regular past tense verbs.
    a. A Story about Pete—[t]
        1) Write on the board:

        > | Pe<u>te</u>:   coo<u>ked</u>   fi<u>xed</u>   tal<u>ked</u>   smo<u>ked</u> |

        2) Say:
           "This is my friend Pete. Yesterday Pete cooked breakfast, he fixed his bicycle, he talked to his sister on the telephone, and he smoked five cigarettes."
        3) Have students tell you what *Pete* did. For example,
           A. What did Pete do yesterday?
           B. He cooked breakfast.
        4) Have students pretend to be *Pete*. Have them tell you everything they did:
           A. Pete, what did you do yesterday?
           B. I cooked breakfast, I fixed my bicycle, I talked to my sister on the telephone, and I smoked five cigarettes.
    b. A Story About Ted—[d]
        1) Write on the board:

        > | Te<u>d</u>:   clean<u>ed</u>   listen<u>ed</u>   play<u>ed</u>   studi<u>ed</u> |

        2) Say:
           "This is my cousin Ted. Yesterday Ted cleaned his apartment, he listened to the radio, he played cards with his sister, and he studied English."
        3) Have students practice talking about *Ted* the same way they did for *Pete.*
    c. A Story About David—[id]
        1) Write on the board:

        > | Da<u>vid</u>:   plant<u>ed</u>   paint<u>ed</u>   rest<u>ed</u>   wait<u>ed</u> |

        2) Say:
           "This is my neighbor David. Yesterday David planted flowers, he painted his living room, and then he rested and waited for a long-distance phone call."
        3) Have students practice talking about *David* the same way they did for *Pete* and *Ted.*

FOCUS

1. Practice using past tense for all persons.
2. Introduction to irregular verbs:

   eat–ate   *drink–drank*
   sing–sang   *sit–sat*

GETTING READY

1. Read all the forms in the *Yesterday* box at the top of the page. Have students repeat chorally. For example,

   "I worked."
   "We worked."
   "You worked."

2. Substitute a few other verbs and practice with all the pronouns. For example,

   talked
   "I talked."
   "We talked."
   "You talked."

PRESENTING THE MODEL

1. Have students look at the model illustration in the book or on the SBS Dialog Visual Card.
2. Set the scene: "Two people are talking about John."
3. Present the model.
4. Full-Class Choral Repetition.
5. Ask students if they have any questions; check understanding of new vocabulary: *all day.*
6. Group Choral Repetition.
7. Choral Conversation.
8. Call on one or two pairs of students to present the dialog.
   (For additional practice, do Choral Conversation in small groups or by rows.)
9. Introduce the expressions: *all morning, all afternoon, all evening, all night.* Have pairs of students practice the model again using these expressions in place of *all day.*

SIDE BY SIDE EXERCISES

Examples:

1.	A.	How does Mary feel?	2.	A.	How does John feel?
	B.	Not so good.		B.	Not so good.
	A.	What's the matter with her?		A.	What's the matter with him?
	B.	She has a backache.		B.	He has an earache.
	A.	Why?		A.	Why?
	B.	Because she danced all day (all morning/afternoon/ evening/night).		B.	Because he listened to the radio all day (all morning/ afternoon/evening/ night).

Key Words for the Exercises:

3. headache—studied
4. sore throat—shouted
5. headache—her baby cried
6. earache—his dog barked
7. backache—played basketball
8. sore throat—talked on the telephone
9. backache—planted flowers

10. toothache—ate candy
11. sore throat—sang
12. toothache—drank soda
13. backache—sat
14. stomachache—ate cookies
15. headache—drank vodka

1. **Exercise 1:** Call on two students to present the dialog. Then do Choral Repetition and Choral Conversation Practice.

2. **Exercise 2:** Same as above.

3. **Exercises 3-9:**

> **New vocabulary:** 5. *baby* 6. *bark* 7. *play basketball*

Either Full-Class Practice or Pair Practice.

4. Introduce the irregular verbs at the top of text page 91. Read the forms and have students repeat chorally and individually.

5. **Exercise 10:** Introduce the new word: *candy*. Call on two students to present the dialog. Then do Choral Repetition and Choral Conversation Practice.

6. **Exercise 11:** Same as above.

7. **Exercises 12-15:**

> **New vocabulary:** 12. *soda* 14. *cookies* 15. *vodka*

Either Full-Class Practice or Pair Practice.

OPTIONAL WRITING PRACTICE

Have students write exercises 2, 5, 9, 10, 11, 12, 13 for homework.

WORKBOOK

Students can now do pages 90, 91, 92.

EXPANSION ACTIVITIES

1. *Role Play:* "How Do You Feel?"
   Have students write and act out original dialogs based on the conversations on text pages 90-91. The dialogs should begin: "How do you feel?"

2. *Students' Stories: Review of Irregular Past Tense Verbs*
   a. Write these verbs on the board:

   > sat   ate   drank   sang

   or use SBS Picture Cards 168-171.

   b. Have each student write a story about what he or she did yesterday using all four verbs.
   Examples:
   "Yesterday I sat in a restaurant all day. I ate cookies, I drank wine, and I sang Spanish songs."
   "Yesterday I sat in my apartment all morning. I ate candy, I drank soda, and I sang."
   Have students tell their stories to the class.

ON YOUR OWN

FOCUS

> Making an appointment with the doctor.
> Review of ailments.
> Review of the past tense.
> Contrast of the past tense (with *yesterday*) and the simple present tense (with *usually*).

Students use the *skeletal model* to create their own conversations using any vocabulary they wish.

1. Introduce the new words and expressions:

> *Hello*
> *How are you?*
> *What seems to be the problem?*
> *Do you have any idea why?*
> *probably*
> *make an appointment*
>
> *When can you see me?*
> *How about _____?*
> *That's fine.*
> *See you tomorrow.*
> *Good-bye.*

2. The students write their conversations for homework and then present them in class the next day.

    Example:

> A. Hello, Doctor Smith. This is Mr. Jones.
> B. Hello, Mr. Jones. How are you?
> A. I don't feel very well today.
> B. I'm sorry to hear that. What seems to be the problem?
> A. I have a TERRIBLE stomachache.
> B. Do you have any idea why?
> A. Well, Doctor . . . . I probably have a terrible stomachache because I ate candy all day yesterday.
> B. Do you USUALLY eat candy all day?
> A. No, I don't. But I ate candy all day YESTERDAY!
> B. Do you want to make an appointment?
> A. Yes, I do. When can you see me?
> B. How about tomorrow at 2:00?
> A. That's fine. Thank you very much.
> B. See you tomorrow.
> A. Good-bye.

EXPANSION ACTIVITY

Practice With Visuals: Contrast Simple Present Tense and Past Tense

1. Put this conversational model on the board.

    > A. What did _____ do yesterday?
    > B. _____ all day.
    > A. Does _____ usually _____ all day?
    > B. No. But _____ all day yesterday!

2. Use your own visuals or SBS Picture Cards of every day and leisure activities to provide cues for pairs of students to create conversations based on the model. For example,

    (visual: A man sitting in the park.)

    A. What did Bill do yesterday?
    B. He sat in the park all day.
    A. Does he usually sit in the park all day?
    B. No. But he sat in the park all day yesterday!

A.   ALL MY FRIENDS ARE SICK

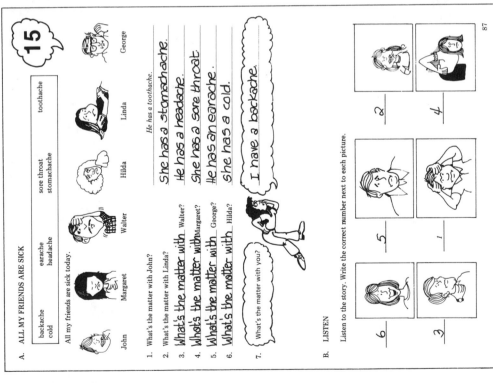

15

| backache | earache | sore throat | toothache |
| cold | headache | stomachache | |

John   Margaret   Walter   Hilda   Linda   George

All my friends are sick today.

He has a toothache.

1. What's the matter with John?
2. What's the matter with Linda?   *She has a stomachache.*
3. What's the matter with Walter?   *He has a headache.*
4. What's the matter with Margaret?   *She has a sore throat.*
5. What's the matter with George?   *He has an earache.*
6. What's the matter with Hilda?   *She has a cold.*

7. What's the matter with you?   *I have a backache.*

B.   LISTEN

Listen to the story. Write the correct number next to each picture.

6   5   2

3   1   4

87

Students practice vocabulary relating to illnesses. In Exercise A, they ask and answer questions. Exercise B is a listening comprehension with the new vocabulary. (text page 88)

Key to Exercise B
Read or play the tape.

Helen is at home today with her family because her sisters and brothers are all sick. What's the matter with them?

1. Her brother David has a very bad headache. He feels terrible.
2. Her sister Patty isn't at school because she has a toothache.
3. Edward has a sore throat.
4. Alice is very upset because she has a backache.
5. What's the matter with Jack? He doesn't know, but he feels terrible.

Helen's family is sick today, but not Helen.

6. Helen feels fine.

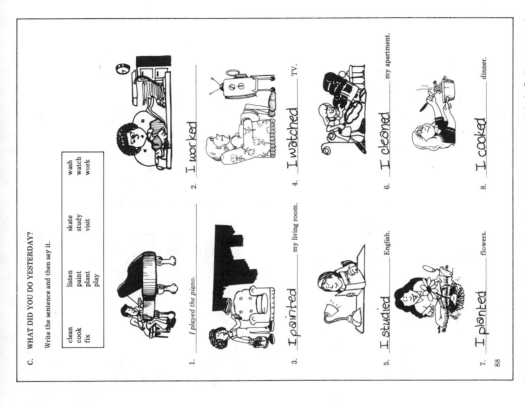

C. **WHAT DID YOU DO YESTERDAY?**

Write the sentence and then say it.

clean	listen	skate	wash
cook	paint	study	watch
fix	plant	visit	work
	play		

1. _I played the piano._

2. I worked

3. I painted _____ my living room.

4. I watched _____ TV.

5. I studied _____ English.

6. I cleaned _____ my apartment.

7. I planted _____ flowers.

8. I cooked _____ dinner.

88

Students practice writing and saying the past tense with *I*. Call on several students for each question to have them practice pronouncing the past tense with [t], [d], and [id]. Note 5: study → studied. (text page 89)

Key to Exercise D
For each sentence, read or play the tape twice.

1. I study.
2. I studied.
3. I smoked.
4. I smoke.
5. I wait for the train.
6. I waited for the bus.
7. I bake.
8. I cooked breakfast.
9. I played cards.
10. I play the piano.
11. I fixed the car.
12. I visited my friends.
13. I work.
14. I rest.
15. I rested.

In Exercise D, students practice listening for past tense endings. They discriminate between sentences in the past and simple present. (text page 89)

E. JOHN'S DAY AT HOME

| bake | cook | fix | paint | plant | rest | wash |

John worked at home all day. His family is very happy.

1. "Thank you John. This is a very good dinner."
2. "This is a wonderful apple pie, John."
3. "The new flowers in the garden are beautiful."
4. "Look at the car. It's really clean. Thank you."
5. "The bedroom looks beautiful. Blue is my favorite color."
6. "The TV isn't broken! I can watch my favorite TV program tonight."

What did John do?

1. *He cooked dinner.*
2. He baked an apple pie.
3. He planted flowers.
4. He washed the car.
5. He painted the bedroom.
6. He fixed the TV.

What did John do after dinner?

7. *He rested.*

F. WHAT DID EVERYBODY DO?

bake	play baseball	wait for the bus
dance	skate	work
paint the bathroom	study	

1. What did David do today?
He worked all day.

2. What did Billy and his father do yesterday?
They played baseball all afternoon.

---

3. What did Fred do yesterday?
He baked cookies all afternoon.

4. What did Mr. and Mrs. Smith do yesterday?
They danced all evening.

5. What did Shirley do today?
She waited for the bus all afternoon.

6. What did you and your husband do yesterday?
We painted the bathroom all afternoon.

7. What did Nancy do today?
She studied English all afternoon.

8. What did Mr. and Mrs. Wilson do yesterday?
They skated all day.

In Exercise E, students use the past tense with *he.* Each numbered conversation is a cue that tells students what John did. (text pages 90-91)
Students practice using the past tense with all persons. In 7 and 8 they also write questions. (text pages 90-91)

CHAPTER FIFTEEN 209

G.   BILL'S WEDDING

Fill in the missing words.

At Bill's wedding last night, my father (play) _played_ the piano, and my mother (sing) _sang_ popular songs. My little sister Sara (eat) _ate_ cookies and candy all night.

My brother Peter is a wonderful dancer. Last night he (dance) _danced_ with all my cousins and all my aunts.

My uncle John never dances, but last night he (drink) _drank_ champagne and vodka, and after that he (dance) _danced_ with every woman in the room.

Aunt Helen and Uncle David always sit and talk at parties. At Bill's wedding they (sit) _sat_ on the sofa together and (talk) _talked_ next to them and (cry) _cried_ about their children all night.

Bill's grandmother (sit) _sat_ next to them and (cry) _cried_.

What did I do at Bill's wedding? I (drink) _drank_ champagne and I (smoke) _smoked_ cigarettes.

H.   THE DAY AFTER BILL'S WEDDING

1.   Peter has a backache this morning. Why?

Because he danced with all his cousins and all his aunts last night.

2.   Sara has a stomachache this morning. Why?

Because she ate cookies and candy all night.

3.   Uncle John is very embarrassed this morning. Why? *Because he drank champagne and vodka, and he danced with every woman in the room.*

4.   Aunt Helen has a sore throat this morning. Why?

Because she talked all night.

5.   I have a headache and a sore throat this morning. Why?

Because you drank champagne and smoked cigarettes.

92

In Exercise G, students fill in the blanks with the past tense of irregular and regular verbs. For additional practice, call on students to read the story aloud. In Exercise H, students answer questions about the story using the past tense. (text page 90-91)

TEACHER'S NOTES

CHAPTER 16 OVERVIEW

TEXT PAGES 93-98

FOCUS

Past Tense

1. Yes/No questions: *Did you brush your hair this morning?*
   No, I didn't. I brushed my teeth.

2. WH- (information) questions: *What did you do last night?*
   Why did your boss shout at you?
   What time did you get up?
   How did you get to class today?

3. More irregular verbs:

go-went	*do-did*
take-took	*steal-stole*
get-got	*forget-forgot*
have-had	*meet-met*
buy-bought	
write-wrote	
read-read	

COMMUNICATIVE SKILLS

1. Expressing past activity:
   I took the bus this morning.
   I arrived late for work.

2. Making excuses:
   Why are you late for class?
   I missed the bus.
   I had to go to the bank before class.

VOCABULARY

an old friend*	How did you get to class?	take the subway
arrive late for work	last night	thief
bananas	meet-met	tomatoes
before	miss the bus	walk
buy	office	What happened?
class	on the way	yesterday afternoon
excuses	on time	yesterday evening
forget-forgot	steal	yesterday morning
girlfriend	take the bus	
go back home		

*This expression refers to a friend one has known for a long time—not a friend who is old.

LANGUAGE NOTES

The present and past tense forms of the verb *read* are spelled the same, but are pronounced differently:

      present tense: [rid]
      past tense: [red]

CULTURE KEY

The expression *on time* is introduced in this chapter and represents an important concept in U.S. culture.

1. Although it is impossible to summarize the rules of etiquette regarding time in the U.S., people are generally expected to arrive *on time* (at the invited or appointed time).

2. On text pages 97 and 98 students practice making excuses for being late; the idea is that one must have a good reason for not being on time.

FOCUS

Yes/No questions with regular verbs in the past tense.

GETTING READY

1. Read the sample sentences in the boxes at the top of the page. Have students repeat each one chorally.

2. Write the framework below on the board and practice it using each of the persons (I, he, she, we, you, they).

> _____ cooked.   Yes, _____ did.
> Did _____ cook?   No, _____ didn't.

a. Read each sentence using a pronoun. For example,
   "He cooked."
   "Did he cook?"
   "Yes, he did."
   "No, he didn't."

b. Have students repeat each line chorally.

PRESENTING THE MODEL

1. Have students look at the model illustration in the book or on the SBS Dialog Visual Card.
2. Set the scene: "A mother is talking to her son."
3. Present the model.
4. Full-Class Choral Repetition.
5. Ask students if they have any questions; check understanding of new vocabulary: *this morning.*
6. Group Choral Repetition.
7. Choral Conversation.
8. Call on one or two pairs of students to present the dialog.
   (For additional practice, do Choral Conversation in small groups or by rows.)
9. Introduce the time expressions under the model. Have pairs of students practice the model again using these expressions in place of *this morning.*

SIDE BY SIDE EXERCISES

Examples:

> 1. A. Did he study English last night?
>   B. No, he didn't. He studied Spanish.
> 2. A. Did she wash her windows this morning?
>   B. No, she didn't. She washed her car.

1. **Exercise 1:** Call on two students to present the dialog. Then do Choral Repetition and Choral Conversation Practice.
2. **Exercise 2:** Same as above.

3. Exercises 3-6:

New vocabulary: 5. *records*

Either Full-Class Practice or Pair Practice.

OPTIONAL WRITING PRACTICE
Have students write exercises 3, 4, 5, 6 for homework.

WORKBOOK
Students can now do pages 93, 94.

EXPANSION ACTIVITIES:

1. *Students Talk About Themselves: Practice With* <u>*Yes, I did. No, I didn't.*</u>
   a. Use your own visuals, SBS Picture Cards, or write these activities on the board:

study _____	listen to _____	work	call _____
wash _____	smoke _____	dance	plant _____
play _____	brush _____	ski	paint _____
		skate	

   b. Have students ask each other *Yes/No* questions about yesterday using the verbs shown on the visuals or on the board. Call on pairs of students. For example,

   A. Did you play cards yesterday?   A. Did you study English yesterday?
   B. No, I didn't.   B. Yes, I did.

2. *Practice With Negative Sentences:* Steve and Bill Story
   a. Say:
   "I have two friends: Steve and Bill. They're very different. I'm going to tell YOU about Steve, and you're going to tell ME about Bill."
   b. Give an example:
   Write the 2 sentences below on the board and read them:
   Steve worked yesterday.
   Bill didn't work yesterday.
   c. Have students listen as you read each statement about *Steve.* Then ask a student, "What about *Bill*?" Have the student change the verb to the negative form and make the statement about *Bill.*
   1. Steve *shaved* yesterday morning.   4. Steve *painted* his garage yesterday.
      (Bill *didn't shave* yesterday morning.)   (Bill *didn't paint* his garage yesterday.)
   2. Steve *cleaned* his apartment.   5. Steve *cooked* dinner last night.
      (Bill *didn't clean* his apartment.)   (Bill *didn't cook* dinner last night.)
   3. Steve *called* his mother yesterday.   6. Steve *danced* at a disco all night.
      (Bill *didn't call* his mother yesterday.)   (Bill *didn't dance* at a disco all night.)
   d. Ask the class, "What did Bill do yesterday?" Have students make up answers using any vocabulary they wish.

3. *Dictation*
   Dictate these sentences to the class. Tell students to listen carefully to the endings of words before they write them.
   1. He worked.   4. Did they study?
   2. Did they work?   5. She studied.
   3. She didn't work.   6. I didn't study.

FOCUS

> Irregular verbs in the past tense:
>
> | | |
> |---|---|
> | *go-went* | *buy-bought* |
> | *take-took* | *write-wrote* |
> | *get-got* | *read-read* |
> | *have-had* | *do-did* |

GETTING READY

1. Introduce the past tense of *go: went.*
2. Read the sample sentences in the boxes at the top of the page. Have students repeat chorally.

PRESENTING THE MODEL

1. Have students look at the model illustration in the book or on the SBS Dialog Visual Card.
2. Set the scene: "Friends are talking."
3. Present the model.
4. Full-Class Choral Repetition.
5. Ask students if they have any questions; check understanding of new vocabulary: *went.*
6. Group Choral Repetition.
7. Choral Conversation.
8. Call on one or two pairs of students to present the dialog.
   (For additional practice, do Choral Conversation in small groups or by rows.)
9. Practice the model with other pronouns. Put on the board:

Sally   Bob   Mr. and Mrs. Jones

Call on pairs of students to practice the model again using these names. For example,
   A. Did Sally go to the bank this afternoon?
   B. No, she didn't. She went to the supermarket.

SIDE BY SIDE EXERCISES

Examples:

> | | | | | |
> |---|---|---|---|---|
> | 1. | A. Did you go skating yesterday? | | 2. | A. Did you take the subway this morning? |
> | | B. No, I didn't. I went skiing. | | | B. No, I didn't. I took the bus. |

1. **Exercise 1:** Call on two students to present the dialog. Then do Choral Repetition and Choral Conversation Practice.
2. **Exercise 2:** Introduce the new vocabulary: *take the subway, take the bus.* Same as above.
3. **Exercises 3-8:**

> **New vocabulary:**   5. *buy, bananas, tomatoes*   6. *girlfriend*

Either Full-Class Practice or Pair Practice.

216   CHAPTER SIXTEEN

OPTIONAL WRITING PRACTICE

Have students write exercises 1-8 for homework.

WORKBOOK

Students can now do pages 95, 96 Exercise E.

EXPANSION ACTIVITIES

1. *Review Irregular Past Tense Forms*
   Say the simple form of the following verbs and have students tell you the past tense forms.

1. eat-ate	4. sit-sat	7. get-got	10. write-wrote
2. drink-drank	5. go-went	8. have-had	11. read-read
3. sing-sang	6. take-took	9. buy-bought	12. do-did

2. *Practice With Irregular Verbs:* Steve and Bill Story

   a. Say: "I'm going to talk about my friend Steve and Bill. I'm going to tell YOU about Bill, and you're gong to tell ME about Steve."

   b. Give an example: Write these sentences on the board and read them:
      Bill didn't get up at 7:00 this morning.
      Steve got up at 7:00.

   c. Have students listen as you read each statement about *Bill*. Then ask a student, "What about Steve?" Have the student change the verb from negative to affirmative and make the statement about *Steve*.

   1. Bill *didn't take* a shower yesterday.
      (Steve *took* a shower yesterday.)
   2. Bill *didn't have* breakfast yesterday.
      (Steve *had* breakfast yesterday.)
   3. Bill *didn't eat* lunch at a restaurant.
      (Steve *ate* lunch at a restaurant.)
   4. Bill *didn't write* to his brother last night.
      (Steve *wrote* to his brother last night.)
   5. Bill *didn't read* a story at night.
      (Steve *read* a story at night.)
   6. Bill *didn't do* his exercises yesterday.
      (Steve *did* his exercises yesterday.)
   7. Bill *didn't have* a good day.
      (Steve *had* a good day.)

3. *Chain Game: Practice With Irregular Verbs*
   Practice the irregular verbs on text page 95 by playing the following game with your students:

   a. Start the chain game by saying:
      A. { I went skiing yesterday.
         { Did *you* go skiing yesterday?

   b. The student you ask must answer, "No, I didn't," make a new statement using the verb *go*, and ask another student, who then continues the *chain*. For example,
      B. { No, I didn't. I went skating.
         { Did *you* go skating?
      C. { No, I didn't. I went bowling.
         { Did *you* go bowling?
              etc.
   The chain can continue as long as students can think of new vocabulary.

Other examples:

1. A. { I got up at 7:00 this morning.
      { Did *you* get up at 7:00?
   B. { No, I didn't. I got up at 7:30 this morning.
      { Did *you* get up at 7:30 this morning?
   C. { No, I didn't. I got up at 8:00 this morning.
      { Did *you* get up at 8:00 this morning.

2. A. { I had a headache yesterday.
      { Did *you* have a headache?
   B. { No, I didn't. I had a
      { stomachache.
      { Did you have a stomachache?
        etc.

TEXT PAGES 96-97 (TOP)

FOCUS

1. Practice with regular and irregular verbs in the past tense.
2. *Why* questions.

PRESENTING THE MODEL

1. Have students look at the model illustrations in the text or on the SBS Dialog Visual Card.
2. Set the scene: "This is a story about Mary."
3. Present the model.
4. Full-Class Choral Repetition.
5. Ask students if they have any questions; check understanding of new vocabulary: *miss the bus, walk, office, arrive late for work.*
6. Call on one or two students to present the model.
   (For additional practice, do Choral Repetition in small groups or by rows.)

SIDE BY SIDE EXERCISES

Mary is talking to a friend about the chain of unfortunate events in her day. In this conversation Mary answers her friend's questions and, in so doing, she retells the story at the top of the page in reverse order.

Answer Key:

A. Hi, Mary! Did you have a good day today?
B. No, I didn't. I had a TERRIBLE day.
A. What happened?
B. I had a terrible headache all afternoon.
A. Why did you have a terrible headache all afternoon?
B. Because my boss shouted at me.
A. Why did your boss shout at you?
B. Because I arrived late for work.
A. Why did you arrive late for work?
B. Because I had to walk to the office.
A. Why did you have to walk to the office?
B. Because I missed the bus.
A. Why did you miss the bus?
B. Because I got up late.
A. Why did you get up late?
B. Because I went to a party last night.

1. Set the scene: "Mary is talking to her friend."
2. With books closed, have students listen as you present the first 8 lines of the dialog.
3. Full-Class Choral Repetition.
4. Have students open their books and look at the dialog. Ask if there are any questions and check understanding of new vocabulary: *What happened?*
5. Group Choral Repetition.
6. Choral Conversation.

218 CHAPTER SIXTEEN

7. Call on one or two pairs of students to present the dialog.
   (For additional practice, do Choral Conversation in small groups or by rows.)
8. Call on one or two pairs of students to complete each of the remaining 4 question-answer sets in the dialog. Do Choral Repetition and Choral Conversation Practice after each.
9. *Pair Practice:* Have all the students practice the dialog in pairs. Then have pairs present the dialog to the class.

ASK ANOTHER STUDENT IN YOUR CLASS (text page 97, top)

1. Read questions 1-6 and have students repeat chorally; introduce the new expressions: *How did you get to class?, on time.*
2. Divide the class into pairs; have each person *interview* the other, using the questions and taking notes.
3. Have each student *report* to the class on the person he or she *interviewed.*
   For example,
   1. Barbara didn't go to a party last night.
   2. She watched TV and studied mathematics.
   3. She didn't get up late today.
   4. She got up at 6:30 this morning.
   5. She took the subway to school.
   6. She arrived on time.

OPTIONAL WRITING PRACTICE

Have students write lines 9-16 of the dialog on text page 96. Also have students write answers to the questions at the top of text page 97.

WORKBOOK

Students can now do page 96 Exercise F.

EXPANSION ACTIVITY

More Practice With Mary's Day
Have students use the SBS Dialog Visual Card about *Mary* (text page 96) or the key words below as cues for the following activities:
   Key words: (Write on the board)
   1. go/party   5. arrive late/work
   2. get up late   6. boss/shout
   3. miss/bus   7. have/terrible headache
   4. walk/office
1. Call on students to retell some or all of the story about Mary.
2. Have students role play the conversation at the bottom of the page. Call on students: One pretends to be *Mary* and another *Mary's friend.*
3. Practice with *she*: Have students create conversations about Mary. They can begin:
      "What happened to Mary?"
      "She had a terrible headache all afternoon."
      "Why did she have a terrible headache all afternoon?"
4. Practice with *he*: Change *Mary* to *Marvin.* Have pairs of students create conversations about *Marvin.* They can begin:
      "What happened to Marvin?"
      "He had a terrible headache all afternoon."

FOCUS

1. Making excuses.
2. Further practice with verbs in the past tense.

EXCUSES! EXCUSES!

This exercise is preparation for the ON YOUR OWN exercise on the next page.

1. Read each excuse using one of the suggestions in parentheses to fill in the blank; have students repeat. Introduce the new words: *before class, forget-forgot, go back home, meet-met, on the way, an old friend, thief, steal-stole.*

2. Call on students to say each excuse using different vocabulary. For example,

    I missed the bus.
    I missed the train.
    I missed the subway.

3. Have students think of additional excuses they might use for being late to class.

4. Discuss the attitude toward time in your culture. When is it important to be on time? When is it acceptable to be late? How late can you be? (See CHAPTER OVERVIEW, Culture Key.)

ON YOUR OWN

PRESENTING THE MODEL

1. Have students look at the model illustration in the book or on the SBS Dialog Visual Card.

2. Set the scene: "A teacher and a student are talking. The teacher is upset because the student is late for class."

3. Present the model.

4. Full-Class Choral Repetition.

5. Ask students if they have any questions; check understanding of new vocabulary: *well, excuses.*

6. Group Choral Repetition.

7. Choral Conversation.

8. Call on one or two pairs of students to present the dialog.

    (For additional practice, do Choral Conversation in small groups or by rows.)

9. For homework, have students write their own conversations based on the model. Students can use any excuses they wish. Have students role play their conversations in the next class. The students playing the part of the teacher should sit at your desk while the one who is late comes in the door.

WORKBOOK

Students can now do page 97.

EXPANSION ACTIVITY

Picture Story: Past Tense
Make up a story about the events in someone's day yesterday.

1. Put times and key words (or stick figures) on the board. For example,

| 7:00 | 8:15 | 12:45 | 5:00 | 6:30 | 8:00 | 10:00 |
| (get up) | (walk to work) | (meet a friend and have lunch) | (go home) | (eat dinner) | (read the newspaper) | (go to bed) |

2. Tell about that person's day. For example,
   1. Jim got up at 7:00 yesterday.
   2. At 8:15 he walked to work.
   3. He met a friend at 12:45 and they had lunch.
   4. He went home at 5:00.
   5. At 6:30 he ate dinner.
   6. At 8:00 he read the newspaper.
   7. He went to bed at 10:00.

3. Ask *What* and *When* questions about *Jim*; then call on pairs of students to ask and answer questions. For example,
   "What time did Jim get up yesterday?"
   "When did he meet a friend?"

A. CORRECT THE SENTENCE

1. My sister fixed the TV this morning.

   She didn't fix the TV.

   She fixed the car.

2. Mr. and Mrs. Nelson painted their bedroom yesterday morning.

   They didn't paint their bedroom.

   They painted their kitchen.

3. William washed the clothes this morning.

   He didn't wash the clothes.

   He washed the windows.

4. Our neighbors played chess yesterday evening.

   They didn't play chess.

   They played cards.

5. Bob talked to his uncle yesterday evening.

   He didn't talk to his uncle.

   He talked to his aunt.

6. Peggy waited for the train this morning.

   She didn't wait for the train.

   She waited for the bus.

7. Maria studied mathematics this evening.

   She didn't study mathematics.

   She studied English.

8. Mr. Jones called the doctor yesterday afternoon.

   He didn't call the doctor.

   He called the plumber.

Hello, Aunt Helen.

93

Students practice writing positive and negative sentences with regular past tense verbs. (text page 94)

Exercise B is a dictation that gives practice with positive and negative sentences in the past. Students decide from the sound and from the context whether or not a verb ends in *ed*. Exercise C gives practice with short answers and *yes/no* questions. Students answer and then ask questions about the dictation. (text page 94)

Key to Exercise B—Sally and Her Brother
Read or play the tape.

Sally is very tired today. She *worked* all day yesterday, and her family didn't *help* her. Yesterday morning she *fixed* the car. Yesterday afternoon she *painted* the bathroom. Yesterday evening she *cleaned* the basement. She didn't *rest* all day.

Sally's brother isn't very tired today. Yesterday he didn't *work*. He didn't *fix* the car. He didn't *paint* the bathroom, and he didn't *clean* the basement. What did he do? He *talked* on the telephone all morning. He *listened* to music all afternoon, and he *rested* in front of the TV all evening.

SALLY AND HER BROTHER

B.   LISTEN

Listen to the story. Write the missing words.

Sally is very tired today. She (1) _worked_ all day yesterday, and her family didn't (2) **help** her. Yesterday morning she (3) **fixed** the car. Yesterday afternoon she (4) **painted** the bathroom. Yesterday evening she (5) **cleaned** the basement. She didn't (6) **rest** all day.

Sally's brother isn't very tired today. Yesterday he didn't (7) **work**. He didn't (8) **fix** the car. He didn't (9) **paint** the bathroom, and he didn't (10) **clean** the basement. What did he do? He (11) **talked** on the telephone all morning. He (12) **listened** to music all afternoon, and he (13) **rested** in front of the TV all evening.

C.   WRITE ABOUT SALLY AND HER BROTHER

1. Did Sally work all day yesterday? _Yes, she did._
2. Did her brother work all day yesterday? **No, he didn't.**
3. Did Sally fix the car yesterday morning? **Yes, she did.**
4. Did her brother talk on the telephone yesterday morning? **Yes, he did.**
5. Did Sally talk on the telephone yesterday morning? **No, she didn't.**
6. _Did_ _Sally_ _fix_ the car yesterday morning? Yes, she did.
7. **Did Sally paint** the bathroom yesterday afternoon? Yes, she did.
8. **Did her brother listen** to music yesterday afternoon? Yes, he did.
9. **Did her brother clean** the basement after dinner? No, he didn't.
10. **Did Sally rest** in front of the TV yesterday evening? No, she didn't.
11. **Did Sally clean** the basement yesterday evening? Yes, she did.

94

D. YESTERDAY

1. Henry usually takes the bus. — He _didn't_ _take_ the bus yesterday. He _took_ the subway.
2. Julie usually buys candy. — She _didn't_ _buy_ candy yesterday. She _bought_ cookies.
3. Mr. and Mrs. Smith usually go jogging. — They _didn't_ _go_ jogging yesterday. They _went_ swimming.
4. Sara usually writes to her mother. — She _didn't_ _write_ to her mother yesterday. She _wrote_ to her father.
5. Peter and George usually get up at 7:00. — They _didn't_ _get_ _up_ at 7:00 yesterday. They _got_ _up_ at 9:00.
6. I usually have dinner at 6:00. — I _didn't_ _have_ dinner at 6:00 yesterday. I _had_ dinner at 8:00.
7. Paul usually reads novels. — He _didn't_ _read_ a novel yesterday. He _read_ poetry.
8. George and Peter usually do their homework at 4:00. — They _didn't_ _do_ their homework at 4:00 yesterday. They _did_ their homework after dinner.
9. Charlie usually eats at home. — He _didn't_ _eat_ at home yesterday. He _ate_ at a Chinese restaurant.
10. I usually drink tea. — I _didn't_ _drink_ tea yesterday. I _drank_ coffee.
11. Walter usually sits next to John. — He _didn't_ _sit_ next to John yesterday. He _sat_ next to Nancy.
12. David and Barbara usually sing popular songs. — They _didn't_ _sing_ popular songs yesterday. They _sang_ old songs.
13. Jane usually takes a shower. — She _didn't_ _take_ a shower yesterday. She _took_ a bath.
14. We usually go to a movie on Saturday. — We _didn't_ _go_ to a movie yesterday. We _went_ to a concert.
15. Mr. and Mrs. Wilson usually buy Mexican coffee. — They _didn't_ _buy_ Mexican coffee yesterday. They _bought_ French coffee.
16. Jim usually has lunch with his brother. — He _didn't_ _have_ lunch with his brother yesterday. He _had_ lunch with his boss.

95

E. WHAT'S THE QUESTION?

1. _Did you go_ to the bank? — No, I didn't. I went to the post office.
2. _Did he buy_ a car? — No, he didn't. He bought a bicycle.
3. _Did they write_ to their uncle? — No, they didn't. They wrote to their sister.
4. _Did she have_ a stomachache? — No, she didn't. She had a cold.
5. _Did you get up_ at 9:00? — No, I didn't. I got up at 11:00.
6. _Did you read_ today's newspaper? — No, I didn't. I read yesterday's newspaper.
7. _Did you go_ bowling? — No, we didn't. We went dancing.
8. _Did they have_ a good time? — No, they didn't. They had a terrible time.
9. _Did you eat_ Italian food? — No, we didn't. We ate Greek food.
10. _Did he buy_ a new shirt? — No, he didn't. He bought a new tie.
11. _Did they drink_ coffee? — No, they didn't. They drank tea.
12. _Did she sing_ French songs? — No, she didn't. She sang German songs.
13. _Did she do_ her Spanish homework? — No, she didn't. She did her English homework.
14. _Did you sit_ next to Robert? — No, I didn't. I sat next to Fred.

F. LISTEN

Listen to each question. Put a circle around the correct answer.

1. a. She goes to the bank on Friday.
   (b.) She went to the bank yesterday.
2. (a.) He studies French.
   b. He studied Spanish.
3. a. He does his homework at 4:00.
   (b.) He did his homework after dinner.
4. a. I buy tomatoes.
   (b.) I bought bananas.
5. (a.) I listen to popular music.
   b. I listened to rock and roll.
6. a. He visits his uncle.
   (b.) He visited his aunt.
7. (a.) She writes to her grandmother every week.
   b. She wrote to her grandmother yesterday.
8. a. They play basketball at school.
   (b.) They played basketball in the park.
9. (a.) They go dancing on Saturday.
   b. They went dancing last night.
10. a. He cleans his room on Friday.
    (b.) He cleaned his room this morning.

96

Students practice positive and negative sentences in the past tense with irregular verbs. The irregular verbs on text page 91 are included in the exercise. (text page 95)

In Exercise F, students listen to questions and practice discriminating between the present tense do and does and the past tense did. (text pages 96, 97)

G. BUT THEY DIDN'T

Bill went to a restaurant yesterday afternoon, but he didn't eat. He drank coffee, and he studied mathematics.

1. Where _did_ Bill _go_ yesterday afternoon? He went _____ to a restaurant.

2. What __did__ he _drink_ ? He drank _____ coffee.

3. What __did__ he _study_ ? He studied _____ mathematics.

Alice went to the supermarket yesterday, but she didn't buy any food. She forgot her pocketbook and had to call her mother.

4. Where __did__ Alice _go_ yesterday? She went _____ to the supermarket.

5. What __did__ she _forget_ ? She forgot _____ her pocketbook.

6. Who __did__ she _call_ ? She called _____ her mother.

Steven and Nancy went to their science class this morning, but they didn't study science. They ate candy and listened to records at a birthday party for their teacher.

7. When __did__ Steven and Nancy _go_ to their science class? They went _____ this morning.

8. What __did__ they _eat_ ? They ate _____ candy.

9. What __did__ they _listen_ to? They listened _____ to records.

Mary went to a discotheque last Saturday, but she didn't dance. She met an old friend, and they talked all night.

10. When __did__ Mary _go_ to a discotheque? She went _____ last Saturday.

11. Who __did__ she _meet_ ? She met _____ an old friend.

12. What __did__ they do? They talked _____ all night.

97

Students practice asking and answering questions in the past tense with regular and irregular verbs. (text pages 97-98)

Key to Exercise F (above, on page 224)
For each question, read or play the tape twice.

1. When did Betty go to the bank?
2. What does Fred study at school?
3. When did Peter do his homework?
4. What did you buy at the store?
5. What kind of music do you listen to?
6. Who did he visit in Paris?
7. When does Nancy write to her grandmother?
8. Where did Alice and Jane play basketball?
9. When do Mr. and Mrs. Johnson go dancing?
10. When did Billy clean his room?

TEXT PAGES 99-104

FOCUS

Past tense of the verb *to be:*
    We were hungry.   *He was tired.*

COMMUNICATIVE SKILLS

1. Describing oneself and one's activities in the past and present:
        I was sick.
        I was at the movies.
        Tom had a big breakfast today. He was hungry.
        Before we were tired. Now we're energetic.

2. Talking about one's childhood:
        I was tall.
        I had curly hair.
        I was two years old when I began to talk.

VOCABULARY

at the movies	dirty	healthy	soap
ballgame	dog food	How about you?	tiny
before	energetic	How old?	too
bread	enormous	ice cream	toothpaste
cereal	family	paint (n)	uncomfortable
clean	floor wax	shiny	unhealthy
comfortable	full	skim milk	vitamin
commercial	furniture		window cleaner

ON YOUR OWN (text page 104)

begin-began	finish	go on a date	remember
childhood	first	hero	spare time
cute	freckles	hobby	start
dimples	games	I was _____ years old.	words

LANGUAGE NOTES

In this chapter there are several words with the [w] sound: *was, were, WHAMMO, William, windows*; also the [h] sound: *happy, hungry, healthy, hat, home, handsome, hair, hobby, hero.*

CULTURE KEY

The exercises on text pages 100-101 are about TV commercials for household products. These exercises are meant to be a humorous exaggeration of the kinds of advertisements which both entertain and irritate people in the U.S.

FOCUS

Introduction of the past tense forms of the verb *to be: was/were.*

GETTING READY

Introduce *was* and *were.* Form sentences using the words in the box at the top of the page. Say each sentence and have students repeat chorally and individually.

PRESENTING THE MODEL

1. Have students look at the model illustration in the book or on the SBS Dialog Visual Card.

2. Set the scene: "This is a TV commercial for WHAMMO Vitamins."

3. Present the model.

4. Full-Class Choral Repetition.

5. Ask students if they have any questions; check understanding of new vocabulary: *commercial, before, family, vitamins, too, energetic, How about you?*

6. Call on one or two students to present the commercial.

    (For additional practice, do Choral Repetition in small groups or by rows.)

SIDE BY SIDE EXERCISES

Examples:

1. Before our family bought WHAMMO Ice Cream, we were always sad.   I was sad.   My wife/husband was sad.   My children were sad, too.   Now we're happy because WE bought WHAMMO Ice Cream.   How about you?
2. Before our family bought WHAMMO Bread, we were always hungry.   I was hungry.   My wife/husband was hungry.   My children were hungry, too.   Now we're full because we bought WHAMMO Bread.   How about you?

1. **Exercise 1:** Introduce the new word: *ice cream.* Call on one or two students to present the commercial. Then do Choral Repetition and Choral Conversation Practice.

2. **Exercise 2:** Introduce the new words: *bread, full.* Same as above.

3. **Exercises 3-5:**

New vocabulary:	3. *soap, dirty, clean*	4. *cereal, healthy*	5. *skim milk*

Either Full-Class Practice or Pair Practice.

4. **Exercise 6:** For homework, have students prepare 2 commercials for other WHAMMO products. Have students *act out* their commercials in class the next day.

OPTIONAL WRITING PRACTICE

Have students write exercises 2, 4 for homework.

WORKBOOK

Students can now do page 98.

EXPANSION ACTIVITIES

1. *Practice* Was *and* Were *With Visuals*

   a. Begin by telling this story:
      "Yesterday I really wanted to see you. I called you on the phone, but you weren't there. I went to your house, but you weren't there.
      "Where were you?"

   b. Use SBS Picture cards, your own visuals, or word cards for places around town. Hold up different visuals as you ask students the questions below. Students answer according to the visuals.
      "Where were you?"
      "I was at the bank."
      "I was at the movies."
      "Where were you and (any name)?"
      "We were at the supermarket."
      "We were at a concert."
      "Where was (male's name)?"
      "He was in the park."
      "He was at Stanley's International Restaurant."
      "Where was (female's name)?"
      "She was at the police station."
      "She was at the zoo."

2. *Talk About The Weather*
   Ask students questions about the weather yesterday, last week, and last month. For example,
      A. How was the weather last week?
      B. It was cloudy and cold.

FOCUS

Contrast of present tense and past tense forms of the verb *to be.*

PRESENTING THE MODEL

1. Have students look at the model illustration in the book or on the SBS Dialog Visual Card.
2. Set the scene: "A woman is talking about WHAMMO Shampoo."
3. Present the model.
4. Full-Class Choral Repetition.
5. Ask students if they have any questions; check understanding of new vocabulary: *shampoo.*
6. Call on one or two students to present the commercial.

    (For additional practice, do Choral Repetition in small groups or by rows.)

SIDE BY SIDE EXERCISES

Examples:

1. Before we bought WHAMMO Toothpaste, our teeth were yellow.
   Now they're white.
2. Before we bought WHAMMO Paint, our house was ugly.
   Now it's beautiful.

1. **Exercise 1:** Introduce the new word: *toothpaste.* Call on a student to tell about WHAMMO Toothpaste. Then do Choral Repetition.
2. **Exercise 2:** Introduce the new word: *paint.* Call on a student to tell about WHAMMO Paint. Then do Choral Repetition.
3. **Exercises 3-6:**

    New vocabulary: 3. *furniture, comfortable, uncomfortable* 4. *dog food, tiny, enormous* 5. *window cleaner* 6. *floor wax, dull, shiny*

    Introduce the new vocabulary one exercise at a time. Call on one or two students to do each exercise. (For more practice, do Choral Repetition.)
4. **Exercise 7:** For homework, have students write 2 commercials based on the model. Have students present their commercials in class the next day. Encourage students to bring in products from home to use as *props.*

OPTIONAL WRITING PRACTICE

Have students write exercises 1-6 for homework.

WORKBOOK

Students can now do page 99.

EXPANSION ACTIVITY

Before/Now Commercials With Real Objects
1. Bring real objects to class and provide key words on the board such as:

    a WHAMMO Watch (late/on time)
    a pair of WHAMMO Shoes (uncomfortable/comfortable)
    (tired/energetic)
    a WHAMMO Exercise Book (thin/heavy)
    a WHAMMO Coat (cold/warm)
    a WHAMMO fan (hot/cool)

2. Give the *products* to students and allow a short time for preparation. Encourage students to expand their commercials and say as much as possible about the *products*.

FOCUS

Negative forms of the verb *to be: wasn't, weren't*

GETTING READY

Introduce *wasn't* and *weren't*. Form sentences with the words in the grammar box at the top of the page. Say each sentence and have students repeat chorally and individually. For example,

"I wasn't at home."
"He wasn't tired."
"They weren't hungry."

PRESENTING THE MODEL

1. Have students look at the model illustration in the book or on the SBS Dialog Visual Card.

2. Set the scene: "Two friends are talking."

3. Present the model.

4. Full-Class Choral Repetition.

5. Ask students if they have any questions; check understanding of new vocabulary: *ballgame*.

6. Group Choral Repetition.

7. Choral Conversation.

8. Call on one or two pairs of students to present the dialog.

   (For additional practice, do Choral Conversation in small groups or by rows.)

SIDE BY SIDE EXERCISES

Examples:

---

1. A. Was it hot yesterday?
   B. No, it wasn't. It was cold.

2. A. Were they at home this morning?
   B. No, they weren't. They were in school.

Answers to Exercises 3-8:

3. No, she wasn't. She was happy.
4. No, he wasn't. He was a chef.
5. No, we weren't. We were at the beach.
6. No, you weren't. You were a noisy baby.

7. No, he wasn't. He was late.
8. No, she wasn't. She was on time.

1. **Exercise 1:** Call on two students to present the dialog. Then do Choral Repetition and Choral Conversation Practice.

2. **Exercise 2:** Same as above.

3. **Exercises 3-8:** Either Full-Class Practice or Pair Practice.

OPTIONAL WRITING PRACTICE

Have students write exercises 1, 4, 5, 6, 7, 8 for homework.

WORKBOOK

Students can now do page 100.

EXPANSION ACTIVITY

Chain Game: Practice Was/Were, Wasn't/Weren't
Use chain games to practice the verb *to be* in the past tense with a variety of vocabulary words.

1. Write on the board:

   I was _____ yesterday.

2. Start the game by saying:
   "I was at the beach yesterday.
   Were YOU at the beach yesterday?"

3. The student you ask must answer, "No, _____," make a new statement, and ask another student:
   "No, I wasn't. I was at the ballgame.
   Were YOU at the ballgame?"

4. Each student thereafter must do the same; the game can continue as long as students can think of new vocabulary to use.

   Another example:

   My grandparents were _____.

Start the game by saying:
   "My grandparents were teachers.
   Were YOUR grandparents teachers?"

FOCUS

> Contrast of simple past tense and past of *to be*.

PRESENTING THE MODEL

There are 2 model conversations. Introduce and practice each separately. For each model:

1. Have students look at the model illustration in the book or on the SBS Dialog Visual Card.
2. Set the scene: "Two people are talking."
3. Present the model.
4. Full-Class Choral Repetition.
5. Ask students if they have any questions.
6. Group Choral Repetition.
7. Choral Conversation.
8. Call on one or two pairs of students to present the dialog.

   (For additional practice, do Choral Conversation in small groups or by rows.)

SIDE BY SIDE EXERCISES

Examples:

> 1. A. Did you sleep well last night?
>   B. Yes, I did. I was tired.
> 2. A. Did Roger sleep well last night?
>   B. No, he didn't. He wasn't tired.

1. **Exercise 1:** Call on two students to present the dialog. Then do Choral Repetition and Choral Conversation.
2. **Exercise 2:** Same as above.
3. **Exercises 3-8:**

   > **New vocabulary:** 5. *finish*

   Either Full-Class Practice or Pair Practice.

OPTIONAL WRITING PRACTICE

Have students write exercises 1, 2, 3, 4, 7, 8 for homework.

WORKBOOK

Students can now do page 101.

EXPANSION ACTIVITY

Students Talk About Themselves

1. Have students ask each other questions about the recent past using a conversational framework and key words on the board.

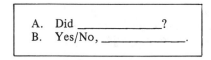

```
A.  Did _____?
B.  Yes/No, _____.
```

eat/big breakfast   go to/doctor
hungry   sick

sleep well   miss/train
tired   late

For example,

    A. Did you have a big breakfast this morning?
    B. Yes, I did. I was hungry.
       Or:
       No, I didn't. I wasn't hungry.

2. Call on pairs of students to create conversations. Encourage students to expand the conversations using any additional vocabulary they wish.

For additional conversations, make up more cues. For example,

boss/shout   have/headache
angry   tired

take/bath   go/restaurant
dirty   hungry

wear/coat   dance all night
cold   energetic

ON YOUR OWN

FOCUS

> Students talk about their childhoods.
> Review of the past tense.

1. Go over the questions. Introduce the new vocabulary:

    > *remember, childhood*   1. *cute, dimples, freckles*   2. *games*
    > 4. *spare time, hobby*   5. *hero*   6. *how old, begin-began,*
    > *I was—years old, first words*   8. *start*   9. *go on a date*

2. For homework, have students write answers to questions 1-9. Also have them think of 3 additional questions to ask other students (10-12).

3. In the next class, have students ask and answer the questions. (They should not refer to their written homework when practicing.)

    This can be Full-Class Practice or Pair Practice. If Pair Practice, have students report back to the class. For example,

    > "Mary was short."
    > "She had black curly hair."

    > "Bill didn't like school."
    > "He liked sports and TV."

    > "George began to walk when he was one year old."
    > "He started school when he was six years old."

WORKBOOK

Students can now do pages 102, 103.

EXPANSION ACTIVITY

How old was he/she?
Use a time line like the one below to talk about someone's childhood.

1. Put the time line on the board:

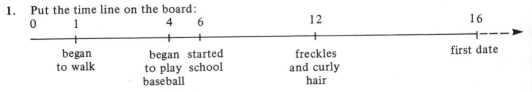

2. Tell about that person. For example,

    "Mary began to walk when she was one year old."

    "When she was four years old she began to play baseball."

    "She started school when she was six years old."

    "When she was twelve years old she had freckles and curly hair."

    "She went on her first date when she was sixteen years old."

3. Ask questions. For example,

    "When did Mary begin to walk?"

    "How old was she when she started school?"

4. Call on pairs of students to ask and answer questions.

In Exercises A and B, students practice *was* and *were*. In Exercise C, they listen for the difference between *is* and *was* and *are* and *were*. (text page 100)

Key to Exercise C
For each sentence, read or play the tape twice.

1. Mary is happy today.
2. Mrs. Wilson was very busy today.
3. The children were very noisy this morning.
4. The weather was beautiful today.
5. John is very hungry this morning.
6. We were very tired this evening.
7. Sally's clothes are always dirty.
8. Anita and Carmen are very sick today.
9. My grandmother was never angry.
10. Our homework is very easy today.
11. My sister and I are very upset.
12. Nancy and Rita were at school today.

A. A TERRIBLE MORNING

was	were

I _was_ very depressed last Monday. The weather _was_ terrible. It _was_ cold and foggy. My husband _was_ sick, and the neighbors _were_ angry because my children _were_ noisy.

The house _was_ dirty. There _were_ dishes in the sink. My children's clothes _were_ on the floor in their bedroom, and our refrigerator _was_ broken. I _was_ tired and hungry all morning.

B. A BEAUTIFUL MORNING

was	were

I _was_ very happy yesterday morning. The weather _was_ beautiful. It _was_ warm and sunny. There _were_ flowers in the garden. There _was_ a bird at the window. My children _were_ at school, and my husband and I _were_ on vacation.

C. LISTEN

Listen to each sentence. Put a circle around the word you hear.

1. is / **was**
2. is / **was**
3. are / **were**
4. is / **was**
5. is / **was**
6. are / **were**
7. are / **were**
8. are / **were**
9. **is** / was
10. **is** / was
11. **are** / were
12. **are** / were

98

D. BEFORE AND NOW

beautiful	expensive	heavy
cold	full	tired
dirty	happy	quiet

1. Before I painted my room, it _was_ ugly.
   Now _it's_ _beautiful_.

2. Before I worked at Stanley's Restaurant, I _was_ thin.
   Now _I'm_ _heavy_.

3. Last week the weather _was_ warm.
   Now _it's_ _cold_.

4. Before Mary met her husband, she _was_ always sad.
   Now _she's_ _happy_.

5. When our children _were_ young,
   they _were_ always noisy.
   Now _they're_ _quiet_.

6. Before we had dinner, we _were_ hungry.
   Now _we're_ _Full_.

7. When I _was_ young, coffee _was_ cheap.
   Now _it's_ _expensive_.

8. Before Jack worked in a garage, his clothes _were_ always clean.
   Now _they're_ _dirty_.

9. Before we got married, you _were_ always energetic.
   Now _you're_ _tired_.

99

E. A THIEF STOLE A CAR

was	were	wasn't	weren't

A thief stole an expensive car from a garage on Main Street last Sunday at 5:00. Mr. and Mrs. Jones _were_ in a restaurant next to the garage. Charlie Green _was_ across the street in a bar.

According to Mr. and Mrs. Jones, the thief _was_ tall and thin. His hair _was_ brown and curly. According to Charlie Green, the thief _was_ young and handsome. His clothes _were_ expensive.

The police are looking for the thief today. They're talking to Frank Harris. He's a tall, thin young man with brown, curly hair.

Police: _Were_ you on Main Street last Sunday at 5:00?
Frank: No, I _wasn't_. I _was_ at home with my wife.
Police: Are you sure?
Frank: Of course I am.
Police: That's strange. Your wife says she _was_ at home all evening, but you _weren't_ there.
Frank: I wasn't? I _wasn't_.
Police: No, you _weren't_.
Frank: Oh, I forgot. Last Sunday at 5:00 I _was_ with my friend Tom.
Police: Where _were_ you and your friend?
Frank: We _were_ here at the police station.
Police: Why _were_ you at the police station?
Frank: We _were_ here because at 4:00 last Sunday a thief stole my friend Tom's car!

1. According to Mr. and Mrs. Jones, was the thief tall and thin? _Yes, he was._
2. Was his hair blond and straight? _No, it wasn't. (It was brown and curly.)_
3. According to Charlie Green, was the thief old? _No, he wasn't. (He was young.)_
4. Were his clothes expensive? _Yes, they were._
5. Was Frank at home at 5:00 last Sunday? _No, he wasn't._
6. Was he with his wife? _No, he wasn't._
7. Who was he with? _He was with his friend Tom._
8. Where were they? _They were at the police station._
9. Why? _Because a thief stole his friend Tom's car._

100

Exercise E is a reading comprehension with focus on the past forms of the verb *to be*. The questions after the story give practice with short answers. For additional practice, have students read the story aloud. (text page 102)

Students practice the past and present of the verb *to be* and opposite adjectives. (text page 101)

CHAPTER SEVENTEEN 239

F. ROBERT'S PARTY

| did | didn't | was | wasn't | were | weren't |

Robert had a big party last night. His friends are talking about the party today.

1. *Was* Mary at the party last night?
   Yes, she **was**, but she **didn't** have a good time.
   Why not?
   Robert **didn't** dance with her.
   She **was** very angry at him.

2. **Did** you have a good time at the party last night?
   No, I **didn't**.
   Why not?
   I **didn't** like the music.
   It **was** very loud.

3. **Were** Fred and Tom at the party?
   No, they **weren't**.
   Why not?
   Fred **didn't** feel well, and Tom **was** busy.

4. Why **were** you upset last night?
   I missed the train, and I **was** late. When I arrived at the party, there **wasn't** any food. I **was** hungry all night.

5. Why **did** Betty leave the party at 7:00?
   She **was** sad because her boyfriend **wasn't** there.

6. What **did** Jane do at the party?
   She sat and smoked. She **didn't** talk, and she **didn't** dance. I think she **was** tired.

7. **Did** you like Robert's party?
   Yes, I **did**. The food and the music **were** wonderful, and all my friends **were** there.

G. JULIE AND HER GRANDPARENTS

Listen to the story. Fill in the missing words.

A. How old *were* you when you *met* Grandmother?
B. I **was** twelve years old, and she **was** eleven.
A. Where **did** you meet?
B. We **went** to school together, and I **sat** next to your grandmother in science class.
A. **Did** you help her with her science homework?
B. No, I **didn't**. She **helped** me. She **was** a very good student, and I **was** very lazy.

1. How old was Julie's grandfather when he met Julie's grandmother?
   He was twelve years old.

2. Where did they meet?
   They went to school together.

3. Where did Julie's grandfather sit in science class?
   He sat next to Julie's grandmother.

4. Did Julie's grandfather help his grandmother with her science homework?
   No, he didn't.

5. Why not? **She helped him. She was a very good student, and he was very lazy.**

H. MISS GAYLORD

Listen to the story. Fill in the missing words.

A. Miss Gaylord. What **did** you **look** like when you **were** a child? **Were** you very beautiful? **Did** you **have** many boyfriends?
B. My **sisters** were pretty, but I **was** short and heavy. I **had** straight brown **hair** and freckles. I **didn't** like boys, and they **didn't** like me. When I **went** to **parties**, I **was** always embarrassed.

These exercises review the past tense and the vocabulary and structures in the text. Each dictation is followed by a set of questions. (text page 104)

In Exercise F, students use *did, was,* and *were* in questions and answers. (text page 103)

G. JULIE AND HER GRANDPARENTS
A. How old *were* you when you *met* Grandmother?
B. I *was twelve* years old, and she *was eleven.*
A. Where *did* you *meet?*
B. We *went* to school together, and I *sat next to* your grandmother in science class.
A. *Did* you *help* her with her science homework?
B. No, I *didn't.* She *helped* me. She *was* a very good student, and I *was* very lazy.

H. MISS GAYLORD
A. Miss Gaylord. What *did* you *look* like when you *were* a child? *Were* you very beautiful? *Did* you *have* many boyfriends?
B. My *sisters* were pretty, but I *was* short and heavy. I *had* straight brown hair and freckles. I *didn't* like boys, and they *didn't like* me. When I went to *parties,* I was always embarrassed.

I. GRANDCHILDREN
A. How *old was* Tommy when he began to *walk?*
B. He *was ten* months old, and I *bought* him his first pair of shoes. When he began *to talk,* his first words *were* "shoes" and "thank you."
A. Really? *Did* I tell you about my grandson Jimmy? He *was eight months* old when he *began to walk.*
B. Yes, you *did,* but that's O.K. I love to hear about Jimmy. *How* old *is* he now?
A. He's *twenty years* old.

---

1. Was Miss Gaylord beautiful when she was young? *No, she wasn't.*
2. Were her sisters pretty? *Yes, they were.*
3. What did Miss Gaylord look like? *She was short and heavy. She had straight brown hair and freckles.*
4. Did she like boys? *No, she didn't.*
5. When was she always embarrassed? *She was always embarrassed when she went to parties.*

I. GRANDCHILDREN

Listen to the story. Fill in the missing words.

A. How *old* *was* Tommy when he began to *walk*?
B. He *was* *ten* months old, and I *bought* him his first pair *of* shoes.
   When he began to *talk*, his first words *were* "*shoes*" and "*thank you*."
A. Really? *Did* I tell you about my grandson Jimmy? He was *eight* *months* old
   when he *began* *to* *walk*?
B. Yes, you *did*, but that's O.K. I love to hear about Jimmy. *How* old *is* he now?
A. He's *twenty* *years* old.

1. How old was Tommy when he began to walk? *He was ten months old.*
2. What were his first words? *His first words were "shoes" and "thank you."*
3. How old was Jimmy when he began to walk? *He was eight months old.*
4. How old is Jimmy now? *He's twenty years old.*

CHECK-UP TEST: Chapters 15–17

A. Fill in the blanks.

| was | were | wasn't | weren't |

1. A. _Was_ John at school yesterday?
   B. No, he _wasn't_. He _was_ sick.
2. A. Why _were_ Jane and Betty upset?
   B. They _were_ upset because the weather _wasn't_ good.
3. A. Where _were_ you and Lois last night? I called you, but you _weren't_ at home.
   B. We _were_ at the movies.

B. Complete the sentences.

Ex. Before we painted the living room, it _was_ ugly. Now _it's beautiful_ .
1. Before I worked at Stanley's Restaurant, I _was_ thin. Now _I'm heavy_ .
2. When Mr. and Mrs. Smith got married, they _were_ poor. Now _they're rich_ .
3. When we _were_ young, we _were_ energetic. Now _were_ always _tired_ .

C. Complete the sentences.

Ex. a. Barbara usually bakes cookies. — *bake* — She _baked_ an apple pie.
Ex. b. Robert usually writes to his father. — *didn't* / *write* — He _didn't write_ to his father yesterday.
1. I usually have lunch at school. — *didn't have* — I _didn't have_ lunch at school.
2. We usually listen to records. — *listen* — We _didn't listen_ to records yesterday.
3. George and Paul usually visit their uncle. — *visit* — They _didn't visit_ their uncle yesterday.
4. Jack usually goes jogging. — *go* — He _didn't go_ jogging yesterday.

D. Write the question.

Ex. _Did you get up_ at 9:00? No, I didn't. I got up at 10:00.
1. _Did she write_ to her uncle? No, she didn't. She wrote to her brother.
2. _Did you play_ baseball? No, I didn't. I played tennis.
3. _Did they have_ a good time? No, they didn't. They had a terrible time.
4. _Did she read_ the newspaper? No, she didn't. She read a book.
5. _Did he go_ to the movies? No, he didn't. He went to a concert.

E. Read the story and then write about yesterday.

Every morning I get up at 7:00. I brush my teeth, and I clean my room. I don't eat breakfast, but I drink coffee. At 8:00 I walk to the drugstore, and I buy a newspaper. I wait at the bus stop in front of the drugstore and take the bus to work.

Yesterday I _got up_ at 7:00. I _brushed_ my teeth, and I _cleaned_ my room. I _didn't eat_ breakfast, but I _drank_ coffee. At 8:00 I _walked_ to the drugstore, and I _bought_ a newspaper. I _waited_ at the bus stop, and I _took_ the bus to work.

F. LISTEN

Listen to each sentence. Put a circle around the word you hear.

Ex. is / (was)
1. (is) / was
2. is / (was)
3. (are) / were
4. are / (were)
5. is / (was)

Key to Part F, Check-Up Test—Chapters 15, 16, 17
For each sentence, read or play the tape twice.
Ex. Sally was very sad this morning.
1. My mother is very tired today.
2. Was Helen busy this morning?
3. John and Judy are very hungry this afternoon.
4. My aunt and uncle were at a concert.
5. Mr. Jones was late.

242 CHAPTER SEVENTEEN

Note About Book Test and Alternative Book Test that Follow: This is a 50-question test. In Part I, each verb is a question. For the rest of the test, each numbered item is a question.

The Additional or Alternative Book Test is scored separately. There are 25 items to be filled in.

Book IA Test Key

A.
1. Her
2. His
3. Their
4. our

B.
1. it
2. him
3. them
4. us

C.
1. When
2. Why
3. Where
4. How many
5. What

D.
1. are
2. does
3. Is
4. Do
5. are

E.
1. They're reading
2. She's listening
3. We're dancing
4. He's fixing
5. I'm calling

F.
1. doesn't drink
2. washes
3. don't eat
4. has

G.
1. These watches are gold.
2. These dresses weren't expensive.
3. Who are those handsome men?
4. Why are those children sad?

H.
1. didn't bake/baked
2. didn't help/helped
3. didn't have/had
4. didn't go/went

I. read, cleaned, ate, took

J.
1. they aren't
2. she wasn't
3. he can't
4. I wasn't
5. there isn't

Teacher Key to Listening Comprehension Part K, on Page 247
Read each question twice:

Ex. What kind of food does Mrs. Jones usually cook?
1. What are Fred and Jane doing?
2. What does Peggy do when she's tired?
3. What did Albert do today?
4. Is Peter happy at school?
5. When does Mr. Johnson go to the park?
6. Where did Alice go on vacation?

K.
1. b
2. b
3. c
4. b
5. a
6. c

Alternative Test

name, a, live, an, in , my, is, cooks, him, not, aren't, go, going to, don't, to, and, played, went, had, are, don't, going to have

243

BOOK 1A TEST

A. Fill in the blanks.

| his | her | its | my | our | their | your |

Ex. I brush _my_ teeth every day.

1. Mary is very beautiful. _____ hair is brown and curly.

2. Where are John's clothes? _____ clothes are on the floor.

3. Where's Mr. and Mrs. Smith's car? _____ car is in the garage.

4. We don't have a dining room, but _____ kitchen is very large.

B. Fill in the blanks.

| her | him | it | me | them | us | you |

Ex. Do you like Mary? Of course I like _her_ .

1. When the sink is broken, I always fix _____.

2. When my brother is at home, I always play with _____.

3. When my neighbors are at home, I always visit _____.

4. When my sister and I are hungry, my mother always feeds _____.

C. Fill in the blanks.

| How many | What | When | Where | Who | Why |

Ex. _____ _Where_ _____ do you live? In Rome.

1. _____ does George go to the bank? On Friday.

2. _____ are they smiling? Because they're happy.

3. _____ are you going? To the supermarket.

4. _____ brothers do you have? Three.

5. _____ are you drinking? Coffee.

D. Fill in the blanks.

| do | does | is | are |

Ex.   _Do_   you like John?

1. Why _____ you crying?

2. When _____ Barbara usually study English?

3. _____ Mary cooking dinner today?

4. _____ you usually clean the house on Monday?

5. What _____ the children doing?

E.   Complete the sentences.

Ex. What's Jane doing?   _____ _She's cleaning_ _____ her room.   That's strange.
                                                                                 She never cleans
                                                                                 her room.

1. What are Bob and Judy   _____ the newspaper.   That's strange.
    doing?   They never read
                                                                            the newspaper.

2. What's Sally doing?   _____ to music.   That's strange.
                                                                            She never listens
                                                                            to music.

3. What are you and your   _____   That's strange.
    sister doing?   You never dance.

4. What's Jack doing?   _____ the car.   That's strange.
                                                                            He never fixes the
                                                                            car.

5. What are you doing?   _____ my uncle.   That's strange.
                                                                            You never call
                                                                            your uncle.

F.   Complete the sentences.

              YES!   NO!

Ex. I play the piano.   I _____ _don't_ _____ _play_ _____ the guitar.

     Robert _speaks_ English.   He doesn't speak French.

1. Helen drinks tea.   She _____ _____ coffee.

2. Johnny _____ the dishes.   He doesn't wash his clothes.

3. Our children eat candy.   They _____ _____ tomatoes.

4. Peter _____ a dog.   He doesn't have a cat.

G. **Write the sentences in the plural.**

Ex. This is a beautiful beach. _____ *These are beautiful beaches.* _____

1. This watch is gold. _____

2. This dress wasn't expensive. _____

3. Who is that handsome man? _____

4. Why is that child sad? _____

H. **Complete the sentences.**

Ex. We usually listen to records.   We _____ *didn't* _____ _____ *listen* _____ to records yesterday.

We _____ *listened* _____ to the radio.

1. I usually bake cookies.   I _____ _____ cookies yesterday.

I _____ an apple pie.

2. Martha usually helps her mother.   She _____ _____ her mother yesterday.

She _____ her father.

3. We usually have dinner at 6:00.   We _____ _____ dinner at 6:00 yesterday.

We _____ dinner at 8:00.

4. George usually goes to the movies on Saturday.   He _____ _____ to the movies yesterday.

He _____ to the beach.

I. **Complete the sentences.**

Every morning I get up at 7:00, I read the newspaper, and I clean my room. At 8:00 I eat breakfast, and at 8:30 I take the bus to work.

Write about yesterday.

Yesterday I _____ *got up* _____ at 7:00, I _____ the newspaper, and I _____ my room. At 8:00 I _____ breakfast, and at 8:30 I _____ the bus to work.

J.   Give short answers.

Ex.   Is Mary tall? No, _____*she isn't.*_____

1.   Are Henry and Frank studying?   No, _____ .

2.   Was Jane at home yesterday?   No, _____ .

3.   Can Mr. Wilson play chess?   No, _____ .

4.   Were you hungry this morning?   No, _____ .

5.   Is there a restaurant in your neighborhood?   No, _____ .

K.   LISTEN

Listen to each question. Put a circle around the correct answer.

Ex. | a.   She's cooking Italian food.
    | b.   She cooks French food.
    | c.   She cooked German food.

1. | a.   They play tennis.
   | b.   They're playing soccer.
   | c.   They played baseball.

4. | a.   Yes, he does.
   | b.   Yes, he is.
   | c.   Yes, he was.

2. | a.   She's reading.
   | b.   She yawns.
   | c.   She rested.

5. | a.   Every day.
   | b.   Yesterday.
   | c.   He feeds the birds.

3. | a.   He studies.
   | b.   He's working.
   | c.   He played all day.

6. | a.   She goes to Paris.
   | b.   She goes in June.
   | c.   She went to Rome.

ADDITIONAL OR ALTERNATIVE BOOK TEST

Fill in the missing words.

My _____ is Linda. I'm _____ teacher. I _____ in _____ apartment _____ New York with _____ husband George. George _____ a chef. He _____ Italian food at a very good restaurant. I sometimes help _____ in the restaurant when I'm _____ busy.

My husband and I _____ working today because we're on vacation. We're going to _____ swimming this afternoon, and this evening we're _____ _____ see a movie. I'm very happy today because I _____ have _____ work.

Yesterday afternoon George _____ I _____ tennis, and yesterday evening we _____ to a concert. We _____ a very good time.

What _____ we going to do tomorrow? I _____ know, but I'm sure we're _____ _____ _____ a wonderful time.

THE "SIDE BY SIDE" METHODOLOGY

A.   PRESENTING MODEL CONVERSATIONS

1.   Have students look at the model illustration in the book or on the SBS Dialog Visual Card.

2.   Set the scene: "_____."

3.   With books closed, have students listen as you present the model or play the tape one or more times.

4.   **Full-Class Choral Repetition**: Model each line and have students repeat.

5.   Have students open their books and look at the dialog. Ask students if they have any questions and check understanding of new vocabulary: _____ *(new words)* _____ .

6.   **Group Choral Repetition**: Divide the class in half. Model line A and have Group 1 repeat; model line B and have Group 2 repeat, and so on.

7.   **Choral Conversation**: Groups 1 and 2 practice the dialog twice, without teacher model. First Group 1 is Speaker A and Group 2 is Speaker B; then reverse.

8.   Call on one or two pairs of students to present the dialog.

   (For additional practice, do Choral Conversation in small groups or by rows.)

B.   SIDE BY SIDE EXERCISES

1.   **Exercise 1**: Introduce any new words. Call on two students to present the dialog. Then do Choral Repetition and Choral Conversation Practice.

2.   **Exercise 2**: Same as above.

3.   **Exercises 3-[ ]** :

   Either

   Full-Class Practice: Call on a pair of students to do each exercise. Introduce new vocabulary one exercise at a time.

   (For more practice, call on other pairs of students, or do Choral Repetition or Choral Conversation.)

   or

   Pair Practice: Introduce all the new vocabulary. Next have students practice all of the exercises in pairs. Then have pairs present the exercises to the class.

   (For more practice, do Choral Repetition or Choral Conversation.)

DIALOG VISUAL CARDS 1 A

SIDE BY SIDE Picture Cards

Numerical List

1.	bedroom	47.	handsome – ugly	93.	blush
2.	bathroom	48.	rich – poor	94.	mechanic
3.	living room	49.	large/big – small/little	95.	violinist
4.	dining room	50.	expensive – cheap	96.	singer
5.	kitchen	51.	sunny	97.	dancer
6.	basement	52.	cloudy	98.	chef
7.	yard	53.	raining	99.	baker
8.	garage	54.	snowing	100.	actor
9.	restaurant	55.	hot	101.	actress
10.	bank	56.	warm	102.	teacher
11.	supermarket	57.	cool	103.	truck driver
12.	library	58.	cold	104.	bus driver
13.	park	59.	school	105.	doctor
14.	movie theater	60.	church	106.	nurse
15.	post office	61.	police station	107.	dentist
16.	zoo	62.	fire station	108.	carpenter
17.	hospital	63.	train station	109.	plumber
18.	read	64.	bus station	110.	scientist
19.	cook	65.	laundromat	111.	policeman
20.	study	66.	gas station	112.	secretary
21.	eat	67.	drugstore	113.	factory worker
22.	watch TV	68.	cafeteria	114.	businessman
23.	sleep	69.	bakery	115.	businesswoman
24.	play the piano	70.	barber shop	116.	salesman
25.	play cards	71.	beauty parlor	117.	saleswoman
26.	play baseball	72.	clinic	118.	computer programmer
27.	drink	73.	department store	119.	mailman
28.	dance	74.	doctor's office	120.	painter
29.	sing	75.	nervous	121.	go to a movie
30.	listen to the radio	76.	sad	122.	go to a baseball game
31.	fix _____ car	77.	happy	123.	have lunch/dinner
32.	fix _____ sink	78.	tired	124.	go swimming/swim
33.	fix _____ TV	79.	sick	125.	go dancing/dance
34.	feed _____ dog	80.	cold	126.	go skating/skate
35.	clean _____ yard	81.	hot	127.	go skiing/ski
36.	clean _____ apartment	82.	hungry	128.	go shopping/shop
37.	paint	83.	thirsty	129.	go bowling/bowl
38.	do _____ exercises	84.	angry	130.	go sailing/sail
39.	wash _____ car	85.	embarrassed	131.	go jogging/ jog
40.	wash _____ clothes	86.	cry	132.	go to the doctor
41.	brush _____ teeth	87.	smile	133.	go to the bank
42.	tall – short	88.	shout	134.	visit a friend in the hospital
43.	young – old	89.	smoke	135.	get up
44.	heavy – thin	90.	shiver	136.	take a bath
45.	new – old	91.	perspire	137.	take a shower
46.	pretty – ugly	92.	yawn	138.	put on clothes

251

139.	write	167.	rest	195.	lettuce
140.	headache	168.	eat	196.	pears
141.	stomachache	169.	sing	197.	celery
142.	toothache	170.	drink	198.	sugar
143.	backache	171.	sit	199.	coffee
144.	earache	172.	tomatoes	200.	salt and pepper
145.	sore throat	173.	eggs	201.	tea
146.	cold	174.	bananas	202.	onions
147.	work	175.	apples	203.	butcher shop
148.	cook	176.	cheese	204.	shoe store
149.	talk on the telephone	177.	milk	205.	high school
150.	fix _____ car	178.	ice cream	206.	university
151.	brush _____ teeth	179.	bread	207.	art museum
152.	dance	180.	crackers	208.	hotel
153.	smoke	181.	beans	209.	playground
154.	watch TV	182.	garlic	210.	parking lot
155.	play cards	183.	rice	211.	airport
156.	study	184.	flour	212.	candy store
157.	shave	185.	cookies	213.	newsstand
158.	smile	186.	yogurt	214.	hardware store
159.	clean	187.	soda	215.	pet shop
160.	cry	188.	orange juice	216.	motel
161.	listen to the radio	189.	jam and jelly	217.	shopping mall
162.	yawn	190.	beer	218.	TV station
163.	shout	191.	mayonnaise	219.	courthouse
164.	paint	192.	butter	220.	concert hall
165.	wait for the bus	193.	wine		
166.	plant flowers	194.	melon		

SIDE BY SIDE Picture Cards

Alphabetical List

a

actor (100)
actress (101)
airport (211)
angry (84)
apples (175)
art museum (207)

b

backache (143)
baker (99)
bakery (69)
bananas (174)
bank (10)
barber shop (70)
basement (6)
bathroom (2)
beans (181)
beauty parlor (71)
bedroom (1)
beer (190)
big (49)
blush (93)
bowl (129)
bread (179)
brush _____ teeth (41, 151)
bus driver (104)
businesswoman (115)
businessman (114)
bus station (64)
butcher shop (203)
butter (192)

c

cafeteria (68)
candy store (212)
carpenter (108)
celery (197)
cheap (50)
cheese (176)
chef (98)
church (60)
clean (159)
clean _____ apartment (36)

clean _____ yard (35)
clinic (72)
cloudy (52)
coffee (199)
cold [adjective] (80)
cold [ailment] (146)
cold [weather] (58)
computer programmer (118)
concert hall (220)
cook (19, 148)
cookies (185)
cool (57)
courthouse (219)
crackers (180)
cry (86, 160)

d

dance (28, 125, 152)
dancer (97)
dentist (107)
department store (73)
dining room (4)
doctor (105)
doctor's office (74)
do _____ exercises (38)
drink (27, 170)
drugstore (67)

e

earache (144)
eat (21, 168)
eggs (173)
embarrassed (85)
expensive (50)

f

factory worker (113)
feed _____ dog (34)
fire station (62)
fix _____ car (31, 150)
fix _____ sink (32)
fix _____ TV (33)
flour (184)

253

r

raining (53)
read (18)
rest (167)
restaurant (9)
rice (183)
rich (48)

s

sad (76)
sail (130)
salesman (116)
saleswoman (117)
salt (200)
school (59)
scientist (110)
secretary (112)
shave (157)
shiver (90)
shoe store (204)
shop (128)
shopping mall (217)
short (42)
shout (88, 163)
sick (79)
sing (29, 169)
singer (96)
sit (171)
skate (126)
ski (127)
sleep (23)
small (49)
smile (87, 158)
smoke (89, 153)
snowing (54)
soda (187)
sore throat (145)
stomachache (141)
study (20, 156)
sugar (198)
sunny (51)
supermarket (11)
swim (124)

t

take a bath (136)
take a shower (137)

talk on the telephone (149)
tall (42)
tea (201)
teacher (102)
thin (44)
thirsty (83)
tired (78)
tomatoes (172)
toothache (142)
train station (63)
truck driver (103)
TV station (218)

u

ugly (46, 47)
university (206)

v

violinist (95)
visit a friend in the hospital (134)

w

wait for the bus (165)
warm (56)
wash _____ car (39)
wash _____ clothes (40)
watch TV (22, 154)
wine (193)
work (147)
write (139)

y

yard (7)
yawn (92, 162)
yogurt (186)
young (43)

z

zoo (16)

SIDE BY SIDE Picture Cards

Categories

Adjectives

angry (84)
big (49)
cheap (50)
cold (80)
embarrassed (85)
expensive (50)
handsome (47)
happy (77)
heavy (44)
hot (81)
hungry (82)
large (49)
little (49)
nervous (75)
new (45)
old (43, 45)
poor (48)
pretty (46)
sad (76)
short (42)
sick (79)
small (49)
tall (42)
thin (44)
thirsty (83)
tired (78)
rich (48)
ugly (46, 47)
young (43)

Ailments

backache (143)
cold (146)
earache (144)
headache (140)
sore throat (145)
stomachache (141)
toothache (142)

Foods

apples (175)
bananas (174)
beans (181)
beer (190)
bread (179)
butter (192)
celery (197)
cheese (176)
coffee (199)
cookies (185)
crackers (180)
eggs (173)
flour (184)
garlic (182)
ice cream (178)
jam and jelly (189)
lettuce (195)
mayonnaise (191)
melon (194)
milk (177)
onions (202)
orange juice (188)
pears (196)
pepper (200)
rice (183)
soda (187)
sugar (198)
tea (201)
tomatoes (172)
wine (193)
yogurt (180)

Community

airport (211)
art museum (207)
bakery (69)
bank (10)
barber shop (70)
beauty parlor (71)
bus station (64)
butcher shop (203)
cafeteria (68)
candy store (212)
church (60)
clinic (72)
concert hall (220)

courthouse (219)
department store (73)
doctor's office (74)
drugstore (67)
fire station (62)
gas station (66)
hardware store (214)
high school (205)
hospital (17)
hotel (208)
laundromat (65)
library (12)
motel (216)
movie theater (14)
newsstand (213)
park (13)
parking lot (210)
pet shop (215)
playground (209)
police station (61)
post office (15)
restaurant (9)
school (59)
shopping mall (217)
supermarket (11)
train station (63)
TV station (218)
university (206)
zoo (16)

Home

basement (6)
bathroom (2)
bedroom (1)
dining room (4)
garage (8)
kitchen (5)
living room (3)
yard (7)

Professions

actor (100)
actress (101)
baker (99)
bus driver (104)
businessman (114)
businesswoman (115)
carpenter (108)

chef (98)
computer programmer (118)
dancer (97)
dentist (107)
doctor (105)
factory worker (113)
mailman (119)
mechanic (94)
nurse (106)
painter (120)
plumber (109)
policeman (111)
salesman (116)
saleswoman (117)
scientist (110)
secretary (112)
singer (96)
teacher (102)
truck driver (103)
violinist (95)

Verbs

blush (93)
bowl (129)
brush _____ teeth (41, 151)
clean (159)
clean _____ apartment (36)
clean _____ yard (35)
cook (19, 148)
cry (86, 160)
dance (28, 125, 152)
do _____ exercises (38)
drink (27, 170)
eat (21, 168)
feed _____ dog (34)
fix _____ car (31, 150)
fix _____ sink (32)
fix _____ TV (33)
get up (135)
go bowling (129)
go dancing (125)
go jogging (131)
go sailing (130)
go shopping (128)
go skating (126)
go skiing (127)
go swimming (124)
go to a baseball game (122)
go to a movie (121)

go to the bank (133)
go to the doctor (132)
have lunch/dinner (123)
jog (131)
listen to the radio (30, 161)
paint (37, 164)
perspire (91)
plant flowers (166)
play baseball (26)
play cards (25, 155)
play the piano (24)
put on clothes (138)
read (18)
rest (167)
sail (130)
shave (157)
shiver (90)
shop (128)
shout (88, 163)
sing (29, 169)
sit (171)
skate (126)
ski (127)
sleep (23)
smile (87, 158)

smoke (89, 153)
study (20, 156)
swim (124)
take a bath (136)
take a shower (137)
talk on the telephone (149)
visit a friend in the hospital (134)
wait for the bus (165)
wash _____ car (39)
wash _____ clothes (40)
watch TV (22, 154)
work (147)
write (139)
yawn (92, 162)

Weather

cloudy (52)
cold (58)
cool (57)
hot (55)
raining (53)
snowing (54)
sunny (51)
warm (56)